CU00927123

LANDSCAPE PROFESSIONAL PRACTICE

Landscape Professional Practice

Hugh Clamp

OBE, VRD, FLI, FRIBA, FCIArb.

Gower Technical Press Ltd

Published by
Gower Technical Press Ltd,
Gower House,
Croft Road,
Aldershot,
Hants GU11 3HR,
England

Gower Publishing Company,
Old Post Road,
Brookfield,
Vermont 05036,
U.S.A.

Revised and reprinted 1989

British Library Cataloguing in Publication Data
Clamp, Hugh
    Landscape professional practice.
    1. Landscape architecture
    I. Title
    712   SB472.3
Library of Congress Cataloging-in-Publication Data
Clamp, Hugh.
    Landscape professional practice / Hugh Clamp.
    p.   cm.
    Bibliography: p.
    Includes index.
    1. Landscape architects—Legal status, laws, etc.—Great Britain.
    2. Landscape protection—Law and legislation—Great Britain.
    3. Landscape architecture—Contracts and specifications—Great
Britain. I.   Title.
    KD2990.L37C53 1988
    344.42h01761712—dc19
    [344.2041761712] 87-33256

ISBN 0 291 39721 2

Printed and bound in Great Britain at
The Camelot Press plc, Southampton

Contents

Illustrations

Tables

Preface

Landscape architects, managers and scientists need, in addition to their academic qualifications and practical experience, to have acquired the necessary minimum standards of professional competence in:

professional conduct and legal responsibilities; a knowledge of both common and statute law in matters affecting the environment; and the efficient management and administration of their projects.

Those who require their services either as a consultant or an employee can then be confident that their interests will be safeguarded and that the work will be competently and expeditiously executed.

This book covers the above aspects of landscape practice in detail and sets out clearly and in a logical sequence the necessary information and procedures. Practical examples for those concerned with the design, management and scientific sides of landscape projects are also given.

1

The Code of Conduct and the Landscape Consultant's Appointment

Code of Professional Conduct

Landscape professional practice is no different from the other professions in that, as distinct from any other occupation, the professional is trusted to put his client's interests above any financial gain to himself. In spite of the fact that the longer a doctor's patient is sick, a lawyer's client's litigation continues, the financial affairs of an accountant's client take to finalize or the value of an engineering project, the greater the financial reward, they must be relied on to cure, or finalize the affairs of their clients at the earliest possible moment and at the minimum cost.

So it is with landscape architects, managers and scientists. Whether they are remunerated on a time or a percentage basis they also are entrusted with ensuring that all the projects on which they are engaged are completed in both the minimum time and cost commensurate with the client's particular requirements.

Earlier professional codes of conduct were drafted as much for the protection of the members of the respective professional institutes as for their clients. There were mandatory minimum scales of charges, but no minimum standards of competence. Professionals were prohibited from advertising their existence or special expertise, except in the most oblique and subtle manner, and certainly did not compete with a fellow member for the same client.

Now, under the threat of legal proceedings from the Office of Fair Trading, all that has been swept away. Fee scales may only be 'recommended', members are encouraged to advertise their services and no one can expect another job from the same client however well the previous one was executed. Landscape consultants no longer compete with their fellow professionals by attempting to offer a better service for the same fee as their competitors. Now they must submit tenders of fees for a professional service, the quality of which is almost impossible to define in writing, on projects the scope of which by their very nature must be unknown at the outset of the commission except in the most general of terms.

It must not be thought that as a consequence Codes of Professional Conduct have disappeared. The need for firmly controlled professional standards of conduct is still as strong as ever. The 1986 edition of the Landscape Institute's Code (Appendix 1) still contains nine clauses and while under Clause 3 members are still required to act impartially and to interpret the conditions of contract fairly between client and contractor, the acceptance of their primary allegiance to their client is undisputed. Not since 1974 have they mistakenly been thought to be 'quasi arbitrators' in the exercise of their landscape contractual duties unless they are disputed by the contractor (when another consultant is appointed as arbitrator) and as a consequence they are no longer immune from charges of professional negligence.

The omission of any references in the obligations of a landscape consultant to anyone or anything other than his client (including the landscape itself) was quite deliberate. While insisting on the provision of the highest standards of professional conduct and self discipline, the landscape consultant is expected to devote all his energies in the best interests of his client. It is quite possible, therefore, for two landscape consultants at a public inquiry each to put forward diametrically opposed but equally valid viewpoints on behalf of their respective clients.

Although there is no restriction on the framework within which they practise their profession, in partnership, as a company (limited or unlimited), as a contractor or as a consultant, any conflict of interest with their client or their shareholders must always have been previously disclosed in writing so that should their advice not be as impartial as might at first have been thought, any conflict of interest has been previously made clear.

By permitting landscape consultants to advertise, i.e. to make a direct approach with the offer of services to a potential but previously unknown client, they are for the first time allowed to 'tout' for work provided that it is done discreetly (Figure 1.1).

As a consequence this also means that they may well be approaching a client who already has the services of a landscape consultant so that (although many may not realize it) they are now in effect permitted to 'poach' another's client, again of course provided it is done discreetly. It is also important to remember that Clause 8 of the code only requires a landscape consultant to notify a member on being approached to proceed with work on which to their knowledge another has been already employed. The obligation is only to 'notify' – no consent of the former landscape consultant is required but it is always prudent to ascertain when so doing that no outstanding fees are due to the former consultant just to make sure this is not the sole reason for the change! In any case, as

Dear Sir

Mr .... has suggested in a letter to us of .... that
we write to you concerning the proposals to .... and
we understand that he has kindly put our name forward for
consideration in the appointment of a landscape architect.

Our practice was established in .... and we presently
employ .... qualified landscape architects and town
planners, ... senior assistants, ... technicians
and .... students.

Please do not hesitate to contact us if you require further
details and, if appropriate, we shall be pleased to attend
an interview and to arrange for you to inspect our offices.

Yours faithfully

Figure 1.1 Pro forma for a letter from a landscape architect in response to an enquiry from a potential client

in any divorce, both sides are rarely blameless and it is wise to remember this fact and to take particular care to ensure the same thing does not happen again.

Equally, while advertising is no longer prohibited and those seeking the services of a landscape consultant need no longer rely on personal recommendation – and provided of course they knew who to go to for such a recommendation, members of the Landscape Institute, in paying for such an advertisement, must still ensure that it is 'factual, relevant and not misleading'. That is to say that while it is perfectly proper to describe past and present projects, although a statement of aims and objectives is not precluded, matters of opinion and comparisons with the work of others is still unacceptable.

Quite what is meant by the prohibition of advertisements 'discreditable' to the profession is less clear. Presumably advertising on television (if it could be afforded and thought to be worth while) would be considered acceptable but not in the back pages of some less than reputable magazine or Soho 'theatre' programme. This also raises the question of reaching the right markets. While it is always gratifying to see one's work illustrated in the pages of *Landscape Design, Horticulture Weekly* or the *Architects Journal* this is less likely to bring in new commissions than publication in *The Local Government News*, the *Estates*

Gazette or *Country Life* depending on one's preference for a particular kind of work or forecast of future demand.

Practice promotion

Landscape consultants have always been able to make the work of their offices more widely known by sending articles and details of work in progress and recently completed jobs to the technical press, provided no payment was made to the journal concerned. The relaxation of the prohibition against advertising has given rise to illustrated professional directories circulated free of charge by the publishers to potential clients. A charge is made for inclusion in such directories. This is a convenient way of ensuring that illustrations of one's work, together with that of one's professional colleagues and competitors, are well publicized but should be used with discretion in view of the cost involved.

Professional standard photographs of all completed jobs are therefore essential and should always be readily available, in black and white and in colour. With modern processing techniques it is no longer necessary to hold large stocks of enlargements of each job and one or two shots enlarged to A4 or A5 with an accompanying description filed separately in the library will usually suffice. 35mm Colour slides are sometimes an advantage but take time to copy and are not essential.

Printed single sheets with a number of photographs of a particular project or type of project are helpful to potential clients as are printed Practice Information sheets and CVs of the partners. Copies of articles in the press including those describing the work of the practice or individual jobs are always of interest to new clients. An illustrated summary of recently completed work prepared on a regular basis and sent not only to existing but also potential clients is also useful.

'Entertaining' clients is often counter productive, particularly when dealing with those in the public sector, but the discussion of mutual problems before or after a meeting in congenial but not ostentatious surroundings perhaps over a meal can sometimes be helpful.

While in a similar way business connections with certain individuals could be seen to be clearly undesirable, this no longer excludes those involved in the landscape contracting and plant producing side of the industry. Landscape architects, managers and scientists have always been able to work within these sectors of the industry provided it was on a salaried or consultancy basis. Now they can be shareholders or directors, participating directly in the profitability of the organization resulting from their own individual efforts. This injection of professional expertise at board level can only be of benefit to the industry, provided there is compliance with the safety checks of disclosure to eliminate any conflict of interests.

Irrespective of any mandatory codes of conduct however, the basic principle of acting with integrity whether as a consultant in the public or private sector, or as a director or employee of a landscape contractor or nurseryman must still apply. To act fairly, even without the protection from legal actions on the grounds of negligence must always be the essential obligation of the landscape practitioner.

Landscape professional services

The essential ingredient of any landscape project is the existence of an atmosphere of trust and goodwill, without which any scheme is doomed to failure. Like other professional codes of conduct, which lay down standards of behaviour without specifying details of compliance, the landscape professional conditions of engagement list the duties of landscape architects, managers and scientists but not how these duties are to be carried out. The conditions are totally silent on the manner in which the work is undertaken and the quality, resources, effort and skills required for any particular project. These are matters which at present rely entirely on the individual concerned and for this reason alone make the present arrangements for fee tendering totally ineffectual unless supplemented with supporting information. One cannot therefore proceed without first agreeing in writing with the client exactly what is being undertaken. Even today, 200 years after the consultancy services offered by Capability Brown, many, if not most, clients (except perhaps those in the public sector and fellow professionals) are unaware of the scope of the services that are available or are necessary for any particular project. For this reason alone, it is a specific requirement of the landscape Code of Conduct that its members confirm the services they are providing (Clause 5). Most litigation between a client and a landscape consultant arises from a lack of a clear understanding between the parties, each thinking the other knew what he himself expected of the other, whereas in fact the other party thought he was required to undertake something quite different and as a result the item in question was never done by either. Had the details been put down in writing beforehand the situation would never have occurred.

Landscape projects are often complex, involve a number of different individuals and extend over a long period of time, due to seasonal planting requirements which usually have to take precedence over the requirements of the individuals concerned and as a result, changed circumstances often involve other changes not envisaged at the outset. It is essential therefore that all agreements make provision for the resolution of such problems.

Conditions of appointment

The fact that this section of the Landscape Institute's Conditions now runs to over 30 Clauses, setting out the conditions under which a landscape consultant is engaged and describing what (but not how) he is to do, emphasizes the importance of getting these matters clearly understood and agreed at the outset.

Professional negligence

It used to be thought that provided consultants exercised reasonable skill, care and diligence in accordance with the normal standards of the profession to comply with their conditions of appointment, they would be able to practise in the confident belief that they would be free of any action for professional negligence. Sadly this seems to be no longer the case with the courts apparently upholding the public belief that in the event of an accident, whatever the circumstances, the recipient should not suffer the financial consequences and someone, preferably with insurance cover, should be found to bear the cost. The final straw was the Civil Liability (Contribution) Act of 1978 which entitles a plaintiff to recover the whole of his loss from a number of defendants and if one or more of them is without the means to pay, possibly if he has conveniently 'ceased trading', the remaining defendants must bear the whole of the cost of the loss themselves.

For this reason the Landscape Institute requires registered practices to take out professional indemnity insurance as do government departments and most statutory and local authorities; it ensures that they have sufficient funds to meet their financial obligations should a case of professional negligence be found against them. In the current climate of public opinion however, it seems no longer necessary to prove lack of a duty of care and landscape consultants would seem now to be held liable for any mistake or error of judgement however carefully they had considered the matter before coming to a decision.

The incidence of claims for 'mistakes', irrespective of the reasonable skill, care and diligence exercised, has resulted in enormously increased insurance premiums, often in excess of 10 per cent of gross fee income. This is not helped by the Property Services Agency (PSA) and some authorities requiring of their consultants proof of insurance cover of an amount equivalent to double the fee income of the individual or practice concerned.

To reduce the risk of claims it is therefore essential to keep the client fully informed, preferably in writing, at all times; particularly when making economies below what would otherwise seem prudent, when considering options or when instructed by a client on a course of action against one's better judgement, and to obtain his authority before initiating or proceeding to another stage of the work.

For the same reason approved proposals should never be altered without the clients' consent nor any variations incorporated particularly those affecting the authorized expenditure or contract period.

Other consultants

While a landscape consultant must neither assign his commission nor subcontract it in whole or part without notifying and obtaining the consent of the client, other consultants may be employed either by the landscape consultant or direct by the client, provided their respective divisions of responsibility are clearly defined. Under these circumstances each must be solely responsible for his own sphere of the work (and suitably insured) notwithstanding any authority the landscape consultant may have to co-ordinate and integrate the others' work into his own. Should any design work be required of a specialist subcontractor or supplier, his responsibility for its efficacy and satisfactory performance to the client and not the landscape consultant, must also be clearly defined.

Contractor's obligations

It cannot be too often repeated that, irrespective of the existence of a landscape consultant, a landscape contractor has a clear obligation 'with due diligence in a good and workmanlike manner to carry out and complete the Works in accordance with the Contract Documents'. While the landscape contractor is also responsible for his own operational methods; the landscape consultant is equally contractually responsible under his own quite separate agreement with the client 'to monitor the progress and quality of the works against the contract documents'. If therefore the quality of the works is not in accordance with the contract documents the client can, and often does, either jointly or severally sue both the landscape consultant and the landscape contractor for breach of their contracts with him.

Quality control

To reduce the chances of being sued two things can be done. First the contract documents may include clauses requiring the contractor to report when certain stages of the work are completed, so that they can be inspected before they are covered up and the work proceeds to the next stage. Second the client may agree to the appointment of and pay for either professional staff and/or a clerk of works to be employed permanently on the site. While this will relieve neither the contractor nor the consultant of their responsibilities, it does at least reduce, but not eliminate the chances of mistakes during the progress of the work. It cannot of course cover deliberate or fraudulent concealment of errors or omissions. It also helps if instructions from the client are received from only one individual on his behalf and equally essential that instructions to the landscape contractor are passed to him only by the landscape consultant.

Copyright

Copyright of the designs in all drawings and documents (unless otherwise agreed) always remains with the landscape consultant. It is common practice however for the client to be able to make use of them *provided that* they are used only for the same site or part of the site for which design was prepared, such as when they are used for subsequent maintenance or management. The law on copyright of drawings begins with the Fine Arts Copyright Act of 1842, followed by the Berne Convention of 1908 and the Copyright Act of 1911, which included under the definition of 'Artistic Works' 'any building or structure having artistic character or design or any model of such building or structure'. Today in any case involving infringement of copyright, reliance is placed on the Copyright Act, 1956 which includes, 'irrespective of artistic quality', drawings:

> reproducing the work of art in any material form,
> publishing the work of art, and
> including the work in a television broadcast.

Drawings are defined as including 'any diagram, map, chart or plan', and works as either 'buildings (including any structure) or models'. Copyright extends for 50 years beyond the calender year in which the 'qualified person', i.e. any British subject, resident or person whose country was a signature to the Berne Convention, died.

Ownership

The ownership of copyright of a drawing resides with the person (either who, or whose employee actually drew the plan) and after his death, to his personal representatives including partners, inheritors or next of kin, unless previously assigned. As far as drawings are concerned the ownership of the paper on which they are drawn passes to the client on payment of his fee, but the 'design' remains with the 'artist' who may wish to use the same details on another project. Photographs, paintings, drawings or engravings of the project, particularly those used subsequently by contractors in advertisements, do not involve infringement of copyright nor do photographs or films of the project used in a television broadcast but copying of the 'artist's' drawings themselves, for whatever purpose, does (unless it is for the purpose of construction of the design). Under the 1956 Act, the Crown is however entitled to the copyright in all artistic work 'made by or under the direction or control of Her Majesty or a government department'.

Infringement

The infringement of copyright occurs when the work copied is known to the copier, i.e. ignorance of the existence of that which was copied is a valid defence although as one would expect the reproduction of a drawing into a building or landscape project does not involve infringement of the copyright of the drawing.

In *Meikle* v. *Maufe* (1941) when Maufe extended the existing Heals building in Tottenham Court Road in 1935 to match the adjoining building built to the design of Smith & Brewer in 1912 (the ownership of this design had by then passed to Meikle) a claim that his copyright had been infringed was upheld. It was considered that there could be no implied consent by Smith and Brewer to the reproduction of their design because they had not known of the possibility of an extension at the outset.

Copyright of partial services

If the client at the outset makes it clear that all he requires of the consultant are drawings to obtain a statutory consent and he then pays for them, then they would be valueless unless the client could then use them to construct the project (even if it had started as a full commission). The client therefore has an implied licence to issue the drawings to a contractor to complete the project as designed.

In *Blair* v. *Osborne and Tompkins* (1971) the architect was instructed and obtained a detailed planning consent for two semi-detached houses at the bottom of Blair's garden but no more. It was held that the client had therefore an implied licence 'to use whatever plans had been prepared at the appropriate stage' for all purposes for which they would usually be used, namely all purposes connected with the erection of the building to which they were related.

Stovin Bradford v. *Volpoint Properties* (1971) concerned the modification of a refused application prepared by their own office for the conversion of an existing warehouse and the erection of six others. The original design included a distinctive diamond design feature in the elevations and when the building was built, in accordance with a revised planning consent granted on appeal, it was held that in view of the 'agreed nominal fee' there had been an infringement of copyright and no implied licence had arisen, as a result of which £500 damages were awarded.

The landscape consultant's appointment should, as a consequence, ensure that the client has an express licence to use the drawings solely for the purpose for which they were prepared and that drawings prepared to obtain a planning consent should not be used to construct the works except with the consultant's express consent.

Injunctions cannot be granted after the construction of the building has started nor can they require the building to be demolished.

Suspension of the project

The LI Conditions of Appointment provide for the client to suspend the appointment of his landscape consultant, having given reasonable notice of his intention, on receipt of which it is prudent for the consultant to ensure that the work is completed to a clearly defined work stage. Equally should circumstances arise which make it impracticable for the consultant to continue with the work, he must notify the client and agree the future course of action. If after six months and in response to a request for instructions the consultant has received no instructions within a further 30 days, the project is considered terminated. If the consultant has died or become incapacitated, the client may be entitled to use all the drawings and documents prepared that far, provided all outstanding fees have been paid.

Disputes between client and consultant

Should a dispute occur, regrettably they sometimes do, and it cannot be resolved by mutual agreement, in addition to recourse to the courts, there are three options open to both client and landscape consultant.

First an agreed joint statement of undisputed facts may be submitted to the President of the Landscape Institute for his ruling which is accepted as final and binding. Second a mediator or conciliator agreed between the disputing parties as being a suitable person and on whose opinion they both agree to abide may be appointed.

Third an arbitrator may be appointed under the Arbitration Acts 1950 and 1979 whose decision is binding and enforceable by law without the right of appeal, unless the existence of misconduct of the arbitrator can be proved.

Fees

There are only three ways of remunerating a self-employed landscape consultant: (1) on a percentage basis based on the cost of the works; (2) on a time basis, and (3) by a lump sum (Figure 1.2).

```
Dear Mr .......
```

```
Following our meeting yesterday I/we are writing to confirm
that I/we shall be very pleased to accept the appointment as
your landscape architect(s) for the above project.

(A)   As I/we mentioned our fee will be on a percentage basis
      in accordance with section 3 of the enclosed LI Conditions
      of Engagement.  In this instance the contract coefficient
      being ........ and the job coefficient being ........ the
      combined coefficient is ........ and on an authorized
      expenditure of £...... the percentage will be .... x ....
      x .... = %.

(B)   As I/we mentioned our fee (for post contract services)
      will be charged on a time basis in accordance with
      section 2.  Accounts will be rendered monthly/quarterly
      in accordance with section 8.1.

Principals' time will be charged at £...... per hour in
accordance with section 7, and VAT at the rate prevailing at
the time.


Yours sincerely
```

Figure 1.2 Pro forma for a letter from a landscape architect to a client confirming his appointment and fees

Percentage basis

Remuneration is traditionally on a percentage basis where landscape consultants are responsible for the work from inception to completion of lump sum and prime cost contracts; the fee being based on the total cost of the work carried out under the consultant's direction. If any work or materials are supplied to the contractor without charge, then their value, (as are increased costs if allowable) is added to the contract sum for the purposes of evaluating the sum on which the percentage fee is based. However, the Landscape Institute recommends fees should be recalculated when the final certificate stating the total construction cost has been issued. When the fee is paid in stages, for example the work stages in the basic service, it is becoming common practice for the fee to be fixed and based on the estimated value at that stage and not readjusted at the end when the final account has been completed. Under this arrangement therefore, the fee at tender stage is based on the lowest tender and only that part of the fee due for post-contract services is based on the final account. The reason for this arrangement arose at a period of high inflation when it seemed unreasonable for landscape consultants' fees for the preparation of tender documents to be increased for no extra work, by basing them not on the contract sum but the final account enhanced by the value of the increased cost of labour and materials. The only advantage to the landscape consultant of this method is that it reduces the chances of overlooking fees due for landscape services for work designed and detailed but not carried out. Fees are not chargeable on any value added tax recoverable by the contractor from the client.

Should any part of the work be considered to involve sufficient repetition to justify a reduction in the fee for the design and detailing of that part of the work, then the amount of any abatement must always be by prior written agreement, as should be the fee for any work carried out on a site other than that for which it was designed when some form of royalty basis might then be appropriate.

As the cost of a landscape architect's services does not increase directly in proportion to the cost of the work, the percentage charged should be greater for the smaller contract and decrease as the cost of the works increase. For this reason the percentage fee is not considered appropriate for projects of a lesser value than £20 000 at 1987 prices.

It is generally accepted that some types of work are more complicated and time consuming than others, without a corresponding increase in the cost of the work and therefore different percentage fees are appropriate for different categories of work. Landscape work involving alterations is more complicated than new work and private gardens more complicated than industrial estates. These differences must be taken into account by the landscape consultant when agreeing with his client a percentage fee based on the cost of the work executed.

Stage payments: when the work is not to be paid in equal regular instalments with an adjusted final payment on completion, the recommended apportionment of fees due on completion of each basic service work stage are as follows:

C	15%	15
D	20%	35
E	20%	55
F,G	20%	75
H–L	25%	100

Time basis

For all classes of work, particularly consultancy and advisory work of some magnitude or intermittent work spread over long periods, fees based on the actual time taken are the most appropriate.

It is essential to keep accurate records for inspection by the client when this method is used; with the grade of staff, dates and time involved clearly identifiable. The hourly rate is normally 18p per £100 of gross annual income, i.e. the hourly rate for an assistant earning £7500 net plus £750 emoluments (£8250 gross) would be £12.30. The gross annual salary of the individual concerned, including bonus, national insurance, pension, medical schemes and other emoluments is charged irrespective of the type of work on which he has been engaged.

Partner's time is normally excluded from this arrangement and is a matter of separate negotiation, rates of £25–45 being normal in 1987, dependant on the experience and qualifications of the partner concerned and the type of work on which he will be engaged.

If staff are engaged through an agency then their rates should be agreed separately, as should resident site staff when hotel and subsistence allowances may or may not be involved. Secretarial and administrative staff time is not normally charged.

Travelling time during office hours is charged at the same rate. Charging for travelling time out of office hours depends on the circumstances, office policy, and distance involved and must be agreed separately. Overtime is not normally recoverable from the client unless carried out at his express instructions.

Hourly rates for principals and staff attending lengthy enquiries and appeals must also take into account that they may well, as a consequence, be unable to devote any time to other projects. Equally, should the requirement for their attendance for which they have reserved time be cancelled at short notice, some recompense is normally due. It is normal when undertaking work solely on a time basis, to give a client a ceiling figure of the anticipated total cost, based on past experience of similar projects, with an undertaking that this will not be exceeded without his prior written approval.

Lump sum

Many clients are unable to enter into an open-ended commitment for fees either on a percentage or time basis. In these circumstances provided the scope, extent and timetable for the work are clear at the outset, then it is always possible to agree a lump sum fee for any work on which a landscape consultant is engaged. It must always be remembered however that should the landscape consultant have underestimated the extent or the cost of the work, he must still continue to complete it properly, although it is then at his own cost and he will not be reimbursed.

Retainers

Where the services of landscape consultants are required on a regular basis, either continuously or intermittently, and for which there may or may not be an identifiable 'cost of the works' a retainer is often the most appropriate on a lump sum or time basis. When the fee is on a lump sum basis it will be paid at monthly, quarterly or annual intervals irrespective of the work required. On a time basis, accounts are rendered when the work has been completed, or at similar agreed intervals, for the actual work involved.

Partial services

For a variety of reasons, including the uncertainty of future funding arrangements, an increasing number of landscape commissions are let on a partial service basis, with either some earlier previously completed or later post contract stage omitted. Under these circumstances special care is necessary to clarify such aspects as copyright, financial and other professional liabilities for work which may have been carried out by others beforehand or in the future. In such cases when the work is carried out on a percentage basis the work stages to be undertaken and fees to be paid are usually an adequate indication of those parts of the work for which the landscape consultant is responsible and liable. When the consultant's work is to be carried out on a time basis – for example, work stage 8 – operations on site, clarification of the individual consultant's responsibilities for design and for inspection are particularly important.

Suspension, resumption and termination

Should a landscape consultant's commission be suspended, fees are charged on a partial services basis for work completed up to that time and for all expenses and disbursements incurred while work is stopped. After six months or if it is terminated, fees, expenses and disbursements are due on all work completed to date.

Should the work be resumed within six months the fees previously received are considered to be payments on account.

Expenses and disbursements

All expenses and disbursements properly incurred by the consultant, to which he may add an administrative charge, are normally recoverable. Those commonly involved are as follows:

Printing
The cost of printing and copying of all drawings and documents provided by the consultant for the project, including those provided free to the contractor, are recoverable from the client including any necessary maps, models and photographs.

Subsistence and hotel expenses
Expenses necessarily incurred for principals and staff while away from the office are either recovered from the client on the basis of the actual expenditure incurred or by an agreed lump sum such as that adopted by PSA (dependent on the time away from the office). The option selected must be agreed with the client beforehand and is not necessarily the same as that paid to the staff involved, i.e. while staff may be reimbursed the actual cost, clients may require a fixed allowance.

Travelling
Clients will normally require public transport to be used particularly for journeys in excess of 100 miles. When however this would involve uneconomically long travelling times, the cost of journeys by private cars is usually allowed on an appropriate mileage basis, arrived at with the addition to petrol costs of a suitable allowance for insurance, road tax, repairs and depreciation.

Postage and telephone
These are usually allowable as recoverable expenses but it is rare to charge for postage costs less than 50p and telephone charges other than

trunk calls. Telex, facsimile, air freight and courier costs are however normally identified and recovered.

Miscellaneous charges

Charges for items such as the cost of models, site, progress and aerial photographs, special drawings and perspectives must be agreed with the client before they are incurred. Fees for planning and Building Regulation applications, if not paid by the client direct, are also recoverable.

Compounding expenses

Expenses and disbursements may be estimated, added and included within the lump sum or percentage fees. Even so they are never 'free' as far as the consultant is concerned.

Additional work

Fees for additional work arising for reasons which could not have been envisaged at the outset or beyond the consultant's control are always recoverable from the client on an agreed basis: for example the need to revise drawings and other documents arising from changes in statutory regulations or the clients requirements; delays or changes for which the contractor, subcontractor or suppliers are responsible; the cost to the landscape consultant of any work arising from claims from the contractor for extension of the contract period or for the reimbursement of direct loss and expenses, particularly if rejected, is recoverable also.

Additional services

Fees for all work other than that included in the basic services, including site surveys, visits to nurseries, quantity surveying, resident site staff and responsibility for the services of other disciplines are always chargeable on the basis of the scales of the profession concerned.

Value added tax on fees

All fees for professional services for work carried out in the United Kingdom, irrespective of the origin of the client, are subject to the surcharge of value added tax, levied under the Finance Act, 1972, except for those consultants whose total fee income is less than the current limit of exemption.

Payment

Landscape consultant's fees become payable at agreed intervals or stages and are considered to be instalments as interim payments on account (Figure 1.3). If not settled within 30 days, consultants are entitled to interest at 2 per cent above the current bank base rate. If any item is disputed or questioned by the client, payment of only the disputed item should be withheld and the remainder settled in full, if interest on the balance outstanding is not to be added.

Working with related professions

Landscape projects often involve working with other disciplines, architects, engineers and surveyors. Their work has then to be integrated with other programmes, timetables, work stages and priorities and it should not be forgotten that these are not necessarily the same as those of the landscape consultant. The work stage and fees for one profession may be quite different from that of another discipline at the same stage. Great care is necessary to ensure that problems are not left unresolved, either because each of the parties thinks that one of the others is dealing with it, or, even more serious, that the one in whose sphere of responsibility the problem arises does not appreciate that the problem exists – for example, a highways engineer responsible for lighting a motorway intersection in the middle of the countryside. Tact and diplomacy are always necessary when a change or certain solution is required which may well involve a different discipline in additional work, for reasons which they themselves do not think justified. This is particularly relevant when the other discipline considers rightly or wrongly that they are the 'lead' consultants.

Work overseas

It is important to remember when engaged on or seeking work overseas for either a UK or foreign based client that professional practice, procedures and codes of conduct are rarely the same as those of the UK. Different economic conditions and ethics create different codes and procedures. It is essential to spell out in great detail the service being offered, and how it is to be provided, in order to eliminate any future misunderstandings particularly those with regard to payment. Ascertain the tender and contract conditions to be adopted in the country in question and whether there are any stipulations as to where the consultant's work is to be carried out. Are the fees to be subject to any local taxes and what arrangements are necessary for them to be transferred to the UK? What

17

```
                         INVOICE
     To: ................................

         ................................

  Your ref:

  Our ref:

  Date:

  Dr to ...............................
```

Interim/Final STATEMENT ....198.. ....198..	To professional services in connection with .... To fees in accordance with LI Conditions of Engagement as agreed .../.../... viz: *contract coefficient x job coefficient .... x .... % = %*

```
                (a) ...% on amount of est. cost/lowest
                    tender/contract/value of work
                    executed of £......                    £ _____

                    ...% due on completion of Stage ...    £

                (b) Time basis as attached Statement       £
                    less previously received on Account
                    dated .../.../... (exclusive of
                    value added tax)                       £

                (c) Additional services                    £ _____

                Balance now due                            £ _____

                Out of pocket expenses (period ......
                to ......)                                  £
                (exclusive of value added tax) as per
                attached statement

                     Printing                              £

                     Travelling                            £

                     Copying                               £

                     Miscellaneous                         £
                                                             _____

                Balance fees and expenses now claimed      £

                Plus VAT15%                                 £

                Disbursements     ...................       £
                                                             _____

                TOTAL NOW DUE                              £
                                                             ========
```

Please note this is not a tax invoice. An authenticated tax
receipt will be forwarded on payment of this account in
accordance with HM Customs and Excise Note 708 Part III para
28 construction services supplied under a contract which
provides for periodic payments.

                                    With compliments

*Note: Calculations to establish the combined coefficient and resulting
percentage due may not be necessary if these have been previously
confirmed with the employer and have not been subsequently varied.

Figure 1.3 Pro forma for a model fee invoice

are the arrangements for the reimbursement of travelling expenses and hotel accommodation? When undertaking work for overseas clients, membership and advice from the British Consultants Bureau (1 Westminster Palace Gardens, Artillery Row, London SW1) is often useful.

Plan of work

Most projects proceed in the following eleven clearly defined stages and landscape consultants should never proceed to the next stage without notifying the client accordingly so that there will be no dispute in the future when the appropriate fees become due.

Preliminary services

Work Stage A. Inception
The assessment of a client's requirements, i.e. his true needs as distinct from what he thinks he wants, can be a lengthy and time consuming business, as can be reconciling the often irreconcilable conflict between the cost of meeting these needs and the amount of money available. Obtaining information on site ownership, boundaries, access and underground services also takes time, as does discussing the timescale and advising on the need for other consultants and specialist advice. Consequently this work, particularly when complex or involved, is almost always charged on a time basis (see p.13).

Work Stage B. Feasibility studies
Having ascertained the client's requirements before outline proposals can be prepared, there follows consideration of their feasibility and consideration of alternative ways of meeting them, the consequential technical and financial implications and the need for planning and other statutory consents. This work is also usually charged on a time basis.

Basic services

Work Stage C. Outline proposals
Once the client's requirements have been ascertained, the site with its constraints and potential identified and the financial cost limits laid down, the way is clear for the landscape consultant to prepare his outline proposals with an approximation of their cost for the client's approval and instructions to proceed to the next stage. These can be in written form but usually involve drawn material as well.

Work Stage D. Sketch scheme proposals

The key factors at this stage are that the consultants should have developed the outline proposals so that they include cost estimates, a programme for the project and 'indicate the size and character of the project, in sufficient detail to enable the client to agree the spatial arrangements, materials and appearance'. It must be obvious therefore at this stage that there must be a considerable input of drawn material. It is also important to emphasize to the client that once approved at this stage, the design becomes frozen and no further changes can be incorporated without delaying the programme and incurring additional fees, not only for the landscape consultant but any other consultants who may be involved. For this reason discussions with the planning and other statutory authorities are essential at this stage and possibly the submission of an outline planning application, if appropriate.

Work Stage E. Detailed proposals

Further detailed design involving selection of the precise materials and standards of workmanship to be used, co-ordinating the proposals of other consultants and specialist contractors or suppliers, including obtaining quotations and cost checks, is involved at this stage, with further approvals from the client and detailed applications for planning building regulations and other such statutory consents as are necessary.

Work Stages F and G. Production information and bills of quantities

At this stage working drawings, schedules and a detailed specification of workmanship and materials are required, all to be in sufficient detail for the preparation of bills of quantities by a quantity surveyor if necessary to enable a contract to be negotiated or competitive tenders invited. It is absolutely essential to allow sufficient time for this stage to be carried out carefully and with meticulous attention to the necessary detail required.

Work Stages H and J. Tender action and contract preparation

Having decided the appropriate type of contract for the particular project e.g. lump sum, cost plus, etc and whether tenders are to be negotiated or invited from a specially selected list, it is necessary to discuss and agree with the client, the contractors to be involved. This having been done, tenders are invited or negotiated, appraised and reported with recommendations to the client. Once approval to proceed is received, the responsibilities of the client, the contractor and the landscape consultant must be explained (and not taken for granted) to all concerned and any further information provided to enable work to start on site.

Work Stage K. Operations on site

The administration of the contract on site by the landscape consultant is time consuming and it is important that it is carried out properly. Although the contract quite clearly states the contractors' obligation to execute the work in accordance with the contract documents, the landscape consultant has an equally clear obligation under the terms of his agreement with the client to 'monitor' the progress and quality of the work against the contract documents. It is for this obligation to the client, in addition to that of inspecting progress, issuing interim certificates for payment, instructing and valuing variations, that he receives one-quarter of his total fee when remunerated on a percentage basis.

Work Stage L. Completion

Giving guidance on maintenance, certifying when practical completion has been achieved, when defects have been made good and the final account, is the last of the landscape consultant's work stages.

Additional services

There are a number of other services that the landscape consultant may be, and often is, called on to perform. In the days before involvement with the Office of Fair Trading and fee tendering, these services were often included with the basic service for no extra fee. Alas those days are no more, since it is clearly unrealistic (clear that is to all but PSA and the Office of Fair Trading) for a client to receive both a reduced fee and additional services at no extra cost.

Examples of additional services that may be necessary are given below.

Surveys and investigations

1 *Site evaluation:* The selection of sites, advice on their suitability and acquisition are additional to the preliminary and basic services.
2 *Measured surveys:* Measuring sites, and existing buildings, taking levels and drawing them out, whether carried out by the consultant or specialist surveyors are recoverable as an additional expense.
3 *Site investigation:* Preparing reports on the nature and conditions of vegetation, soil and other features is an additional service.
4 *Maintenance and management:* Cost in use studies, management and site maintenance studies are not included in the preliminary and basic services.
5 *Environmental studies:* The assessment of the impact on the

21

environment of development proposals, following the recent EEC directive, is now obligatory for certain schemes and optional on others.

6   *Development plans:* Where only part of the site will be developed initially, but that part must be designed to take into account future development, the design of the future part merits an additional fee.

7   *Demolition:* Services in connection with demolitions are not included in the basic service.

8   *Special drawings and models:* Prepared for use in connection with applications for consents, approvals or negotiations with authorities, mortgages, conveyancing or other legal services attract an additional fee.

9   *Prototypes:* If designed for repetitive use and agreed beforehand they can be covered on a royalty basis.

10 *Site furniture and equipment:* Design and advice on the selection, inspection during fabrication, trials and instructions on use are not included.

11 *Multidisciplinary meetings:* Although co-ordination of the proposals of other consultants is included in the basic service, provision is also made for extra fees to be charged for attending multidisciplinary meetings.

12 *Public meetings:* The often time-consuming work of preparing material and attending public meetings to hear and/or give evidence is additional to the basic service.

13 *Works of art:* Any advice required on the selection, commissioning and installation of works of art are chargeable separately.

14 *Scientific development:* If research or trials are necessary to overcome problems where traditional systems are inadequate, this is considered additional to the basic service.

15 *Visits to nurseries:* The cost of visiting nurseries to check on the quality, size and health of plants, when time permits is always well worth while and is a recoverable extra.

Cost estimating and financial advice

While financial cost checks and approximate estimates, to ensure the cost of a project remains within the authorized expenditure, are included in the basic service, any detailed cost planning and cash flow analyses are not, neither are the preparation of schedules, bills of quantities or the re-measurement of work executed. The inspection of damage and negotiation of claims for the cost of reinstatement and making applications are all considered to be extra to the basic service.

Planning negotiations

Any exceptionally prolonged and detailed planning negotiations and all work in connection with the preparation and submission of appeals, including submission of proofs of evidence and appearing as an expert witness, are not part of the basic service, nor are submissions to other organizations such as the Royal Fine Art Commission, ground landlords and other matters such as those affecting rights of way, support and wayleaves.

Extra contract administration

While the work involved in advising the client on progress and compliance with the contract documents, issuing certificates, instructing and valuing variations is included in the basic service, frequent or constant attendance on site, the administration of other than lump sum contracts, the preparation of 'record' drawings and landscape management plans are not, or assisting a client's legal advisors in preparing and giving evidence, attending on solicitors, counsel and the courts in connection with litigation and arbitration.

Other consultants

Landscape consultants services are frequently included with those of other professions such as architects, engineers and quantity surveyors, when it is important to ensure that where these are provided from within the same organization, the fees charged are in accordance with those recommended by the relevant professional body.

Many of these additional services would in the past have been provided by the landscape consultant at no extra cost to the client, when obliged to follow the mandatory minimum fee scales. Now to comply with the mistaken belief of the Office of Fair Trading that these were not in the public interest and must now be no more than 'recommended', coupled with the insistence of PSA and some authorities that fees must be tendered in competition with other consultants, it is essential that whenever the need for any of these additional services arises or is thought likely to arise, it is pointed out to the client and a proper basis of remuneration agreed before the work is put in hand.

Forms of practice

Having qualified, landscape architects, managers and scientists have the choice of working in the public or private sector as an employee or in the case of the latter in a self-employed capacity. Most choose to work as an employee at least initially until they have consolidated their academic learning and gained further experience.

Public sector

The technical work of a landscape consultant either as a principal or an employee is no different in the public or private sector. The conditions under which the work is carried out do however differ in a few respects. In the public sector the services of landscape architects, managers and scientists are required in Central Government Offices such as PSA and DHSS and the Department of Transport, in the statutory authorities such as CEGB and health authorities, in development corporations, new towns and in local government at both county council and district level.

In the latter case chief officers are responsible to committees of elected members who lay down priorities, allocate funds and whose approval is necessary on all schemes before the work is put in hand. These committees and the staff in their respective departments have to comply with established council procedures and standing orders, particularly those affecting the invitation and acceptance of tenders, with alternatives and limits dependent on the amount of the expenditure involved (private consultants engaged by the council having also to follow the same procedures). The various committees, e.g. planning, housing, recreation, highways etc. are therefore the 'client', professional advice being provided either from employees working within the department concerned or more usually from a department of technical services including architects, engineers and quantity surveyors either working in single or multidisciplinary teams.

It is usually assumed that public sector projects are for the good of the community as a whole, free of individual and commercial interests and because of their responsibility for subsequent upkeep and maintenance, designed with due regard to both capital and revenue running costs.

Contracts of employment for all salaried staff are now required by law and to comply with the Contracts of Employment Act 1972 should cover at least:

1 The names of firm and individual concerned
2 Starting date of employment

3 Any probationary period
4 Job description and responsibilities
5 Salary and any other remuneration
6 Holidays
7 Pension scheme, LV and professional indemnity details
8 Sick leave entitlement
9 Reimbursable expenses
10 Trade union rights
11 Continuous professional development training and course entitlements
12 Competitions and spare time work
13 Copyright and royalties
14 Notice and references
15 Disciplinary rules
16 Grievances
17 Any other conditions.

If and when employees have sufficient continuity of private work to enable them to go into practice on a self-employed basis landscape consultants have a choice of six ways of practice.

As a sole practitioner

This is the only option when there is insufficient fee income envisaged to support more than one individual. The difficulty inherent in this arrangement (although often there is initially no alternative) is that due to fluctuations in work load or the postponement of projects there may well be long periods of inactivity which can only be overcome by taking in work subcontracted from other more busy practices, with the consequent legal problems that may arise as a consequence, not the least of which being the question of professional indemnity insurance.

There are however considerable tax advantages from the greater tax deductible expenses and allowances to the self-employed (even when working from home using only the kitchen table). Working on a self-employed full or even part-time basis does not necessarily have to start from the beginning of the fiscal year in April and the advice of a tax consultant is always advisable, even on this point alone, it often being advantageous to start later in the year.

Practice as a partnership

To even out the peaks in work load and to take advantage of the tax concessions most consultants arrange to practise, as soon as they can, as a 'partnership'. This is defined in the Partnership Act of 1980 as: 'the relationship which subsists between two or more persons carrying on a business in common with a view to profit'. This is not to say that they must 'make' a profit, indeed it is not unknown, although regrettable, for some partnerships from time to time to make a loss and still continue in being. The only legal requirement is the intention to make a profit. Sharing an office or staff does not necessarily constitute a partnership. Practising in partnership with another or others, who do not necessarily have to have the same qualifications or disciplines is also possible (provided they are not activities incompatible with their individual codes of professional conduct) and enables a practice to provide a more comprehensive service. Their liabilities in law however are total and to the full extent of their financial assets, property and homes without restriction of the limits of their liability individually or collectively in any way, it being considered this 'to concentrate the mind' in respect to their proper duty of care.

The main advantages of a partnership over practising as an individual are:

1 Financial responsibilities are spread over more than one individual.
2 Peaks and troughs in individual work loads can be evened out and executed more economically.
3 Accommodation, equipment, technical and secretarial resources can be shared.
4 Greater capital can be provided for work in progress and to minimize overdraft requirements.
5 The costs of 'practice promotion' can be shared.
6 Different skills and abilities can be incorporated into the practice at partnership level.

Partners cannot by definition draw a salary but must rely for remuneration on a share of the profits (which does not have to be on an equal basis) which may or may not be directly related to the capital they have in the firm. Often new partners joining an existing practice may agree to leave a proportion of their share of the profit in the firm to build up any capital they may have put in initially until they have gained parity with the existing partners and before they can become entitled to an equal share of the profit although this is not always compulsory.

Only when the capital in the firm is unequal is it normal for it to attract interest.

Salaried associates, even if entitled to a bonus or share of the profit by definition if receiving any salary, are not in law 'partners' even as 'junior' partners, the phrase 'salaried partner' being a legal contradiction in terms.

When the names of associates are included in the letterhead, to give due recognition of their status, they must be identified separately in the same way as should consultants, who are often retired partners, receiving a retainer or smaller share of the profit, and who are no longer legally liable for the actions of the partnership subsequent to their departure. They are however still liable for any actions by the partnership prior to their departure and so professional indemnity insurance must be maintained either by themselves or by the partnership to cover any claims that may subsequently be made even years later.

If the names of all the partners are not included in the name of the partnership it is advisable but no longer obligatory for the name of the practice to be registered as a business name.

Partnership agreements like any other contract should (if for no other reason than to establish their existence with the Inspector of Taxes) but do not have to, be in writing and should cover *inter alia:*

1 The name of the practice
2 Its address or addresses
3 Its bankers and who may sign cheques on the practice's behalf
4 Its accountants, whose opinion is usually final and binding in the event of any dispute between the partners and if not, to whom the matter should be referred
5 The minimum period of the partnership and arrangements for its dissolution in the event of an earlier disagreement
6 The initial capital to be provided by each partner and arrangements for the payment of interest if any
7 The division of profits and limit of monthly drawings
8 Prohibition or allowance for other activities if any
9 Maximum time off for holidays and illness
10 Any pension payments and arrangements for senior or retired partners
11 The exclusion of 'goodwill' from the assets of the practice (for tax reasons) and
12 Arrangements for any property to be used by the partnership.

The custom of including restrictions on the subsequent setting up in practice after dissolution within a certain distance is of no value, but arrangements for the retention of any clients introduced by a partner prior to his retirement (if they can be identified) may be useful.

Co-operatives

Similar in most respects to partnerships, co-operatives (in effect all members of the firm, either including or excluding secretarial staff)

27

would seem to offer advantages in encouraging individual identification with the financial prosperity of the practice but are difficult although not impossible to put into practice. There are a number of practical problems such as size, requirements for capital and distribution of profits, professional liability and indemnity insurance etc., but for those who value equal ownership, control, community needs and job satisfaction above the size of earnings and output, the effort to overcome them is often worthwhile.

Co-operatives are of two types: either those based on 'common' ownership principles where no one can build up any equity in the enterprise which they can sell or take away when they leave. These are the most common and are usually based on the Industrial Common Ownership Movement (ICOM) model rules.

Alternatively they are run under 'co-ownership' principles in which members acquire shares which earn a dividend but without earning additional voting rights and which members can sell back when they leave. Model rules have been produced by the Co-operative Development Agency (CDA) and Job Ownership Ltd (JOL) in which shareholdings can alter in value.

Both types of co-operative can be legalized by registering with the Registrar of Friendly Societies under the Industrial and Provident Societies Acts or with the Registrar of Companies as a company limited by guarantee of £1 per member (or if appropriate by shares). Both types of co-operative provide limitation of liability protection.

Group practice and consortia

Similar advantages in sharing economies in accommodation and administrative costs, sometimes by setting up a separate company solely for this purpose, are achieved by group practices and consortia. Each practice retains its individual identity but this arrangement does not have the advantages (or disadvantages!) of sharing profits and work load. Members of the Landscape Institute must not however misrepresent themselves as being qualified to perform the work of another division or grade of the Institute. Consortia are usually formed from practices of different disciplines, i.e. landscape consultants, architects, engineers and surveyors, each retaining the separate identity and practising as such from separate addresses in order to provide a client with a wider range of disciplines but with a single responsibility in the event of something going wrong and for a single fee. In both cases meticulous care is necessary in clarification of responsibilities in respect of professional indemnity insurance.

Practice as a company

Architects, solicitors and accountants have always been able to practise as a private company but until recently they have been prohibited from limiting their liability to their shareholding. The increasing number and value of professional indemnity claims, together with the enactment of the Latent Damage Act, 1986, has resulted in many consultants giving serious consideration to practising as a limited liability company in the UK in a similar way to that which has always been permitted overseas. Practising as a limited liability company does not however give automatic immunity from claims, a company still being liable to the full extent of its assets and individual directors still being personally liable if they can be identified (not difficult in the case of a professional practice).

There are however other advantages (although there are an equal number of disadvantages), the most important being that changing a partnership into a company is relatively easy, while reversing the process is often time consuming and painful. Companies must be registered under the Companies Act, 1948–81 with the Register of Companies which costs £50 and takes up to three months. They are distinct and separate entities who must submit their annual accounts to the Registrar and are entirely separate from their directors who are paid a salary, usually fixed by themselves, subject to PAYE. Not surprisingly they are responsible to their shareholders who in the case of a private company are limited to the directors themselves, each director being responsible to the extent of his own individual shareholding. This may be less than £100 but in the case of a landscape 'company' is usually equivalent to its capital, rarely less than £10 000 and often in excess of £50 000. The main advantage to a landscape practice is that when operating as a company it does not have to distribute all its profits (and therefore pay tax on them) to its directors. It does however have to pay tax, possibly at 60 per cent as corporation tax on undistributed profits. However, when operating as a partnership, practices have to include in their accounts an amount for the estimated value of 'work in progress' which in certain circumstances can achieve the same effect of evening out the peaks and troughs of annual fee income.

The actual management of a practice run as a company will probably be little different from that run as a partnership. Monthly meetings of partners chaired by a senior partner are replaced by monthly board meetings of the directors under the chairman assisted by a 'company' secretary with an annual general meeting of shareholders in accordance with the Companies Act.

Partners and directors are usually working partners and executive directors and rarely are decisions made on the basis of voting rights, it being usual to rely on a consensus view.

It is unlikely that the ability to practise as a limited company, with non-executive directors and shareholders providing capital from the listed or unlisted securities market, will arise in the landscape professions for all but the largest practices (as is beginning to occur with architects) for some years to come.

Simultaneous practice

Members of the Landscape Institute, while always being permitted to work on a salaried basis, or as consultants on a fee basis, for landscape contractors may now also be directors without loss of professional status or membership, 'provided always that they inform the client in writing at the outset of the full extent of their interest.' This means that they can at the same time be both landscape consultants and directors of a company or organization trading for example as landscape contractors (particularly those offering a design and build service) or nurserymen. Since they can also, and sometimes must, appear with their professional qualifications on the notepaper of each, it is considered advisable for there to be two quite separate notepapers so that the client is fully aware without any possible doubt of the particular responsibilities and loyalties of the person with whom he is dealing at any one time.

2
The Law Relating to the Landscape

Common Law

The general principles of law and legal concepts

English law has its origins in a combination of Saxon and Norman law (as distinct from the law in France and Scotland which is derived from Roman Law). 'Common Law' has never been written down or enacted but following the Norman Conquest in 1066 derived from Henry II developing a system common to the whole country. It was based on the judicial decisions of itinerant judges and where Common Law was inapplicable, the concept of Equity was applied by the application of rules requiring a specific performance of a remedy when the payment of damages would not result in an adequate solution to the problem, i.e. to achieve an 'equitable solution'. Both Common Law and Equity are still applicable today although there are no longer different courts for each, and the judgements of both are based on previous decisions of the courts i.e. 'Case' law.

Changes in the basis on which these judgements are made can however be brought about by enabling Acts of Parliament which may lay down general principles leaving the meaning of the words they contain to be interpreted where necessary by the courts, but who do not however have the power to change the words themselves. The English courts work on the basis of contestorial procedures and do not themselves conduct an inquiry to ascertain the facts. Everyone is subject to the same laws.

Criminal offences are against the State, whether damage has arisen or not, and involve prosecution and punishment by fine or imprisonment, to be decided by a magistrate or crown court judge depending on the severity of the alleged offence. *Civil cases* on the other hand affect an individual whose rights have been infringed and whose claim following the issue of a writ may result in his receiving such compensation as the county, crown or High Court may decide he is entitled to. In the latter cases, a jury may be involved with the right of appeal to the Court of Appeal and the House of Lords.

Personal property only affects goods, the possession of which can be proof of ownership, whereas real property is land of which possession is not prima-facie proof of ownership, and which may involve intangible interests such as a right of way.

Easement interests may however be acquired by an easement, either orally or in writing, covering, for example, such items as drain runs, footpaths and daylight over another's land (but not views or privacy), any infringement of which constitutes a nuisance and can be remedied by an application to the courts for an injunction restraining the offender. Conversely the establishment of an interest can be prevented by restrictions under a covenant, which once entered into can rarely be easily set aside.

Natural rights

Common Law recognizes three natural rights protecting the land against nuisance, the right of support from neighbouring land, the right to prevent interference with the supply of water by either pollution or excessive extraction and the right to light.

The right to support

The right to support includes the restriction on loss of support from adjoining land including that arising from excavation, recontouring or the foundations of adjoining buildings although this does not extend to loads imposed by a new building, i.e. while support of the land from an adjoining site is protected that of an adjoining building is not, neither can there be any restriction on an alteration to the existing water table by pumping. These restrictions however refer only to natural rights which are always subject to amendments by mutually agreed easements permitting the limited use of another's land without actually taking part of it.

Rights to water

Rights to water are protected provided it runs in a defined channel, otherwise a landowner can extract as much as he requires for ordinary purposes (provided he returns the same quantity and quality) irrespective of the effect on adjoining land. Rights of water are however often modified by statutes imposed by Acts of Parliament such as the Rivers Act, 1951 and the Water Resources Act, 1963. This inevitably affects such activities as horticultural irrigation and to a lesser degree water cooling but not uses such as electrical generation.

The right to light

A landowner cannot normally prevent the erection of buildings which overlook his property or spoil his view. These can only be secured by a covenant and to prevent the acquisition of a right to light he must now register an objection under the Rights of Light Act, 1959 instead of erecting a screen as was previously necessary. In any case an adjoining owner is only entitled to sufficient uninterrupted light such as that which is required for the ordinary purposes of inhabitants or any business of the tenement according to the ordinary notions of mankind (*Colls* v. *Home and Colonial Stores*, 1906). In similar circumstances – a neighbour was required to remove a caravan and a closeboarded fence which blocked the light to a greenhouse in a garden in Rochdale (*Allen* v. *Greenwood*, 1980).

Nuisance

This, whether public, private or statutory, involves an 'indirect' interference to people's rights or property. 'Public' nuisance is a criminal offence and 'has to involve a sufficient number of persons to constitute a class of the public' (Lord Denning) when either the Attorney General, local authority, or an individual, can bring the proceedings provided they can prove that the nuisance was foreseeable.

'Private nuisance' covers the effect on the reasonable enjoyment of the land of a single individual by another individual from nuisances such as smell, noise, or the vibrations from an industrial process, a nearby disco or shop. The court will decide if the interference is unreasonable and, if appropriate, what compensation is due.

'Statutory nuisance' arises when the alleged offence is controlled by statute, e.g. the Public Health Act of 1936, the Clean Air Acts of 1956 and 1968 and the Control of Pollution Act of 1974. Again the action can be brought by the Crown or an individual, but it is more usually the local authority.

Trespass

This arises if the interference with the rights of an individual is 'direct', i.e. actual entry or an encroachment, and involves direct 'injury' to people, their goods, or more usually land – it must be done intentionally, even if in the mistaken belief that no trespass was involved and no actual harm has been caused. Dumping rubbish, encroachment of a building over a boundary, leaning a ladder against another's building, growing a

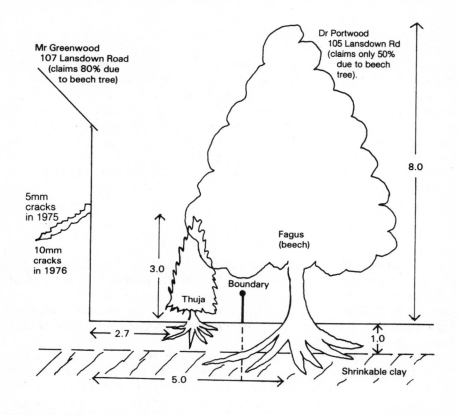

Mr Greenwood
107 Lansdown Road
(claims 80% due
to beech tree)

Dr Portwood
105 Lansdown Rd
(claims only 50%
due to beech
tree).

8.0

5mm
cracks
in 1975

10mm
cracks
in 1976

Fagus
(beech)

3.0

Boundary

Thuja

← 2.7 →

1.0

← 5.0 →

Shrinkable clay

Figure 2.1 Trespass by tree roots

creeper on another's wall, fixing to or painting are all examples of
trespass. Trespass with branches growing over an adjoining owner's
boundary or roots growing under cause special problems in that the
adjoining owner may cut off the offending branches or roots without
prior reference to the owner providing he does not go onto the owner's
land without permission.

An interesting example of trespass resulting in damage to an adjoining
owner's property arising from tree roots and the establishment of legal
responsibility is that of Mr Greenwood (see Figure 2.1). Mr Greenwood
bought his house in 1971 and after the dry summer of 1975, 5mm cracks
appeared in the walls, following the dry winter and further dry summer,
in 1976 these cracks increased to 10mm. This damage resulted in the
need for remedial works to the foundations costing £11 382 which were

carried out in 1979. Mr Greenwood had a 3m high Thuja growing 2.7m from his house, but the adjoining owner, who had lived there since 1965 had an 8m high beech tree growing 5m away from the house. Unknown to both of them, there was a layer of shrinkable clay 1m beneath the surface of the ground.

The case came before Judge Fallon in the High Court in Bristol in 1985, who, having accepted evidence that because of the Thuja only 50 per cent of the damage was due to the Fagus, ruled that because there was no way in which either of the owners could have known of the risk, there was therefore no reason for any of them to have taken any precautions to prevent the damage that occurred. Under the circumstances therefore the respective insurance companies involved should share the cost of the necessary repairs to the foundations equally between them.

Negligence

Contractual negligence can only arise when damage can be proven as a consequence of the breach of a contractual duty of care. The obligations of a landscape consultant and a landscape contractor under contract, written or oral, are relatively simple, being covered by the meaning of the words expressly stated or implied in the contract concerned, or occasionally the meaning behind them or arising from common usage.

Tortuous negligence arises as a civil wrong covering a legal duty owed to people generally. The position under 'tort' is complicated being derived from principles going back many years and is enshrined in a series of cases starting with *Rylands* v. *Fletcher* in 1866, when two Lancashire mill owners had a reservoir built and the water escaped flooding an adjoining colliery.

It was then held that if it can be established firstly that there was an 'escape of a dangerous thing' onto another's land (such as water, spoil, inflammable substances and vibration) and secondly the thing or operation was man made, then the liability was a 'strict liability' and it was not necessary to prove negligence or lack of duty of care. This liability was not however 'absolute' as it would be if it arose from an act of God, or the negligence of the plaintiff. To establish 'strict' liability it is therefore necessary to prove that:

(*a*) there must be an accumulation and escape of the nuisance,
(*b*) it must be man made, and
(*c*) it must be potentially damaging,

even if the perpetrator did not know of the danger and nor was he negligent. In all other cases reliance must be placed on liability under statute or proven lack of the duty of care.

Liability under tort was taken further by *Donohue* v. *Stevenson* in 1932 when, as a result of Mrs Donohue having drunk some ginger beer made by Stevenson in Paisley, from a bottle with a decomposed snail in it, it was held that everyone owes a duty to take all reasonable precautions to ensure the safety of anyone else who might be likely to be affected by his actions whether they were in a contractual relationship or not.

The responsibility for negligent acts was extended in 1964 when notwithstanding an express disclaimer of responsibility in *Hedley Byrne* v. *Heller* a firm of merchant bankers, Heller, was held to be responsible to a firm of advertising agents, Hedley Byrne, for the economic loss caused not only by a negligent act, but for careless advice as well.

The responsibility of local authorities for compliance with Building Regulations was established in 1971 with *Dutton* v. *Bognor Regis* when Mrs Dutton, the second purchaser of a house built on a rubbish tip, not being therefore able to sue in contract, sued Bognor Regis Council in tort for defective foundations which they themselves had inspected and approved, both the plans and on site, for a previous owner. This was confirmed in the House of Lords in 1977 by *Anns* v. *LB of Merton,* but may now be less certain in view of the opinion expressed in *Sir Lindsay Parkinson* v. *Peabody* (1985) that a building inspector employed by a local authority has only a duty of care to the occupant and not an absentee building owner. The case of *IBA* v. *EMI Electronics BICC* (1980), in an appeal to the House of Lords, established that there was an implied responsibility on the main contractor (EMI) for the provision of the complete structure, including the design, of a television mast which had been built and designed by a subcontractor (BICC) and which had subsequently collapsed in a storm. This was confirmed a year later in 1981 by Judge Newey in *Holland, Hannen and Cubitt* v. *WHTO* with regard to defective windows that 'there were implied terms of the contract that the building work should be carried out in a good and workmanlike manner with proper skill and care, with materials reasonably fit for their purpose'.

In 1982 in the case between *Junior Books Ltd* and *Veitchi CI Ltd* a specialist flooring contractor, who had laid a floor in a book factory in Grangemouth in 1970 and which broke up after two years, was held to be liable in tort to Junior Books Ltd, since although there was no direct contract between them, they were sufficiently close and that there was no limitation of liability in existence. It also established that in spite of there being no physical harm, they were entitled to any economic loss they could prove they had suffered.

Pirelli v. *Oscar Faber* in 1982 covered a different, if not more important aspect, when a factory chimney designed and erected in 1969 was found to be defective. The House of Lords held that an action in tort was statute barred because more than six years had elapsed since the defects had occurred in 1970, not withstanding the fact that they had not been discovered until 1978.

Limitation

There is no limitation on the right of action in tort or contract law, but it may be raised by a defendant. The Limitation Act, 1980 provides that an action on a simple contract must be brought within six years and under seal within twelve years, from the date on which the breach of contract occurred (three years in the case of personal injury).

In the case of tort however, the cause of action arises not from the date when the contractor finished the defective work and not the date on which the owner became aware or ought to have become aware of damage, but the date on which the damage came into existence (*Pirelli* v. *Oscar Faber*, 1983). The courts having come to this decision however considered it to be unsatisfactory and enacted the Latent Damage Act, 1986.

The Latent Damage Act, 1986

Although stated as intended to cover all forms of latent damage, it was clear from the examples used during the debates, both in the House of Commons and the House of Lords that the primary intention of the Act, was to cover the construction industry. Under this Act, for claims that cannot be made under contract, claimants now have a longstop of 15 years in which to claim from the date of discovery of the breach of the duty of care (not completion of the works) while defendants now have the protection of the limitation of six years from the date of damage and three years from the date of discovery of a latent defect.

Restrictive covenants

Restrictive covenants occur when the owner of one piece of land or building agrees (covenants) that it will not now or in the future be used for particular purposes, the restriction being for the benefit of those who own or occupy another in the vicinity. For instance in the transfer or conveyance to state that they might not carry out any business in a private residence, not put up a shed in the garden without consent, nor park a car, caravan, or boat in the front garden, which might not be covered by existing planning legislation. Restrictive covenants do not become incorporated in the title of a property and are principally only an agreement between the vendor and present and future purchasers. As such, covenants may be removed by agreement for which consideration may be given, but it is necessary to establish that they are no longer applicable or relevant. This is often difficult and the originators are often difficult to trace. It has therefore become common practice now to insure against the risk of a subsequent action by a beneficiary unexpectedly appearing and attempting to enforce the covenant or demand compensation.

Detailed provisions for the common good both criminal and civil are covered by the government Acts of Parliament or statutes which in most cases cover only the general principles, leaving the detailed legislation and procedures to be covered by other regulations, statutory instruments and general development orders.

Statute Law

The Town and Country Planning Act, 1971

Although there has been planning legislation in existence in the UK since 1947 and subsequent Acts were passed in 1959, 1962 and 1968, current legislation is covered by the 1971 Act. In this, permission is required for any development of land, development being defined in draconian terms in section 22(1) as:

1 the carrying out of building operations, engineering operations, mining operations or other operations in, or over, or under land; or
2 making any material change in use of any buildings or other land.

Section 290 defines building operations as including 'rebuilding operations, structural alterations to buildings and other operations normally undertaken by a person carrying on business as a builder' and a building as including 'any structure or erection and any part of a building but does not include plant or machinery'.

Under such definitions, it can be seen that there is little that can be undertaken without the necessity of a planning application for consent for development.

Building operations
Section 22 states that certain building operations within a building do not constitute development, i.e. if they are internal and do not affect the exterior of a building or buildings within the curtilage (i.e. site boundaries)

of a dwelling house; those that are incidental to its enjoyment, such as for pets, a car, or a caravan in the garden, or a room used as an office; or denotations on the use of land for agriculture or forestry including the use of any buildings, for such purposes. Therefore erecting a 16-foot coal hopper on wheels; repairs and maintenance such as repointing, retiling and repainting; and the removal of cornices and garden ornaments (with certain exceptions) are not building operations but laying tarmac on a forecourt, erecting a flagpole or building a model village are.

Engineering operations (other than the formation or laying out of means of access to highways) are not defined, but any works involving large-scale earth moving, such as are involved in golf courses and water features are clearly included, as was that of the Georgian ha-ha in Richmond Old Deer Park in 1957; widening an existing access a few inches by 'shifting a few cubic yards of soil with a digger and a lorry' was not (Lord Pearson, *Coleshill District Investments* v. *MOHLG*, 1969). Mining operations are not defined other than to exclude peat, but top soil, gravel, sand, clay and stone extraction are considered to be development as are excavations from old tips, slag heaps and railway embankments.

Enforcement proceedings to stop unauthorized operations must be brought by the planning authority within four years, but there is no such immunity for material change of use except where the change involves a single dwelling house.

Material change in use
Section 22 lists three instances of a material change of use: 1, if a building is used as two or more separate dwelling houses; 2, if the deposit of refuse or waste material on land, already used for that purpose, covers more of the surface area or increases the height above that of the land adjoining the site, and 3, to display advertisements on any external part of a building not normally used for that purpose.

In 1972 the Use Classes Order (SI 1972 No. 1385) was brought into effect classifying into 18 different categories the various uses of buildings and land to which they could be put, and within which changes could be made without the need for planning consent, unless as the result of an application the authority restricted its use to one particular activity. These use classes were revised in 1987 to provide more flexibility in the use of business premises in industrial and commercial areas, with new provisions for snack bars, cafes and 'take aways' and regulating the use of open land.

It was left to the planning authorities to decide if the change of use was material or not as a question of fact, if there was:

1 A physical change in the use of the land
2 A significant alteration in the quantity or quality of the activity, or
3 A change relevant from the viewpoint of planning.

This covered not only a physical alteration in site boundaries but also a significant intensification of use in proportion to the site as a whole and the period of time involved.

Permitted development

De minimis non curat lex – the law does not concern itself with trifles. To reduce the burden on planning authorities, the government introduced a general development order SI 1977 No. 289 – 'Permitted Development'. This set out development which was to be permitted without the necessity for a formal application for planning and consent:

1 Limited enlargement or improvement of a dwelling house
2 Forming, laying out, and constructing a means of access to a highway
3 Painting the exterior of any building or work other than for the purposes of advertisement, announcement or direction

followed by 23 different classes of work.

Class I: Development within the curtilage of a dwelling house of not more than 50m³ which does not increase the size above 115m³, the height above the highest part of the roof and does not project beyond the front wall facing the highway. This includes a garage, stable, loose box, coach house and a building for domestic poultry, bees, pets, animals, birds and other livestock not more than 3 metres high or 4 metres to the ridge, porches not more than 2m² not less than 2 metres from the front boundary, a hardstanding for vehicles and oil storage tanks less than 3 metres high and containing less than 3500 litres.

Class II: Sundry minor operations covering new gates, fences, walls and other means of enclosure not more than 1 metre high adjoining a vehicular highway and 2 metres high else-where; the maintenance, improvement or alteration of other gates, fences, walls and means of enclosure, provided they do not increase the height above that which is appropriate.

The remaining permitted 21 classes cover certain changes of use, temporary buildings, recreational organizations, agricultural buildings, industrial development, repairs to private roads and services, war damaged buildings, local authority and private Acts, drainage, highway, water, sewerage authorities and statutory undertakers, mineral workings, the National Coal Board, aerodromes and caravan sites.

Development plans

It is sometimes unkindly said that the activities of planning authorities are entirely negative. This is certainly untrue in the case of their obligation to produce a structure plan laying down their policy and strategy for the area and their ability to prepare local plans to show development proposals of any part within the area. These do not however have to be followed slavishly and planning authorities have the discretion to diverge from the plan if circumstances change or they consider there to be good planning reasons for so doing.

The preparation of structure plans began in 1971, and took 14 years until 1985 for county and district authorities to complete, during which time less than 10 per cent of the country was covered by local plans. The DoE has since suggested that structure plans should now be abolished and sole responsibility for both structure and local plans be transferred to the district councils.

Planning applications

Applications for permission to develop land are made on a prescribed form provided by the planning authority. Since the Local Government Planning and Land Act (1980) this must be accompanied by a fee calculated in accordance with SI 1985 No. 1182, Town and Country Planning (Fees for Applications and Deemed Applications) Regulations 1985, the period within which a decision must be given not starting to run until the correct amount has been paid. Planning authorities then have eight weeks in which to approve or reject the application, in the absence of which, applicants may 'deem the application refused' and appeal to the Secretary of State for the Environment to decide on the application instead of the planning authority. Once having done this the matter is taken out of the hands of the planning authority who are not then allowed to issue a consent even if they would otherwise have done so. Applicants may however agree to the period being extended, if so requested by the planning authority and in practice planning authorities usually assume this to be the case unless they are told otherwise by the applicant. Planning applications may be made either in full or in outline. In the case of the latter the application for consent is for the principle only leaving aspects such as siting, design, landscaping, external appearance or means of access to be considered as 'reserved matters', the consent being granted subject to the condition that these are subsequently submitted for approval. Once a planning consent has been granted the benefit attaches to the land and any subsequent owners, but the development must usually be started within five years unless other time limits are laid down.

Planning conditions

DoE Circular 1/85 gives guidance to planning authorities and gives standard clauses for use in such instances including clauses 20 and 21, dealing specifically with landscape matters. Should the applicant object to any of the conditions or a refusal by the planning authority to approve any reserved matters subsequently submitted to discharge a condition imposed, the applicant may appeal to the Secretary of State in the same way as he can against the refusal of consent. Conditions must not be unreasonable and, to be enforceable, the applicant must have the power to comply with them. Authorities may however enter into special statutory covenants to cover items for which they cannot impose conditions within the consent. Provision for such an agreement is covered in section 52 of the 1971 Act which are therefore commonly known as 'Section 52 Agreements'!

Appeals

Appeals against the refusal of an application or the imposition of conditions must be made to the Secretary of State within six months. He then considers the whole application as if it had been submitted to him direct in the first place, and he can attach an entirely different set of conditions if he so chooses. The Secretary of State, who has a separate department in DoE to deal with appeals, as soon as he has received an appeal form appoints an inspector who issues directions for a public or private hearing, or for written representations only if after consultation with the parties it is considered these will suffice. The rules for the conduct of the appeals are laid down in SI 1971 Nos. 419 and 420. They provide for any interested party to give evidence in support of or against the application if they so wish. After the hearing the inspector visits the sites, accompanied by the parties, who can then only draw his attention to facts and are not permitted at that stage to express an opinion, after which he makes his decision in writing. Appeals take up to six months for a decision depending on the complexity of the case which is final and binding save only for an appeal to the High Court on a point of law.

Listed buildings

Part I of the Civic Amenities Act, 1967 provided for the listing of buildings of special historic or amenity value built before 1939. This was provided for in section 54(1) of the 1971 Town and Country Planning (T&CP) Act and further elaborated by the T&CP Listed Buildings and Buildings in Conservation Areas: SI 1972 No. 1362. This prevented any work to the interior or exterior of a building so listed which would affect its character without prior consent involving a special separate application to the local authority (other than work of purely maintenance, repair and reinstatement and buildings in use for ecclesiastical purposes).

The lists were revised in 1986 and now include over 360 000 buildings in three grades. Grade I covers buildings of exceptional interest (about 2 per cent of those listed), Grade II* of particular importance and more than of special interest (about 4 per cent) and Grade II of special interest warranting every effort being made to preserve them. All buildings built before 1700, most of those before 1840 and some of those built before 1914 which are of definite quality and character are included.

Special regard has to be paid not only to the building, but its setting also. Planning officers must therefore be consulted before making any alteration including landscape work within the curtilage (i.e. the site) of a listed building. Buildings are chosen for architectural, planning, social and economic or historic reason, because of technical innovation, or their group value.

Conservation areas

The Civic Amenities Act, 1967 also provided for the establishment of 'areas of special architectural or historic interest the character of which it is desirable to preserve or enhance'. This was incorporated in section 277 of the 1971 Town and Country Planning Act and requires permission to be applied for to demolish buildings in such areas. Provision is also made in article 4 for the exclusion of permitted development in conservation areas if the planning authority so decides. This is normally done in consultation with local amenity societies and residents, the latter often being understandably reluctant to accept the restriction on the freedom of their ability to alter the colour of their front doors, park cars in their front gardens and convert their roof spaces into extra bedrooms.

Part II of the 1967 Civic Amenities Act provided also for the protection of trees against 'cutting down, topping, lopping, wilfully damaging or destroying' and later 'uprooting' a tree, unless the authority had been notified in writing six weeks previously and had then raised no objection. This enabled an authority to initiate procedure to protect a tree by making a tree preservation order. If a tree was indicated as to be removed on a drawing included in a planning application in a conservation area then the removal of the tree is deemed to be granted also.

Highways Act, 1980

The ordinary citizen has a right to navigate and fish in tidal waters and freedom to travel on the public highway whether it is a motorway or just a footpath on public or private land and Part X of the Act therefore restricts the right of a farmer to plough up a public footpath. Extinguishment or diversion of public rights of way can be affected under either the 1980 Highways Act or the 1971 Town and Country Planning Act. In the case of the Highways Act an extinguishing order can only be made if it appears expedient on the grounds that pedestrian or vehicular access is not needed for public use. A diversion order can be made if it is expedient to do so either in the interests of the owner of the land, the lessee or occupier or the public so long as it is not substantially less convenient to the public. Powers are however granted to local authorities under the Town and Country Planning Acts in respect of footpaths and bridleways to make orders to stop up or divert public rights of way affected by development for which planning permission has been granted. Footpaths or byways affected by a local planning authority development order require notification to and confirmation by the Secretary of State if they are opposed.

Tree preservation orders

Detailed procedures were set out in SI 1969 No. 17, T&CP Tree Preservation Order Regulations and excludes fruit trees (is a walnut tree – Juglans regia – a fruit tree?) and those whose main stem is less than 75mm in diameter, measured 1 metre above the ground. Breach of a tree preservation order may be dealt with as a criminal offence summarily or on indictment. This was included in section 60 1971 T&CP Act permitting local authorities to make tree preservation orders on individual trees, groups of trees or woodlands in the interests of amenity. No consent is needed however for work on dying, dead or dangerous protected trees or for work necessary to prevent or relieve a nuisance. It must be appreciated however that what an applicant considers to be a nuisance may not be considered in the same way by the local authority.

Scheduled monument consent

Under the Ancient Monuments and Archaeological Areas Act, 1971, Part II, the Secretary of State keeps a schedule of monuments and areas where work cannot be carried out without the prior consent of the DoE Monuments are considered to be buildings unoccupied except by a caretaker and include the remains of buildings and caves. Archaeological areas present particular difficulties since the occupier may be unaware of their existence and landscape consultants should always take particular care to check with the local authority before commencing work on open land where they may possibly exist. Section 35 of the Act requires anyone intending to disturb the ground, or carry out flooding or tipping to give the district council six weeks' notice of an intention to commence 'operations' which includes 'ground disturbance, flooding and tipping'. The local authority then has to reply within four weeks if it intends to carry out any archaeological excavation itself which must be completed within a further four and a half months. This has been interpreted to include also planting of trees and shrubs when schedules of plant material may need to be submitted for approval.

The Historic Gardens Register

The National Heritage Act, 1983, combined the Historic Buildings Council, Ancient Monuments Board and the DoE Department of Ancient Monuments and Historic Buildings into the Historic Buildings and Monuments Commission for England, now known as 'English Heritage'. It also provided for the preparation of a Historic Gardens Register to be completed on a county basis by the end of 1986. Inclusion on the Register, which grades gardens dating before 1939 into Grade I – of exceptional interest, Grade II* – of great quality and Grade II – of special interest, is similar to those for listed buildings; but it does not have to be the same grade as the building it surrounds and does not have to have the same planning restrictions. Its purpose is only to identify their merit to owners, local authorities and government departments and to assist in conservation measures and grant aid to which it might not otherwise be thought they were entitled.

Building Regulations

Originating from the earlier Victorian and the Public Health Acts 1936 and 1961, the current building regulations are now covered by the enabling 1984 Building Act implemented by the much shorter Building Regulations, SI 1985 No. 1065. They now lay down only the principles necessary to achieve reasonable requirements for public health and safety, incorporating by reference 'approved documents' e.g. British Standards and Codes of Practice, 'deemed to satisfy provisions' and certificates of compliance by 'approved persons' other than the local authority.

The regulations cover the erection, extensions and material alterations to buildings including alterations to services and fittings and repairs (i.e. the replacement or making good of existing parts of buildings). Seven classes of exempt buildings are set out in schedule 3 (similar to but not the same as permitted planning development). These include buildings controlled under other legislation, buildings not frequented by people, such as garages, greenhouses and agricultural buildings, temporary buildings and mobile homes, ancillary buildings, small detached buildings and extensions. Buildings by statutory undertakers, school buildings, buildings for mines and quarries and those for government departments were originally exempt from the provisions (although expected to comply with the principles), but this has now been changed.

Notice of an intention to carry out work covered by the regulations must be given to the local authority under regulation 12 at least 48 hours in advance (except for shops and offices). Alternatively full plans may be deposited under regulation 13. Applicants do not have to wait until plans have been passed before starting work and more plans may be asked for to assist in the inspection of the work on site. Plans must be passed in whole or rejected within five weeks (or if agreed within a further three weeks). Work that contravenes the regulations must be taken down or altered to comply unless it has been built in accordance with plans that have already been passed.

Irrespective of what is shown on the contract (as distinct from building regulations) drawings, the obligation to comply with the regulations is always with the contractor, but most standard forms require the contractor to notify the consultant if he finds any divergence and for the cost of all alterations to comply with the regulations to be recoverable from the client.

Value added tax

With very few exceptions all landscape construction work is liable to value added tax at the standard rate including, as from 1 June 1984, work of alterations and improvements (except alterations to listed buildings which are still exempt). HM Customs and Excise Note 708 – 'Construction Industry' was revised and reissued in October 1987 and in addition to detailed guidance to differentiate between new work to buildings (zero rated) and alterations (standard rated), listed in addition to construction and alteration work within the grounds or garden of a private residence, the construction or alterations of swimming pools and tennis courts already taxed at the standard rate. Although 'site restoration' defined as 'the clearance of rubble, levelling, providing top soil and laying grass' on zero rated projects was also zero rated, 'planting trees, shrubs and elaborate ornamental work' was specifically identified as taxable. Several new sections have been added and described in detail: 'Garden Buildings' in section 7, constructing fish ponds and rockeries added to 'landscaping; planting of flowers, shrubs and trees', in section 13, and formal gardens to domestic civil engineering in section 16.

Since April 1989, VAT at the standard rate has become due on all building and civil engineering work, alterations, repairs and maintenance and new buildings except individual houses and flats, buildings used for communal residential purposes, buildings used by charities for non business purposes including new churches and 'approved' alterations to listed buildings. The revised arrangements are set out in the revised HM Customs & Excise Note No 708/2/89.

3

The Law Relating to the Protection of the Countryside

The Alkali and Works Regulations Act, 1906

This provided for the supervision of any industrial premises likely to emit specific noxious or offensive gases but did not become really effective until the creation of the Health and Safety at Work Executive and its inspectorate under the Health and Safety at Work Act of 1974.

The Public Health Act, 1936

The control of pollution was originally effected by the 1936 Public Health Act covering buildings, the condition of which caused a hazard to the health of the occupants and the emission of industrial dust or effluvia. If in the opinion of the district authority this occurs, it may serve an abatement notice on the perpetrator under section 93, requiring him to take such action as is necessary to deal with it. If he does not comply a magistrates court can fine the offender and make a nuisance order requiring him to take the necessary action and impose further fines for each day the nuisance continues, following which, the authority may take such steps as are necessary to control the nuisance and recover the cost from the perpetrator. This procedure is also available to any member of the public even if the perpetrator is the local authority itself and can apply to anything from the smell from pig swill to damp in a local authority flat.

National Parks and Access to the Countryside Act, 1949

National Parks only came into existence with the National Parks and Access to the Countryside Act in 1949, creating a National Parks Commission (now the Countryside Commission) under a Chairman appointed by the Secretary of State for the Environment. It is responsible for:

> extensive tracts of country in England and Wales designated for their natural beauty and the opportunities which they offer for public open air recreation – having regard both to their character and their position in relation to centres of population.

The first National Park was the Peak District designated in 1950, followed by Brecon Beacons in 1955. As the British National Parks remain largely in private hands the Commission exercises its responsibilities by stricter planning controls (changes of use authorized by SI 1971 No. 289 are not allowed) and by access arrangements. In 1981 these were strengthened by SI No. 246 restricting height and volumes. Part IV of the Act makes provision for the creation of long-distance recreational routes and Part V for public access to open country consisting wholly or predominantly of mountain, moor, heath, down, cliff or foreshore including any banks, barriers, dune, flat or other land adjacent to the foreshore for which the authority must prepare maps.

Under section 60, agreements and orders can be made permitting the public to enter the land concerned without the owner being as responsible as he would be for other authorized visitors and who become liable for trespass only if they damage walls, fences, hedges, gates or engage in activities which would harm livestock, wild animals or plants, deposit rubbish, light fires or drive vehicles on to his land.

Areas of Outstanding Natural Beauty (AONBs)

Section 87 of the Act also authorized AONBs and as a consequence large areas of the countryside, The Chilterns, Cotswolds, Dorset and the Norfolk Broads, were designated, much to the irritation of local farmers. It provides similar restrictions on development, and for management agreements to control farming methods. Local and county authorities are required also to consult the Countryside Commission before preparing development plans which cover any of the areas designated.

The Clean Air Acts, 1956 and 1968

These covered the prevention of 'dark' smoke from private homes and industrial premises by the creation of smokeless control areas in which burning non-smokeless fuel was an offence. By the inclusion of grants covering the cost of converting grates from one type of fuel to another this was largely effective in bringing about the disappearance of the dense fogs of Victorian times and smoke stained buildings from the inner cities.

The Weeds Act, 1959

This provides powers for the Ministry of Agriculture to instruct occupiers of land to eliminate noxious weeds such as thistles, ragwort and docks from their land and to recover the cost from those responsible.

The Caravan and Control of Development Act, 1960

This provides for sites on which planning consent has been given to be maintained so that they are fit for habitation. Licences can improve conditions in the interests of the occupants, any other classes of persons or the public at large by imposing restrictions on the number and sizes of the caravans and their position (but not construction), fire, safety and sanitary provisions and 'any steps for preserving or enhancing the amenity of the site including the planting and replanting of trees and bushes'.

Commons Registration Act, 1965

This required all Common Land to be registered including both urban public open space and rural village greens and for land not claimed under the Act to be taken over by the local authority concerned.

The Countryside Act, 1968

This gives local authorities power to create country parks on their own land or that which they may compulsorily acquire, and to provide amenities on common land particularly encouraging 'water recreation' including not only rivers, canals and expanses of water through which they run but also sufficient land for access on foot, by boat and for picnicking.

The Water Act, 1973

Following the reorganization of local authorities in 1972 all water authorities were combined in ten authorities based on the natural watershed, irrespective of local authority boundaries. They are responsible also for sewerage although delegating local sewerage collection to the district councils and local distribution to the private statutory water companies.

Land drainage is covered separately by the Land Drainage Act, 1976. The Water Resources Act, 1963 restricts fishing and any abstraction in excess of 1000 gallons only to those who have been so licensed.

The Control of Pollution Act, 1974

This Act was intended to cover water pollution but as the relevant sections have not yet been brought into force, this is still left to be covered by the Rivers (Prevention of Pollution) Acts, 1951 and 1962.

Its primary effect has therefore been the control of noise particularly that emanating from building sites whereby district councils may issue noise abatement notices, which if not complied with can be enforced by a magistrates noise abatement order, as can an application by a member of the public. District councils may also create noise abatement zones, setting maximum noise levels enforced by noise restriction notices.

The Wildlife and Countryside Act, 1981 (Sites of Special Scientific Interest)

This Act excluded major development from AONBs and gave greater prominence to Sites of Special Scientific Interest (SSSIs) designated under the National Parks and Access to the Countryside Act 1949 by making the Nature Conservancy Council responsible for identifying and notifying local authorities, the Secretary of State, owners and occupiers, of areas of land of SSSI for flora, fauna or geological reasons. It requires listing any 'operations' which may damage the features and requires the occupier to give three months' notice of his intention to carry out any such operation. A planning consent overrides any restriction but the Secretary of State has powers to forbid any operations threatening the survival of any animal or plant of national interest or covered by international obligations. It is a pity he does not seem to have considered badgers within this category, whose survival still seems threatened by MAFF.

The Act also enables the Nature Conservancy Council to designate areas of foreshore or sea-bed as marine nature reserves to be managed by the Council for conservation or research.

Under Part III of the Act, county and borough councils are required to maintain definitive maps and descriptions of public rights of way including bridle-ways and public footpaths over private land. The maps are conclusive evidence of an existing right of way which may be extended and new ones created by the public, and which the local authority must record. Section 59 of the Act makes it an offence to keep on land crossed by a public right of way, bulls, older than ten months unless they are non-dairy breed left at large with cows or heifers.

Local Government and Planning (Amendment) Act, 1981

Amends existing provisions to enforce tree planting by developers to ameliorate the effect on the locality.

Town and Country Planning (Minerals) Act, 1981

Provides a planning authority with additional powers of control of the landscaping of current postponed and completed mineral workings, including their maintenance up to five years after planting.

Derelict Land Act, 1982

Amends the 1949 National Parks and Access to the Countryside Act to provide grants to enable urban and rural derelict land to be reclaimed for environmental and economic reasons.

Litter Act, 1983

Requires local authority to provide and empty litter bins in streets and public places.

Town and Country Planning Act, 1984
Town and Country Planning (Compensation) Act, 1985
Town and Country Planning (Amendment) Act, 1985

Three short Acts: the first allows the Crown to apply for planning consent to the development of land it wishes to sell; the second restricts the circumstances in which compensation is payable; and the third provides for the replacement of an equal number of trees to those which are to be removed.

Food and Environment Protection Act, 1985

Part 3 controls the use of pesticides in order to safeguard the environment.

The Wildlife and Countryside (Amendment) Act, 1985

Provides for the Countryside Commission to direct the protection of Areas of Outstanding Natural Beauty and Sites of Special Scientific Interest.

Housing and Planning Act, 1986

The simplification of the Zones laid down in the 1971 Act are set out in Part 2. Financial assistance of urban regeneration grants is covered in Part 3, and special provisions for conservation and other such amenity areas, with restrictions or prohibition of advertisements, are set out in Part 4. Part 5 covers opencast mining and Part 6 listed buildings, conservation areas and revised controls of advertisements.

Forestry Act, 1986

Enables the Forestry Commission to replace trees, other than those covered by a TPO, felled without authority.

Agriculture Act, 1986

Environmentally sensitive areas can be designated to ensure that agricultural and horticultural economic requirements do not result in the destruction of the natural beauty of the countryside including its flora, fauna, archaeological and amenity aspects.

The Control of Pesticide Regulations, 1986 (SI 1986 No. 1510)

These came into effect in 1986 affecting all those who advertised, sold, supplied, stored or used pesticides (including aerial sprays), householders, and employers of those who used them. From 1 January 1987 advertising and certificates of competence for storage were controlled; from 1 July 1987 controls were applied to anti-fouling paints and surface coatings and from 1 January 1988 those who sell or supply pesticides require users to 'take all reasonable precautions to protect the health of human beings, creatures and plants to safeguard the environment and in particular to avoid the pollution of water'.

Environmental impact assessment

The Council of Environment Ministers of the European Communities adopted in 1985 a directive 'on the assessment of the effects of certain public and private projects on the environment' generally known as the 'Environmental Assessment Directive'. Compliance by member states was required by 1988. The Directive provides that for certain types of projects listed in the Annexe, developers must collect certain information about the environmental effects of the project which has to be taken into consideration by the authority before giving consent to the development. The information to be provided, also set out in an Annexe, includes a description of those aspects of the environment likely to be significantly affected by the proposed project, in particular population, fauna, flora, soil, water, air, climatic factors, and material assets (including the architectural and archaeological heritage), landscape and the inter-related spaces between them. Also required is a description of the measures envisaged to prevent, reduce and where possible offset any significant adverse effects on the environment. Other bodies with environmental responsibilities are to be given the opportunity to comment before consent is given and the information is given to the public.

This information can already be demanded by the planning authority under section 5(1) and (4) of the General Development Order SI 1977 No 289. No common format has as yet been laid down, nor is it clear whether assessments should be made available to the public before the various issues have been identified. The options in terms of type of process and location must of course be prepared on an objective and factual basis, free of matters of opinion with the advantages and disadvantages of each option set out.

These Acts of Parliament are implemented by a number of Statutory Instruments and Regulations issued subsequently, the most important recent ones being set out in Appendix 5.

4

Practice Management

All offices irrespective of size require good personnel, an efficient financial and management structure and the ability to profit from past experience for current and future projects.

Financial control

The basic essential for any office and the cornerstone of any accounting system is the cash book. In its simplest form it includes all receipts entered with the date, origin and amount, identifying separately fees, expenses and VAT on the one side and all expenditure broken down into ten or more headings on the other (Figure 4.1). In landscape practices these usually include such categories as: salaries and consultancy fees, rent, heating, light and cleaning, office stationery materials and equipment, telephone and post, project expenses such as printing, travelling, photography and models, furniture and equipment, insurance and sundries including items of single annual expenditure.

This one book with supporting receipts, invoices and bank statements is often sufficient for the preparation of an annual statement of accounts and balance sheet at the end of each financial year for audit and tax purposes. Most mini and micro computer hardware now have an appropriate software system to enable this to be achieved automatically and subject to the incorporation of audit trails and careful checking for errors, provide accurate and up-to-date information at short notice.

It is not sufficient to rely only on accurate records of past and even current income and expenditure (Figure 4.2) without giving some thought to the future, and the preparation of an 'Annual Budget Forecast of Fee Income' is essential even if it relies mainly on inspired guess work in the calculation of the amount of the interim payments of fees and the dates when it is anticipated they will become due (Figure 4.3).

A similar 'Monthly Summary of Income and Expenditure' can also be prepared forecasting monthly expenditure with updated monthly subtotals taken from the cash book and the monthly figures taken from the fee income forecast (Figure 4.4).

INCOME

INV. NO.	DATE	JOB	JOB NO.	1 TOTAL	2 SUB-TOTAL	3 FEES EXP.	5 SUNDRIES	6 VAT	7

EXPENDITURE

CHEQUE NO.	PAID TO:	1 DATE	TOTAL	2 VAT	3 SALS. ACCOM.	5 CONSLTS FEES	6 GENERAL	7 PROJECT EXP.	8 BOOKS PUBS. STAT.	9 TRAVEL SUBS ENT.	10 PETTY CASH	11 FINANCE, BANK CHARGES	12 PARTNERS DRWGS	13 MISC.

Figure 4.1 A page from a simple cash book

56

A few hours spent at the beginning of each year and a few minutes each month to keep it up to date, substituting more accurate estimates when they are known and actual receipts and payments when they are made, will pay handsome dividends to ensure the future financial stability of the practice and is absolutely essential when negotiating any necessary overdraft facilities with the bank.

Staff

It used to be said that one-third of the income of a practice was expended on technical staff salaries, one-third on rent and overheads, leaving one-third for the remuneration of the working partner or partners, but today the proportion is nearer one-half, one-third, one-sixth, many partners earning little more than their most senior assistants. With the greatest single expenditure of an office being on staff, the careful husbanding and deployment of their resources must therefore be of primary importance.

It is often convenient to divide technical staff into four categories of responsibility and remunerate them accordingly.

1 *Technical (junior) assistants* – Unqualified and graduate (year out) assistants capable of performing simple jobs under strict supervision. Work at this level is not the job of a qualified consultant, but will normally be that of students in training.
2 *Assistants* – Fully qualified assistant consultants capable of handling, under supervision, small jobs. They might also be members of a team working on a larger project. The work at this level should be seen as the task of junior staff, in their early years after qualification.
3 *Senior assistants* – Assistants capable of taking responsibility for large jobs or of acting as team leaders in charge of a number of assistants engaged on either a large project or a series of smaller projects. This level should be regarded as the professional career grade and should normally be reached after some five years or so experience and practical knowledge. Professional competence is misused if staff have not had the opportunity of undertaking work at this level of responsibility by their mid-thirties at the latest.
4 *Associates* – Assistants capable of directing the activities of a number of teams. Work at this level will be found mainly in the larger offices and is the level to which more able staff achieve promotion; they should expect to have influence in the framing of office policy in design and construction matters.

ON
CASH FLOW FORECAST
Financial year: 1987
Date: 10th August 1987

	Year 1986	Jan	Feb	Mar	Apr	May	Jun	Jul	Aug	Sep	Oct	Nov	Dec	TOTAL
Month (1987)		ACTUAL	ACTUAL	ACTUAL	ACTUAL	ACTUAL	ACTUAL	ACTUAL						
RECEIPTS														
Fees/expenses received		81,342	149,237	36,015	70,676	100,455	29,682	24,501	59,000	29,000	21,300	28,100	48,000	677,308
Total		81,342	149,237	36,015	70,676	100,455	29,682	24,501	59,000	29,000	21,300	28,100	48,000	677,308
PAYMENTS														
Project expenses		8,631	14,512	7,796	5,826	14,424	8,269	8,232	11,000	11,000	11,000	11,000	11,000	122,690
Consultants fees		10,414	8,504	3,999	12,956	7,629	2,312	4,782	3,000	3,000	3,000	3,000	3,000	65,596
Salaries		23,866	26,990	21,780	21,522	20,972	22,472	25,129	18,000	18,000	18,000	18,000	22,000	256,731
Superannuation		10,262	2,809	4,709	1,292	6,263	7,972	3,361	2,500	3,000	3,000	3,000	3,000	51,168
Bank charges				5,459			3,875	250		4,000			4,000	17,584
VAT (net)		14,519	5,435	1,502	27,193	3,579	1,383	20,447	2,500	1,500	16,000	1,500	1,500	97,058
Partnership tax							16,033						16,000	32,033
Professional indemnity			16,785		16,785			16,785						50,355
Partners drawings		4,896	4,060	4,060	4,675	4,062	4,061	4,667	4,060	4,060	4,700	4,060	4,060	51,421
Pension		6,165												6,165
Total		78,753	79,095	49,305	90,249	56,929	66,377	83,653	41,060	44,560	55,700	40,560	64,560	750,801
Receipts less expenses		(2,589)	(70,142)	13,290	19,573	(43,526)	36,695	59,152	(17,940)	15,560	34,400	12,460	16,560	
Bank balance b/fwd		175,900	173,311	103,169	116,459	136,032	92,506	129,201	188,353	170,413	185,973	220,373	232,833	
Bank balance c/fwd		173,311	103,169	116,459	136,032	92,506	129,201	188,353	170,413	185,973	220,373	232,833	249,393	

Figure 4.2 A typical statement of consultant's income and expenditure

JOB NO.	JOB NAME	1987 1Jan ACTUAL	1Feb ACTUAL	1Mar ACTUAL	1Apr ACTUAL	1May ACTUAL	1Jun ACTUAL	1Jul ACTUAL	1Aug ACTUAL	1Sep	1Oct	1Nov	1Dec	1988 1JFMA
941	Lectures			1,029	88	450		257			500			
1077	A Cope		1,027	1,995										
1086	Getwell Hospital										2,000	4,500		
1219	Iron Court													
1226	Shepherds Hill		247	745										
1245	Hasel Grove													
1251	Lime Close								12,420					
1253	Select Square									3,000				
1261	Ivy Green				16,348									
1285	Norborough	4,580												
1289	Treadwell	3,917												
1292	Daniels										500		3,600	
1305	The Bothy										1,700			
1309	Berry Farm		34,702				6,385							
1310	Faraway Borough			815										
1321	Contour Survey					59,961								
1323	The Studio										300	3,600		
1324	Primrose Cottage		2,747				2,070							
1329	Treadwell Green	52,173												
1330	Gnomes Homes	8,425												
1331	Gravel Court			10,623										
1334	Puddle Lane	7,545									2,800		1,800	
1342	Old Manor House										3,200			
1345	Cherry Avenue										100			
1346	Leafy Lane													
1347	Robins Row		91											
1349	Hollywell	1,437	1,506											
1350	Linden Crescent													
1355	Ridge & Cope										4,500			
1356	The Square, Nettleshire								9,044					
1357	Willow Close									15,000				
1361	The Cover										2,500			
1366	Templars		2,981						12,219	15,000				
1368	The Bungalow												600	
1369	Rainbow Build												17,000	
1372	Redhill Farm		47,245						16,695					

Figure 4.3 Typical fees forecast

59

MONTHLY SUMMARY OF RECEIPTS AND PAYMENTS

Last Year		This year to date	Forecast to date
	INCOME		
. . . .	Fees received	. . . .	. . . .
. . . .	Expenses received	. . . .	. . . .
. . . .	VAT received	. . . .	. . . .
. . . .	Sundry receipts	. . . .	. . . .
. . . .	Transfer from deposit	. . . .	. . . .
£ _____		£ _____	£ _____
	EXPENDITURE		
. . . .	VAT inputs incl. HMC & Ex	. . . .	. . . .
. . . .	Wages, salaries and staff pensions	. . . .	. . . .
. . . .	Consultants fees	. . . .	. . . .
. . . .	Rent, rates, ins., htng, ltng, clng	. . . .	. . . .
. . . .	Books, stationery, materials, telephone, post	. . . .	. . . .
. . . .	Non-recoverable pract. exp., i.e. photos & models	. . . .	. . . .
. . . .	Recoverable pract. exp., i.e. printing, travel, xerox, maps etc.	. . . .	. . . .
. . . .	Subs, indemnity ins., bank charges, sundry finance	. . . .	. . . .
. . . .	Petty cash	. . . .	. . . .
. . . .	Sundry items	. . . .	. . . .
£ _____		£ _____	£ _____
. . . .	Repairs, furniture & fittings	. . . .	. . . .
. . . .	Partners regular drawings, pensions	. . . .	. . . .
. . . .	Partners irregular drawings, i.e. Tax Reserve Cert., capital drawings & tax	. . . .	. . . .
£ _____	TOTAL	£ _____	£ _____
	CASH		

Figure 4.4 Monthly summary of income and expenditure

Resource allocation and job costing

Irrespective of being reimbursed by the client on a percentage fee or on a time basis, accurate job costing from up-to-date time sheets prepared regularly by partners and staff is essential. When staff are used on projects where the practice is remunerated on a time basis weekly time sheets, recording the number of hours each day they have devoted to the job in question, are essential so that a detailed statement can be prepared to accompany the fee submission to the client. Although the hourly rate may be charged to the client on the basis of £0.15p per £100 gross annual salary, it is often advisable (if not essential) to work out the actual rate by adding to their gross salary actual overheads and dividing the total by the actual hours worked full or part time (Figure 4.5).

Office staff organization

Without imposing unnecessary disciplines and bureaucratic procedures, at the risk of damaging the creative spirit and vitality of the office, it is necessary at the outset to decide if the practice is to operate on a centralized specialist basis, i.e. one group of staff preparing all design drawings which are then handed to another group to prepare working drawings, specification and tender documents which are then handed to a third group for post-contract administration and site inspections. This is certainly the most efficient and still adopted by some of the larger practices. Most practices today however choose to work on a dispersed or federal basis, each group being responsible for a project from conception to completion on site. The belief is that this arrangement encourages a greater spirit of creative design, personal involvement and more efficient management, while still enabling the composition of the groups within the office to change as and when necessary to suit peaks in work load, even if this means their employment on tasks of lesser responsibility than their greater experience would otherwise suggest. The organizaton of the office has a direct effect on the quality of its output. A good organization is essential if staff are to work congenially with their employer and other colleagues. No partner can usually manage more than 15–20 staff and the larger office will usually require, in addition to associates, senior and junior qualified and unqualified staff and an equivalent hierarchy of secretarial staff, a bookkeeper and librarian. It is also important to remember that internal public relations are just as important as external, and the need for staff meetings to keep office staff informed of the work

		hours	hours	hours	hours	hours	hours
compiled							
staff grade							
Part 1: Time							
Standard working hours	hrs/Yr						
Total hours this individual (if part time employed)	hrs/Yr						

Part 2: Costs		£	p	£	p	£	p	£	p	£	p	£	p
Basic annual salary	£/Yr												
Add : employer's contribution NHI	£/Yr												
Add : employer's contribution graduated pension	£/Yr												
Add : employer's contribution supplementary pension	£/Yr												
Add : cost to employer of canteen facilities/individual	£/Yr												
Add : other payments by employer (eg bonus)	£/Yr												
Add : ditto	£/Yr												
Sub total items 4 to 9 Emloyers' other costs	£/Yr												
Item 3 + item 10 = total annual gross salary	£/Yr												
Estimated overheads for the year (transferred from Form A1, line 4)	£/Yr												

Part 3 : Job costing							
$\dfrac{\text{Item }11+\text{Item }12}{\text{Item }2}$ = Job costing rate (transferred to Form F2)	£/Hr						

Part 4 : Billing charges scale 5.11							
$\dfrac{\text{Item }11}{100}\times 0.15$ = rate for full time personnel	£/Hr						
$\left[\dfrac{(\text{Item }3\times\text{item }1)+\text{Item }10}{\text{Item }2}\right]\times\dfrac{1}{100}\times 0.15$ = rate for part-time personnel	£/Hr						

Figure 4.5 Time sheet for job costing
(Reproduced with the permission of RIBA Publications Ltd)

of the office other than their own and possible new projects on which they might be employed, should not be overlooked. Social occasions such as at Christmas and mid-summer are equally important to engender a congenial spirit within the office.

Office organization

Apart from the usual typing of letters, specifications, minutes and the other post-contract administrative services, there are many other supporting activities necessary for the efficient running of the office and it is often useful for the partners to delegate responsibility for certain items such as:

the acquisition of drawing office stationery and materials,
the office library of technical literature,
records and photographs of completed jobs for future publicity,
office furniture and equipment, and
office repairs and redecorations,

in whole or in part to other members of staff.

Premises

The location of a landscape consultant's office accommodation in the centre of a city is no longer an essential requirement, if indeed it ever was, but most clients nevertheless feel the need for relatively simple close personal contact. Good communications by letter, drawing, telephone and in person are essential and the ability to achieve this is an important requirement in the choice of the location of an office, whether at home or in a block of offices, in the city centre, the suburbs or in the country. The disposition of existing major clients and those in the future who might have need of a consultant's services in the type of work in which they are particularly successful must also be considered. An office in London is of little use to one interested in forestry in the Highlands and an office in Inverness will inevitably prove to be a handicap for those whose particular interest or connections are those involved in atria offices for international conglomerates.

Irrespective of location the ability to adapt to changing circumstances is equally essential, particularly with regard to the need to expand or contract in response to a fluctuating work-load with the consequent increase or decrease in staff numbers and the effect on the amount of office space required. Facilities at home may only be a short-term expedient and the choice is often between sharing space with other practices, and renting, leasing or purchasing the freehold of one's own. Whatever the solution, temporary or long term, it is always better to have too much than too little space as this can subsequently be sublet if necessary. Remember also that

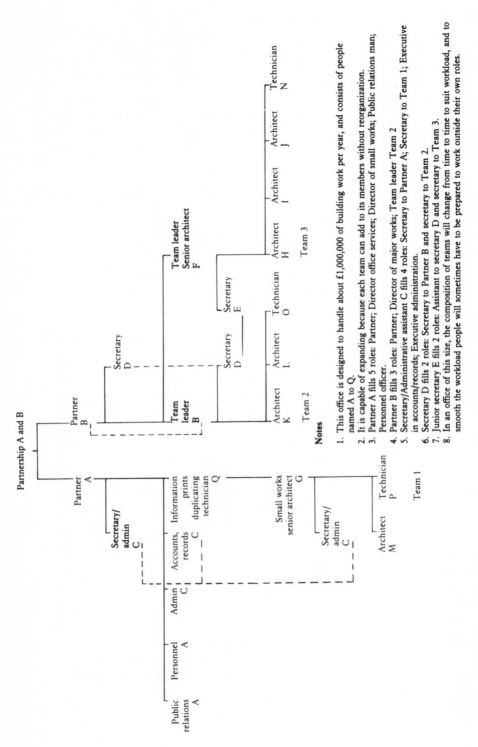

Notes

1. This office is designed to handle about £1,000,000 of building work per year, and consists of people named A to Q.
2. It is capable of expanding because each team can add to its members without reorganization.
3. Partner A fills 5 roles: Partner; Director office services; Director of small works; Public relations man; Personnel officer.
4. Partner B fills 3 roles: Partner; Director of major works; Team leader Team 2.
5. Secretary/Administrative assistant C fills 4 roles: Secretary to Partner A; Secretary to Team 1; Executive in accounts/records; Executive administration.
6. Secretary D fills 2 roles: Secretary to Partner B and secretary to Team 2.
7. Junior secretary E fills 2 roles: Assistant to secretary D and secretary to Team 3.
8. In an office of this size, the composition of teams will change from time to time to suit workload, and to smooth the workload people will sometimes have to be prepared to work outside their own roles.

Figure 4.6 Staff organization
(Reproduced with the permission of RIBA Publications Ltd)

one often expands into surplus space simply because it is available and then finds it hard to contract again when it becomes necessary and also the problem of assigning the end of short leases or long leases in unattractive areas or offices which are difficult to subdivide.

Not only is there the need for enough drawing board space but don't forget adequate accommodation for meetings, secretarial staff, lavatories and tea making facilities. Remember also the need to make the necessary arrangements for cleaning the office, the cost of rates, insurance against fire and theft, the statutory employers' liability insurance against personal accidents to visitors and staff and the need for the offices to comply with the Offices, Shops and Railway Premises Act, 1963 and the employer with the Health and Safety at Work Act, 1974.

Office administration

The extent of administration involved in running even the smallest office can easily be underestimated. Not only are there salaries, PAYE, VAT and national insurance to be paid, but also bills have to be checked and paid, fee invoices issued, chased and receipted when paid, staff records to be maintained, vacancies to be advertised, interviews arranged, and correspondence with accountants, the bank manager, auditors and solicitors to be maintained.

Office stationery

Headed notepaper and envelopes (usually A4) must be clear, legible when photocopied and not only attempt to reflect the 'style' of the office and incorporate the name, address, telephone and fax numbers, names and qualifications of all partners, associates and retired 'consultants' but must also leave space for the letter itself! Most offices also have printed continuation and copy letter sheets, memoranda of meetings, with compliments and drawing enclosure sheets. They may also have printed or photocopied time sheets, and telephone message pads. Bulk purchases of notepads, ball-pens, carbon paper, correcting fluid and other items of office stationery are usually ordered from travelling sales representatives.

Office administrative equipment

Typewriters
The major item of equipment is of course one or more typewriters, at least one with a memory, VDU, justification, variable pitch, word processing facilities for ease of correction, editing and accuracy in

copying. It is important always to obtain the best that one can afford, both from the quality of typing and the impression created by the typeface chosen.

Photocopier

These are now virtually indispensable in any office and should always be A3 with at least a reduction, if not enlargement, facility to enable it to be used by the drawing office also. The choice of hire, lease or outright purchase is a matter of individual preference and cash flow. For larger sizes, coloured copying and large numbers of copies, e.g. specifications, the use of an agency is usually advisable and saves office time, particularly when the cost is recoverable.

Telephones

These are now available on hire or purchase from sources other than BT. Again the facility for future expansion of not only extensions but also the number of outside lines is advisable. Nothing is more irritating to clients and staff than having to wait for an outside line or getting a continuously engaged tone when trying to call in. For the same reason a pleasant polite and helpful telephonist/receptionist with a good telephone manner is essential to create the correct impression of any office large or small. Landscape consultants are entitled to recover the cost of telephone calls, the installation of call logging equipment usually shows the costs, few offices making more than a handful of calls costing more than 50p in any one day other than in exceptional circumstances. Answerphones are however an essential facility if only for clients wishing to contact the office and leave messages before 9, during lunch time and after 6.

Facsimile copiers:

These are rapidly superseding telex and have become an essential adjunct for any office for the instant day or night transmission of both written and drawn information between client, consultant and contractor, but separate telephone lines are required. A4 machines are mostly used, B3 being available only either by enlargement or reduction with the consequent danger of mistakes in scale when used for drawn information.

Office furniture

In addition to drawing boards, now normally melamine faced with parallel motion stands and padded seats with back and footrests, staff involved in practice and project administration also require desks with drawers and chairs both for themselves and visitors. Chests for the storage of negatives, horizontally or vertically, and filing cabinets should always be fire resistant.

Drawing office equipment

Dyeline printing
Still the norm for any drawing larger than A3. Opinions are divided on the advantages of installing in-house equipment, but with the present 3-hour collection and delivery offered by most firms for all but the most unusual orders this can rarely be justified.

Microcomputers
Not only are microcomputers invaluable for the financial management of a practice they are also becoming increasingly useful for project management. Software for most makes of microcomputers is now available for the preparation of project specifications from an office library of standard specification clauses either on disk or on tape and can be prepared directly by the member of staff himself without the assistance of secretarial staff. Computerized plant selection cannot be far away although to date few if any programs suitable for the smaller office are available. As far as computer aided draughting (CAD) and product data are concerned, there is rarely sufficient repetition involved in all but the largest of surveying or earthmoving projects to make it practicable.

Drawing office stationery
Printed cut sheets of tracing paper, especially A1 and A3 with name and address of the firm, name of job, and drawing, scale, date, author and drawing number are now the norm.

Most offices also provide pencils, pens, ink, Letraset, erasing machines or rubbers, colouring equipment, curves and templates; staff providing their own instruments, scales and set squares.

Levelling equipment
It is often better, quicker and more accurate and economical to arrange for site surveys to be prepared by specialist surveyors but most offices have dumpy levels and staffs of their own to save hiring them in the case of emergencies or when a contractor's equipment is not available.

Insurance

Apart from the insurance of the office premises, the furniture, fixtures and fittings against damage from fire and theft etc., including the cost of renting alternative accommodation, replacing lost or destroyed drawings and even loss of profit, insurance must be taken out against any accidental injury to staff and visitors while on the premises. Consideration should also be given to the possibility of accidents to staff going to, during and while travelling back to the office from site visits; long-term staff illness or disablement; any private medical insurance for partners or staff; and retirement pensions for long-serving staff, even if in the circumstances the cost of the insurance premiums are not justified.

Technical library

A good technical reference library, next to competent staff, is probably the most important resource an office can have. It is not however a 'loan' library with essential technical literature hidden away or forgotten beneath the drawing board of one member of the staff and denied to the remainder. Where a particular item of technical information is required for one particular job and needs to be referred to frequently, duplicates or photocopies should be obtained. Even when removed from the library for only a short time, a note should be left behind of its whereabouts, often a tedious chore but really only good manners on the part of the borrower. Staff should however be encouraged always to seek information through the 'librarian' and only in his or her absence seek out the information for themselves.

Equally landscape technical libraries must be more than a collection of unsolicited technical literature, passively received in the daily post and filed haphazardly irrespective of value or relevance (if any). Even valuable existing information must be kept up to date and ideally checked at regular intervals with the manufacturer concerned, to confirm that it is still current and has not been superseded. Literature filed since the library was first set up and never since updated is worse than no information at all, indeed some offices rely on trade information sought anew as necessary for each individual job, accepting the delays that this may sometimes cause. Technical libraries are however more than just shelves of technical literature, libraries are also for books and should at least contain the essential technical references from the Landscape Institute(LI) book list.

Other types of technical literature no landscape consultants library should be without are copies of the essential 15 or so British Standards and the National Building Specification Library of standard clauses for landscape works. As with trade literature, it is equally essential that these are kept up to date either by constant vigilance, or by subscription or membership to such as the Barbour Microfile or Royal Institute of British Architects (RIBA) Product Data subscription services. Much information is today available on microfiche and ideally not only a reader/printer but a photocopier should be installed in the library so that hard copy is readily available when required.

Libraries should also be the point of access to other sources of material, either directly or by telephone with or without FAX. Not only technical libraries such as the Royal Horticultural Society, Wisley, the LI, the RIBA, the Building Research Establishment (BRE) and the Building Centre, but also local public authority libraries are usually only too willing to help in tracing and acquiring historical and technical information.

Most offices subscribe to at least one or more technical journals and periodicals and their receipt, distribution and subsequent disposal is also one of the librarian's responsibilities. In all but the smallest office distribution to members of staff, one after the other, can take weeks/ months to circulate around the whole office and it is probably better for the librarian to identify and forward those items of interest to a particular member of staff, to circulate a monthly summary of acquisitions and items of general interest to all members of staff on a regular basis.

Not to be forgotten is other non-technical information such as professional directories of members' names and addresses not only of the LI but also of the RIBA, Royal Institution of Chartered Surveyors (RICS) and the Institute of Chartered Engineers, not to mention train time-tables, hotel and good food guides. While not strictly within his duties some offices make the librarian responsible for preparing and filing photographs and articles of recently completed jobs.

5
Tender and Contract Documents

Pre-contract project and tendering procedures

Freezing the design

The outline, sketch and detailed proposals having been completed and approved by the client, it is essential that the design is now considered to be 'frozen' – indeed having been approved by the client the landscape consultant has no authority to make any material changes other than those specifically requested by the client. It is equally essential to point out to the client after the design has been frozen that, although changes can subsequently be made, when necessary, to suit changing circumstances or to incorporate better ideas, these changes frequently incur payment of additional fees due to the landscape consultant to incorporate the changes and possibly also to any other consultants involved.

Production information and bills of quantities

The design having been finalized, it is now necessary to put in hand the preparation of the necessary information both drawn and written in order to select a contractor to be entrusted with carrying out the work on site. The way in which the contractor is selected depends entirely on the client's priorities with regard to the date by which the landscape works must be completed, the cost control, the need for a finite or contractual authorized expenditure, the time available to ascertain the client's detailed requirements and the scope of the work required. Irrespective of these priorities it is almost certain that in the majority of cases drawings, specifications and details of the contract conditions (covering dates for commencement and completion, control of the works, payment, compliance with statutory obligations with regard to insurance against injury to persons and damage to property) will have to be prepared.

The work of a landscape consultant is achieved and created on site 'rather like painting a portrait by numbers with the contractor holding the brush and the consultant trying to tell him what colours to use and where to put them'. Unless this can be achieved effectively the project is doomed to failure from the start.

The translation of the design into instructions to the landscape contractor, so that he can implement the design and be remunerated accordingly, is covered contractually in four different documents.

1 *Illustrative:* Drawings illustrating the layout and assembly of the materials and components specified.
2 *Qualitative:* A detailed description of the standards of materials and workmanship required.
3 *Quantitative:* Schedules and bills itemizing the labour and materials required.
4 *Conditions of contract:* The legal document covering the conditions under which the work described in the other documents is to be executed and paid for.

All these aspects must of necessity be included in the contract documents prepared by the consultant and signed by the client and the contractor.

Illustrative (landscape drawings)

The Foreword to BS 1192:Part 4:1984 Landscape Drawing Practice states the intention of drawn information to be:

> to provide communication with accuracy, clarity, economy and consistency of presentation between all concerned with the construction industry . . . . Familiarity with commonly accepted forms of presentation is likely to result in greater efficiency with the preparation of landscape drawings and minimise the risk of confusion on site.

Figures 5.1 and 5.2 give examples of landscape drawings.

Graphic symbols

The need for common and easily understood graphic symbols to convey the consultant's intentions cannot be over emphasised. BS 1192:Part 4: 1984 provides a comprehensive range of 50 conventions which should meet the majority of requirements and should convey the maximum information with the minimum time and effort (Figure 5.3). It is difficult to remember that the benefits of photocopying and dyeline techniques have been with us for less than half a century and that the drawings of Nesfield and Olstead let alone Bridgeman and Brown had all to be laboriously copied by hand.

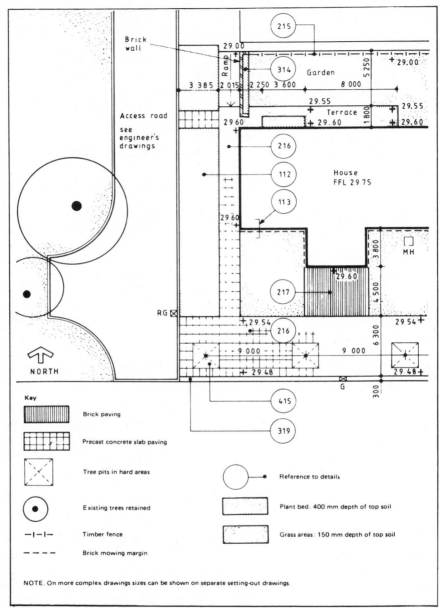

Figure 5.1 A hard-landscape drawing
(Extracts from BS 1192: Part 4: 1984 are reproduced by permission of BSI.
Complete copies can be obtained from them at Linford Wood, Milton Keynes,
MK14 6LE.)

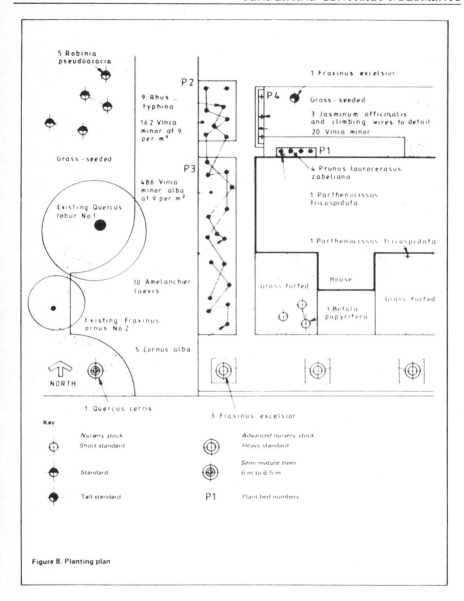

Figure 8. Planting plan

Figure 5.2 A planting drawing
(Extracts from BS 1192: Part 4: 1984 are reproduced by permission of BSI.
Complete copies can be obtained from them at Linford Wood, Milton Keynes,
MK14 6LE.)

73

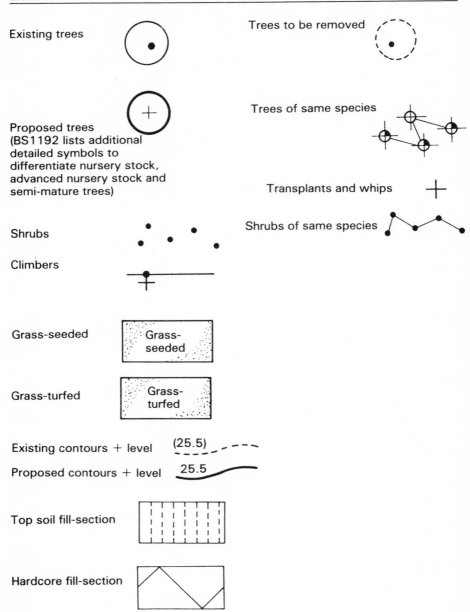

Figure 5.3 The basic British Standard graphic symbols
(Extracts from BS 1192: Part 4: 1984 are reproduced by permission of BSI. Complete copies can be obtained from them at Linford Wood, Milton Keynes, MK14 6LE.)

Copying

Today, contractors take it for granted they are entitled to as many copies as they need and for this reason if no other, colour, other than on single copies with a felt pen, rarely has a place in contract documentation. Colouring drawings is costly and time consuming and the chances of error directly related to the number of copies required. The increased availability of copiers which reduce and enlarge drawings suggest that the reintroduction of the use of drawn scales on drawings is overdue. Even before the increasingly common use of facsimile transmission of drawings and letters by telephone, the thickness of lines, symbols, dimensions, figures and text must always follow the recommendations of BS 1192 to ensure that they are capable of clear and legible reproduction.

Size

Drawings produced for use by the contractor must always be of a size capable of being handled easily on site, irrespective of the size of the project and should rarely on any one project be more than two or three, at the most, different sizes if the possibility of their being mislaid or misfiled is to be minimized. For most projects therefore A1 and A2 size standard sheets are the most appropriate for location, site, setting out and layout plans at scales down to 1:100 and A3 and A4 for component and assembly drawings from 1:50 to 1:5.

Content

No rules exist at present regarding the minimum content of drawings required by a contractor for any one project and it is difficult to see how they could be prepared. BS 1192 does however attempt to indicate how the information should be shown and includes a check list of the information required on various types of drawing. It also lays down three categories of drawings as 1, layout, 2, component and 3, assembly. Landscape consultants will find it helpful if they conform to this discipline.

Drawings should rarely duplicate information to be found elsewhere or on other drawings, since this not only increases the risk of error but involves additional work when changes are made. In spite of a written warning 'Always work to the largest scale drawing' contractors often find it more convenient to work to the one containing the most information i.e. the ones drawn to the smaller scales.

Layout drawings

Often on A1 and A2 size sheets, they must rigorously exclude design information and resist the temptation to show trees and shrubs fully grown and in leaf. The use of overlay draughting techniques whereby different elements of the work are shown on separate sheets (e.g. site clearance, setting out, foundations, drainage and site services) is particularly applicable to landscape projects with one basic drawing from which overlays or copies are made before adding the other information, the addition of which may be essential, useful or just confusing depending on the circumstances. Sections always assist in the calculation of areas and reduction of errors when cut and fill is involved and indicating the location of the additional component and assembly details for the particular area, with the drawing reference number enclosed within a circle, is especially important.

Any restrictions on the location of the contractors' site huts, the position of his spoil heaps and any limitations on access should always be clearly indicated. Setting out dimensions should always be related to an existing alignment, building, road or site boundary. Curves drawn from templates are rarely satisfactory and should always be capable of being accurately set out on site from clearly dimensioned centres and tangent points in the case of circular curves which should be used wherever possible, even if this means the combination of a number of different radii. When irregular curves relying on dimensioned offsets are unavoidable, they must be closely spaced with their origins clearly indicated. Scaling curves, radii and offsets from drawings inevitably involves much time wasting trial and error on site and is rarely satisfactory. A clear and accurate indication of levels is equally important on landscape (as indeed it is on any other) drawings. Contours both proposed and existing are very useful to indicate the intention of the landscape consultant and must be clearly differentiated. Contractors usually also require spot levels at precisely identifiable locations. The convention of new levels being shown unenclosed and existing levels in brackets or boxes should always be followed as should that of arrows, like tadpoles, always pointing 'uphill'.

Component details

These are usually on the smaller A3 and A4 size sheets, may sometimes rely on a manufacturer's drawn catalogue information but most often relate to special components e.g. gates, seats, precast components, or street furniture to be manufactured on or off site (Figure 5.4).

Assembly details

Assembly details relating to the fixing of components, their tolerances and relationship with adjoining work and components, often seeming to be of little interest to the manufacturer or supplier (by others) should not be overlooked. Many offices have 'standard' details indicating their own solution for any particular requirement, e.g. external steps, curbs, paving or fencing, which may be issued as a photocopy with or without the name of the particular project inserted in the job title panel. Alternatively they

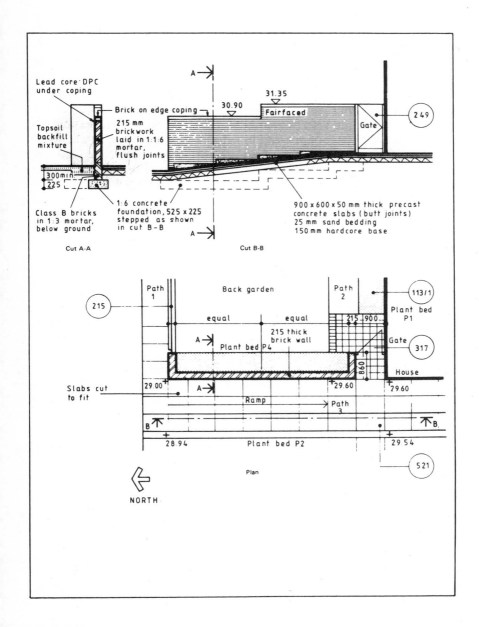

Figure 5.4 Component detail for a hard landscape
(Extracts from BS 1192: Part 4: 1984 are reproduced by permission of BSI. Complete copies can be obtained from them at Linford Wood, Milton Keynes, MK14 6LE.)

may be traced or photocopied on to a larger sheet and included as a contract drawing. Inclusion by reference to a library of standard details only is a false economy and rarely satisfactory, particularly if they are subsequently amended.

It is essential that as many drawings as possible are made available to the contractor and included in the contract documents at the time of tender, since any delay in their issue to the contractor during the contract period may well give rise to a delay in progress and a justifiable claim by the contractor for the reimbursement of the direct loss and expense he has incurred as a consequence and to which he is entitled. Such additions to the contract sum arising from delays caused by the landscape consultant are rarely appreciated by the client, nor do they encourage the consultant's involvement in any of the client's subsequent projects.

Qualitative (landscape specifications)

In addition to information on the layout and assembly of the materials and components to be provided by the landscape contractor, the landscape consultant has also to inform him of the quality of workmanship and materials required. This is usually referred to as a specification or trade preambles in the bills of quantity. The detailed description of the construction, workmanship and materials to be provided by the contractor are clearly a matter for the landscape consultant and are to be included in the contract between the client and the contractor, as one of the documents describing the work which the contractor has undertaken to provide for the contract sum.

In addition to being set out in a recognizable and orderly way the requirements of the specifier must be immediately recognized, understood and priced accordingly by the estimator so that he can allow in his tender no more and no less than he considers necessary to satisfy the requirements of the consultant. When bills of quantities are included in the contract documents it is important to ensure that all reference to the quality of workmanship and materials e.g. the name of the manufacturers of the paving bricks, is excluded from the measured items and covered only in the trade preambles, otherwise the contractor may refer only to the measured items and ignore the specification in the day-to-day arrangements of the work on site.

Standard clauses
For these reasons it is clear that there are great advantages in the use of

standard clauses which the estimator will immediately recognize. From past experience he will know the cost involved without the need for a careful line by line consideration to ensure that there are no ambiguities which he can only allow for in his tender by including such a hidden contingency sum within his rate as he considers will cover the risk involved. Both the Property Services Agency (PSA) and the National Building Specification (NBS) have prepared standard specification clauses to cover most if not all the items likely to arise on building works, including those specially written for site preparation, the planting of trees, shrubs, grass and their subsequent upkeep, likely to arise in connection with landscape works.

While each office can select from these clauses only those options which they require for all their projects, even then they cannot select a 'standard' specification for all projects since they will rarely if ever be on the same site and never therefore exactly the same and requiring exactly the same clauses. All offices require a regularly updated 'library' of standard specification clauses from which they select for each project only those applicable in that instance. If specifications are only based on a previous project, the possibility of error, not only that of including an inappropriate clause from the previous project, but also from omitting those that are necessary for the new project but were not covered by the previous one is almost inevitable.

Phraseology

Specification clauses must be written clearly and concisely using words that communicate the consultants' intentions simply and unambiguously by using the same words and phrases consistently throughout. Clauses should always start with a key word 'TOP SOIL' 'WEEDS' 'HERBICIDES' etc. followed by a verb in the imperative e.g. 'to be', 'provide', 'lay', 'plant', etc. Vague phrases such as 'in all respects' 'the best of their respective kinds, free from all faults and the like' should be avoided in case they are interpreted (as they should be) literally, beyond the limits of that which is practicable or involve exorbitant costs to achieve standards far higher than the specifier intended. Describing operations in great detail or requiring an accuracy or tolerance that is unnecessary or impossible to achieve should always be avoided. Clauses should not only be capable of being carried out but also be capable of being checked for compliance by the specifier either visually or by testing, otherwise unscrupulous contractors in the knowledge that they cannot be checked up on will leave the work undone, to the detriment of the conscientious contractor who has priced the work properly and included it in his tender, which is then not the lowest submitted.

The common arrangement

A joint committee comprising representatives of all sides of the building industry was set up in 1979 at the request of the Department of the Environment who had previously carried out a pilot study to establish the need to co-ordinate the presentation of project information (Co-ordinating Committee for Project Information – CCPI). As a first step 200 work sections were established grouped into 60 or so categories and brought together under the 10–15 broad headings similar to those used in the Standard Method of Measurement (SMM), but in this case applicable to drawings, specification and bills of quantities, the two most relevant to the landscape industry were Group D – Groundwork and Group Q – Site surfacing, planting and fencing including Q30 seeding/turfing and Q31 planting (Table 5.1).

Specifications are usually written in two parts – the first being the 'pre-liminaries' section covering the responsibilities of the parties to the contract, the procedures to be followed, a description of the scope of the work, the site and any special restrictions with regard to access, sequence of work, hours or working rules. The second part of the specification describes the materials and workmanship required. They are now normally listed separately and include reference to the location, accuracy, tolerances and fit of the various elements in the scheme and note any special requirements for appearance, performance test on or off site and for the submission and retention of samples.

Clause selection

Selecting the right clauses requires skill and judgement on the part of the specifier often only achieved by experience. Nothing shows up lack of experience or competence more quickly than a specification which includes inapplicable clauses or those incapable of achievement. It is important also to achieve a balance in the specification, dealing only in great detail with those items which are important or of which there are large amounts and which form a significant part of the work, with only a brief but nevertheless accurate reference to the less important items.

With the increased use of microcomputers and word processors there is no longer an excuse for not producing an individual specification using a selection of the appropriate standard clauses for each project. Specifying by reference 'The contractor is to allow for all workmanship and materials to be in accordance with the relevant clauses in the . . . standard specification' or even just listing the reference numbers of the clauses required is not good enough. 'Mark up' facilities are now available for both PSA and NBS Libraries of standard clauses. By ringing the reference numbers of the clauses required and returning the marked up draft to the originator, with office and project special and non-standard clauses coded

Table 5.1
Common arrangement work sections

D11
Soil stabilization

Stabilization or improvement of bearing capacity or slip resistance of existing ground by injecting or otherwise introducing stabilizing materials, by power vibrating or by ground anchors.

Included

Cement or chemical grouting

Electrochemical stabilization

Sand stowing

Forming regular pattern of holes, compacting surrounding soil, and filling with aggregates or hard fill, all by means of power vibrators

Ground anchors

Dynamic compaction

Freezing of ground water and sub-soil where specified

Stabilizing soil in situ by incorporating cement with a rotovator

Excluded

Stabilization by temporary lowering of water table
(Relevant section, D12 or D20)

Consolidating and compacting existing ground/formation levels
(Excavating and filling, D20)

Soil-cement sub-bases to roads and pavings
(Hardcore/Granular/Cement bound bases/sub-bases to roads/pavings, Q10)

Stabilization by permanent ground water drainage
(Drainage below ground, R12)

D12
Site dewatering

Temporarily lowering the ground water level over the whole or significantly large parts of the site to facilitate construction, the work being required to be executed by a specialist firm.

Included

Forming well points

Gravel or other filling

Installing and removing drain tubes and ring mains

Excavating sumps

Pumps and pumping

Off site disposal of water

Excluded

Removing ground, surface or storm water by pumping from open sumps in basements, trenches, pits or similar excavations, the work not being required to be executed by a specialist firm
(Excavating and filling, D20)

Land drainage, R13

D20
Excavating and filling

Forming bulk, pit, trench and surface area excavations other than for services supplies, m and e services and drainage. Filling holes and excavations other than for ditto. Making up levels by bulk filling or in layers, including hardcore but excluding bases and sub-bases to roads and pavings.

Included

Information regarding site conditions and water levels

Applying herbicides to soil before excavating

Excavating topsoil, subsoil, made ground or rock

Breaking out existing substructures

Breaking out existing hard pavings

Removing existing underground storage tanks and services

Removing existing trees, shrubs, undergrowth and turf

Consolidating bottoms of excavations

Trimming excavations to accurate shape and dimensions

Keeping the excavations free of water (other than site dewatering)

Temporary diversion of waterways and drains

Benching sloping ground to receive filling

Making stockpiles of excavated material

Disposing of surplus excavated material

Earthwork support

Filling with and compacting:
  Excavated material (including selected)
  Imported material
  Rock
  Hardcore and granular material

Consolidating/compacting general areas

Blinding surface of filling with fine material

Preparing subsoil by ripping, grading, etc. before spreading topsoil

Transporting from stockpiles or importing and spreading topsoil

Filling external planters, beds, roof gardens with soil and drainage layers, including filter mats

Excluded

Excavating and filling for temporary roads and other temporary works
(Preliminaries)

Ground investigation, D10, but not information on the results

Soil stabilization, D11

Stabilizing soil in situ by incorporating cement with a rotovator
(Soil stabilization, D11)

Site dewatering required to be executed by a specialist firm
(Site dewatering, D12)

Excavating and backfilling for underpinning
(Underpinning, D50)

Filling internal plant containers
(Interior planting, N14)

Excavating and backfilling for engineering services and service supplies
(Trenches/Pipeways/Pits for buried engineering services, P30)

Hardcore/Granular/cement bound bases to roads/pavings, Q10

Gravel/Hoggin roads/pavings, Q22

Cultivating and final fine grading of soil for seeding, turfing or planting
(Relevant sections, Q30, Q31)

Spreading peat, compost, mulch, fertilizer, soil ameliorants, including working in
(Relevant sections, Q30, Q31)

Excavating and filling treepits
(Planting, Q31)

Table 5.1 *(concluded)*

Q30
Seeding/Turfing

Preparing soil and seeding or turfing to form lawns and general grassed areas.

Included

Applying herbicides

Cultivating topsoil, including removing large stones and weeds

Fine grading topsoil

Providing, spreading and working in peat, manure, compost, mulch, fertilizer, soil ameliorants, sand, etc.

Edging strips for lawn areas

Mesh reinforcement for grass areas

Seeding and rolling

Turfing, including turf edges to seeded areas

Hydro-seeding

Grass cutting

Work to existing grassed areas, including scarifying, forking, fertilizing, applying selective weedkillers, local re-seeding or re-turfing, rolling, edging, etc.

Protecting new and existing grassed and planted areas with temporary fencing, etc.

Watering, including during Defects Liability Period

Work specified to be executed during the Defects Liability Period

Replacement seeding and turfing

Excluded

Earthworks and other preparation:
  Clearing existing vegetation
  Removing existing hard paving and obstructions
  Removing existing topsoil and stockpiling
  General site contouring and adjusting levels
  Transporting from stockpiles or importing and spreading topsoil
  Filling external planters, beds, roof gardens with soil and drainage layers
(Excavation and filling, D20)

Grass block paving:
  Sub-base
  (Granular/Cement bound bases/sub-bases to roads/pavings, Q20)
  Blocks and bedding
  (Slab/Brick/Block etc. pavings, Q25)

Special surfacings/pavings for sport, Q26

Land drainage, R13

Irrigation, S14

Maintenance (as distinct from making good defects) other than that specified to be carried out during the Defects Liability Period

Q31
Planting

Preparing soil and planting herbaceous and other plants, trees and shrubs.

Included

Applying herbicides

Cultivating topsoil, including removing large stones and weeds

Fine grading topsoil

Forming raised or sunken beds, borders, etc.

Providing and spreading peat, manure, compost, mulch, fertilizer, soil ameliorants and working in if required.

Planting herbaceous plants and bulbs

Planting shrubs and hedges

Planting nursery stock and semi-mature trees

Excavating and backfilling tree pits

Fence supports for hedges

Support wires, etc. for climbers

Tree stakes, tree guards, tree guys

Wrapping and other protection of trees, shrubs and plants

Labelling

Applying anti-desiccants

Tree surgery, thinning and pruning

Protecting new and existing grassed and planted areas with temporary fencing, etc.

Watering, including during Defects Liability Period

Work specified to be carried out during the Defects Liability Period

Replacement planting

Excluded

Earthworks and other preparation:
  Clearing existing vegetation
  Removing existing hard paving and obstructions
  Removing existing topsoil and stockpiling
  General site contouring and adjusting levels
  Transporting from stockpiles or importing and spreading topsoil
  Filling external planters, beds, roof gardens with soil and drainage layers
(Excavation and filling, D20)

Interior landscape, N14

Tree grilles
(Slab/Brick/Block/Sett/Cobble pavings, Q24)

Seeding/Turfing, Q30

Fencing, Q40

External prefabricated plant containers
(Site/Street furniture/equipment, Q50)

Land drainage, R13

Irrigation, S14

Maintenance (as distinct from making good defects) other than that specified to be carried out during the Defects Liability Period

---

(Reproduced with permission of NBS Services Ltd.)

and inserted, the copies of the finished specification can be expected to be printed and returned within 2–3 days. It is also possible to prepare one's own computerized office library of standard specification clauses on disc or tape for use within the office but this needs constant vigilance to ensure that it is regularly up-dated to incorporate the latest Regulations, British Standards and Codes of Practice.

Table 5.2
Examples of National Building Specification clauses

Under the following headings
1. Generally
2. Preparing subsoil
3. Spreading/preparing topsoil

W11:1 *GENERALLY*

1051 EXCAVATION AND FILLING: to be as specified in sections C12 and C21.

1101 PLANTING AREAS: clearly mark boundaries of planting areas and obtain approval before commencing work.

1151 WORK NEAR TREES which are to be retained:
1. Do not carry out ploughing, ripping or tipping of soil within the branch spread.
2. Do not vary level of ground within an area up to 3m beyond the branch spread.

1201, 1202
Alternative clauses

1201 HERBICIDES: do not use.

1202 HERBICIDES: apply strictly in accordance with manufacturer's recommendations, observing all precautions. Remove containers from site immediately they are no longer required.

W11:2 *PREPARING SUBSOIL*

2051 PERENNIAL WEEDS: apply herbicide and allow period of time recommended by manufacturer to elapse before grading.

2101
Finished levels of topsoil should be shown on drawings with contours where necessary.

Levels in areas of existing topsoil can often be adjusted by local grading without removal of the topsoil, provided the minimum required depth of topsoil is maintained (See clause 3301). Precise instructions to this effect should be given on drawings.

83

Table 5.2 *(concluded)*

The maximum gradient will be limited by the stability of the soil and for grass banks by the difficulty of cutting:

- hand maintenance   1:1   • special bank machines   1:2
- small machines   1:1½ • suitable tractor-drawn mowers   1:3

2101 GRADE subsoil to smooth flowing contours and to achieve the tolerances specified for the finished level of the topsoil. Excavate locally as necessary for areas of thicker topsoil.

2151, 2152 These will normally be alternative clauses

2151 LOOSEN light, non-cohesive subsoils with a 3 tine ripper, 300mm deep at 600mm centres.

2152 LOOSEN stiff clays and other cohesive subsoils with a single-tine ripper, 450mm deep at 1m centres.

W11:3 *SPREADING/PREPARING TOPSOIL*

3051, 3052, 3053
These clauses can be used on jobs where the distribution of topsoil about the site is very simple and clear. When this is not the case show the information on drawings.

3051 EXISTING TOPSOIL: areas covered by undisturbed in situ topsoil.

3052 EXISTING TOPSOIL: areas covered by topsoil spread by the Main Contractor.

3053 EXISTING TOPSOIL: spoil heaps of topsoil.

3101
Provisional quantities of topsoil required to make up deficiencies should be given in the Bill of Quantities.

3101 IMPORTED TOPSOIL: provide as necessary to make up any deficiency of topsoil existing on site and to complete the work.

3151 CONTAMINATION: do not use topsoil contaminated with subsoil, rubbish, oil based products, or other materials toxic to plant life. Dispose of contaminated topsoil as instructed.

(Reproduced with permission of NBS Services Ltd.)

Specifying materials

Materials can be specified in one of three ways:

By type

Provided the quality and minimum standard required can be clearly described, it is always in the employers' interest to allow a contractor the maximum freedom of choice in the selection of the sources of the materials required. In the case of plants an indication of which of the dimensions of height, stem girth, and container size are to have priority, is essential.

By British Standards

Even when these exist for the material in question it is important to remember a range of options and sizes is almost invariably included within the one standard e.g. the stem circumference of extra heavy advanced nursery stock to BS 5236 can range from 12–20cm and the height from 4.25 to 6.0m (Table 5.3).

By naming

Listing three suppliers, restricting the contractor to one or more from whom he must obtain the plants (or sometimes even a single source), while never to be used unnecessarily, is often the only way of ensuring delivery of plants of an adequate size, condition and state of health. Although this restricts the element of competition of pricing by the contractor of the items concerned, it does at least ensure the minimum standard of the plants to be provided and the comparability of this part of the tender. When naming a single source it may be necessary to add the words 'or equal and approved' to comply with standing orders, in which case it is essential to check preferably by inspection, that what is being offered is indeed equal. It is also advisable to include in the specification the requirement that 'approval of the alternative source must be obtained in writing from the specifier at least 7 days before the latest date for the submission of tenders' to prevent a contractor submitting a very low tender by incorporating prices obtained from an alternative sub-standard supplier.

Specifying workmanship

By finished effect

By far the best method wherever possible, since it tells the contractor what is wanted but leaves it to his expertise as to how he is to achieve it and for which he is entirely responsible should things go wrong.

By British Standard Codes of Practice.

BS 4428 Landscape Operations lays down in general terms the minimum

Table 5.3
Essential Landscape British Standards

There are 83 British Standards for gardening, horticulture and landscape work listed in the February 1983 Sectional List of British Standards (available free from BSI at Milton Keynes, Tel. 0908 320066), 49 of them, i.e. 60 per cent, are available in summary form.

Fifteen British Standards are considered essential references for all those concerned with landscape work.

1. NURSERY STOCK (FAC/1)
   BS 3936 parts 1–10 Specification for trees and shrubs etc.
Part	1.	Trees and shrubs
Part	2.	Roses
Part	3.	Fruit
Part	4.	Forest tree
Part	5.	Poplars and willows
Part	6.	not used
Part	7.	Bedding plants
Part	8.	not used
Part	9.	Bulbs, corms and tubers
Part	10.	Ground cover plants
Part	11.	Culinary herbs in containers

2. OPERATIONS   BDB/5
BS 3998:1966	Recommendations for tree work.
BS 4043:1978	Recommendations for transplanting semi-mature trees.
BS 4428:1968	Recommendations for General Landscape operations.
BS 5236:1975	Recommendations for cultivation and planting trees in the extra large nursery stock category.
BS 5837:1980	Code of Practice for trees in relation to construction.
BS -	Ground Maintenance (EPC/2)

3. MATERIALS   FAC/2
BS 3882:1965(78)	Recommendations and classification for topsoil.
BS 3969:1965(78)	Recommendations for turf for general landscape purposes.
BS 4156:1967(79)	Peat
*BS 5581:1981	Fertilizers

4. TERMINOLOGY
BS 881/589:1974	Nomenclature of commercial hardwoods and softwoods.
*BS 1831:1969	Recommended common names for pesticides.
*BS 2468:1963	Glossary of terms relating to agricultural machinery.
BS 3975:1966/69	Glossary for landscape work part 4 plant description, part 5 Horticultural practice.
BS 1192:1984	Part 4 Recommendations for Landscape drawings.

* Not in *Construction Digest Handbook*

standards of workmanship for earthworks, topsoil, preparation, seeding, laying turf, planting trees, shrubs and herbaceous plants. Site conditions or the requirements of the project frequently require more than the minimum and reliance solely on the requirement to comply with BS 4428 is rarely sufficient except for the simplest work.

By method
In some ways the easiest method of specifying workmanship, to ensure the contractor prices and provides exactly what is required. It does however relieve him of any responsibility should the work subsequently be found to be defective. The requirement 'to supply and fix' a semimature tree without reference to the size and content of its tree pit is clearly inadequate but specifying the sequence and time of its planting could certainly relieve the contractor of his responsibilities for its subsequent survival.

Plant protection
Temporary fencing of trees and shrub borders until they become established must always be described in detail and its provision insisted on. Phrases such as 'Provide such temporary fencing as is necessary and remove on completion of the Defects Liability period' are quite inadequate and only indicate to the contractor that the specifier does not consider this to be very important and is unlikely to enforce its provision. The estimator will therefore only allow a nominal amount for this item in the hope that it will not be insisted on and thus enable him to submit the lowest tender. Since the protection may be required for longer than the length of the defects liability period, it is often advisable to specify that it is to remain in the ownership of the employer. The question of the enclosure of the site for the protection of the public and the plants from vandalism during the progress of the works, is of course quite a different matter and should be left entirely to the discretion of the contractor.

Watering
It is equally insufficient just to specify that the contractor is to water the plants 'as and when necessary during the defects liability period'. The specification must state not only the quantity of water to be provided, depending on the needs of the particular species and subsoil conditions but the number of visits to be allowed for. It can still be left to the contractor to suggest to the consultant when these visits are required and should the total number not have been necessary by the end of the defects liability period, the contract sum will be adjusted accordingly.

A clause should also be included in the specification requiring the contractor to inform the consultant if he is unable to water the plants when necessary because the water supply is restricted by emergency legislation as the result of drought conditions and for him to ascertain the availability and cost of second-class water from a sewage works or other approved source. The consultant can then issue such instructions to the contractor as he considers necessary.

Quantitative (schedules and bills of quantity)

The primary objectives of any set of tender and contract documents are to ensure that the contractor is provided with all the information necessary for him to include in his tender all that is required for the proper completion of the works and that the tender of the lowest is strictly comparable with those of the competitors. It has to be accepted that if competitive tenders are being invited the lowest tenderer will usually be the one who has included no more than the minimum standards specified. The secondary objective is to provide comparable rates for the landscape consultant to use for the evaluation of variation and interim and final certificates.

The Joint Council for Landscape Industries' (JCLI) contract and all other standard forms of contract therefore contain an obligation for the contractor, whether tendering on the basis of a specification and drawings, schedules, schedules of rates or bills of quantities to the contractor, to break down his tender. This breakdown will provide the necessary details of build up, lump sum or otherwise, for the landscape consultant to be able to check that the tender contains no significant errors and for the valuation of variations and interim certificates.

Tenders based on specification and drawings

Even when the tenderer has to take off his own quantities from a specification and drawings it is essential to ensure that even if no quantities are given, the tender is at least broken down so that the landscape consultant is given details of the cost of the individual components of preliminaries, soil preparation, grassing, shrubs, trees and elements of hard landscape. Tenderer's individual circumstances may result in a wide range of different prices for the various elements of the work, while the totals may not be dissimilar but the breakdown of tenders in this way always indicates areas where in the event of a large divergence, at least checks can be made. Wherever possible even on small projects it is always advisable in tender summaries, to include an approximation of the total area involved for each element, so that all tenders are submitted on the same basis. One tender in which the estimator has measured 55m^2 of grass and 45m^2 of shrub border can never be comparable with one which has allowed for 45m^2 of grass and 55m^2 of shrub border.

Schedules

BS 1192:Part 4 defines schedules as 'Tabulated information on a range of similar items' and gives as examples those for tree work, planting shrubs and climbers, with various columns for the numbers involved, i.e. name, type, size, position, unit rate and total cost.

Name	Type	Size	Location	Unit rate No	Total cost

Schedule of rates

It should be noted the JCLI contract provides the option of either schedules or schedules of rates to be included in the contract documents. This enables the contract to be used not only for lump sum contracts but also for those based on schedules of rates where the actual work required is not known at the outset and is remeasured and valued only when it has been completed. A comprehensive schedule of rates including all that is likely to be required may often be little less than a bill of quantities without the quantities. Under such circumstances, it is often useful to include 'notional' quantities based on an approximation of the area or volume envisaged, which although must be remeasured on completion, at least encourages the inclusion of a more accurate tender rate.

Bills of quantities

Clearly tenders will be more accurate if submitted on the basis of full bills of quantities prepared by the landscape consultant or quantity surveyor and paid for by the client direct. The cost of this can rarely be seen to be justified on landscape contracts or sub-contracts of a lesser value than £10 000. On the larger contracts however bills of quantities are essential for proper cost control.

To provide a uniform basis for measuring building work, an independent committee (The Standing Joint Committee) of builders and quantity surveyors was set up in 1922 which has ensured that the minimum information necessary to define the nature and extent of the work are provided to estimators in a standard sequence and format. This enables them to submit an accurately priced tender. Any departures from the standard measurement conventions must be specifically drawn to the attention of the tenderer.

Standard Method of Measurement of Building Works (SMM7)

As far as landscape works are concerned however landscape contractors are particularly badly served. Landscape operations were covered in the earlier edition, SMM6 dated March 1979, by only 48 words in section D44 – Landscaping:

> Soiling, cultivating, seeding, treating top surface, fertilising and turfing to surfaces shall be given separately in square metres, stating the thickness of soil and the quantity per square metre of the seed or fertiliser. Any requirements for watering, weeding, cutting, settlement, reseeding and the like shall be stated.

SMM6 was said to be an interim measure pending a simpler but more radical re-arrangement. The new SMM7 published in 1988 is based on the Common Arrangement, adopted also for drawings and specifications, to produce a co-ordinated set of documents. In addition to the bills of quantity being used for tendering, evaluating interim certificates and variations, it was hoped that the new format would enable them to be used for production planning, ordering materials, cost control and analyses. This information was available in the initial stages of taking off the quantities from the drawings but was lost by the time the measurements had been collated and worked up and printed into the measured items in the bills of quantity. It remains to be seen whether these objectives have been achieved in practice.

The JCLI Method of Measurement for Landscape Works

This was published in 1978 in an attempt to amplify the inadequate 48 words in SMM6. It comprises some 65 rules grouped under the following seven headings:

1 Introduction
2 Preambles
3 Cultivation and preparation of ground for growing material
4 Seeding and turfing
5 Planting including tree and shrub planting
6 Thinning, pruning, tree surgery and grass improvement
7 Protection of existing artefacts and growing material during construction.

The first two sections cover the provision of additional information, the remaining five the work to be included under the various headings and how it is to be measured, so that contractors being sent tender documents from a wide variety of sources will receive them on the same familiar sequence format. JCLI has now redrafted these rules into the same format as SMM7 so that they are compatible both with the Co-ordinating Committee for Project Information (CCPI) Common Arrangement and SMM7 itself.

Civil engineering contracts

Landscape contracts let in accordance with the provisions of the Institution of Civil Engineers (ICE) Form, in which the work is paid for on a remeasurement basis, have similar and simpler, but not identical, rules for the preparation of civil engineering and planting measurements with more items grouped together.

Tender procedures

When the drawings, specification and if necessary bills of quantities are approaching completion, provided that it has not been decided to negotiate a tender with a single contractor, it is necessary to give consideration to which firms are to be invited to tender in competition for the work, either by submission of rates or a lump sum. In either case it is necessary to ascertain, beforehand, if the tenderers are interested and willing to submit a tender in competition.

Inviting tenders

When the details of the work to be included in the contract have been finalized and fully set out in the documents on which the landscape contractor is to be invited to tender, it is then necessary to select a suitable firm to whom the work can be entrusted, and to negotiate or invite competitive tenders from those firms considered to be most appropriate.

'Open' tendering, when tender documents are sent to any contractor replying in response to an advertisement by a local authority in the local and technical press, is neither considered to be good practice nor is it recommended by government departments. Where an authority's standing orders still require it, they can best be complied with by, having made the necessary advertisement, inviting tenders only from a limited number of those best qualified from those applying, taking care to include in the list only firms of the same size and standards of competence. It is unrealistic to expect Rolls Royce to quote a cheap price for repairing a Ford nor will Ford provide workmanship of the same standard as Rolls Royce. Their quotes will be comparable neither in quality nor price.

Strict adherence to the proper procedures in preparing tender documents and inviting tenders is essential if they are to be submitted expeditiously and accurately. Depending on the time available, scope of work and type of contract selected, a choice has to be made between remeasurement contracts based solely on schedules of rates which only require the contractor to quote his percentage additions to the RICS labour, materials and plant rates (which include overheads, travelling time, emoluments and holidays with pay etc.) or as lump sum tenders based on drawings and specifications alone or with full bills of quantities prepared and paid for by the client.

In either case the same tendering procedures will apply. Those for the building industry are set out in the National Joint Consultative Council (NJCC) for Building Codes of Procedure for Single and Two Stage Tendering and are equally applicable to the landscape industry.

Selective tender lists must always be prepared in consultation with the client using only those firms known to the consultant to be of proven ability, either from personal experience or from references from other consultants, or who have satisfactorily executed similar work for the client in the past.

The NJCC Code, having been agreed by all parties concerned (the contractors and client representatives including local authorities and the DoE) lays down precise requirements for the maximum number of contractors from whom tenders are to be invited, dependent on the estimated contract sum (five for contracts up to £50 000, six for between £50 000 and £250 000, and eight for between £250 000 and £1 000 000). Five is normally also the minimum number to allow for contractors returning tender documents by return due to changed circumstances and for tenders submitted after the tender date (or not at all). It is essential to ensure that at least three bona fide tenders are received and reported to the client. Any fewer tenders often results in a completely new tender invitation, to include additional contractors, with the delay that this inevitably causes.

To minimize the risk of this happening the Code provides for all those it is intended to include in the tender list to be written to or telephoned beforehand, informing them of:

1 the location and scope of the work;
2 the consultants involved;
3 the composition of the tender documents (i.e. if quantities prepared on behalf of the client will be provided);
4 the form of contract to be used; and
5 the proposed dates for the invitation and submission of tenders;

asking that they confirm their willingness and ability to submit a tender by the date and time stated.

The tender documents must always state if the tender is to be on a fixed price or fluctuations basis and state the contract period during which the work must be completed. The Code provides for tenders to remain open for acceptance within 28 days, or in exceptional circumstances, if the approval of a funding authority such as the Housing Corporation or a government department is involved, 56 days. If these requirements are complied with, subject to an arithmetic check on the tender rates, the choice of contractor will be a relatively simple matter, almost invariably being automatically the lowest tender submitted, since all are on a

Dear Sirs

Following your acceptance of the invitation to tender for the above, I/we now have pleasure in enclosing the following:

(a) two copies of the bill(s) of quantities;

(b) two copies of the general arrangement drawings indicating the general character and shape and disposition of the works;

(c) two copies of the form of tender;

(d) addressed envelopes for the return of the tender (and priced bill(s)[†]) and instructions relating thereto.

Will you please also note:

1 drawings and details may be inspected at ....;

2 the site may be inspected by arrangement with the employer/ architect (1);

3 tendering procedures will be in accordance with the principles of the Code of Procedure for Single Stage Selective Tendering 1977;

4 examination and adjustment of priced bill(s) (Section 6 of the Code) Alternative 1/Alternative 2 (1) will apply.

The completed form of tender is to be sealed in the endorsed envelope provided and delivered or sent by post to reach .... not later than .... hours on .... the ..... day of .... 19....

*The completed form of tender and the priced bill(s) of quantities sealed in separate endorsed envelopes provided are to be lodged not later than ...... hours on .... the .... day of .... 19.... The envelope containing the tender should be endorsed with the job title: that containing the bill(s) of quantities should be endorsed with the job title and tenderer's name.

Will you please acknowledge receipt of this letter and enclosures and confirm that you are able to submit a tender in accordance with these instructions?

Yours faithfully
Architect/Quantity Surveyor (1)

[1] Delete as appropriate before issuing.

 * Applicable in Scotland only in which case the preceding sentence would not be used.

 † Applicable in Scotland only.

Figure 5.5 An example of a covering letter for tender documents

comparable basis. If any bona fide errors in the tender are discovered the Code provides for them to be corrected in one of two alternative ways, the choice of which is also confirmed in the Form of Tender. Alternative 1 requires the contractor to stand by his lump sum tender and the error to be covered subsequently by a percentage correction to all his rates. This is the option normally adopted by local authorities and in the event of the error being such that the contractor is unable or unwilling to stand by his tender (often the wisest course from both the client's and contractors' point of view, if the error is substantial) the next lowest tender being accepted.

Alternative 2 is normally chosen on private sector projects, the amount of the error being added to or subtracted from the tender sum and the contract being let in the revised amount. This gets over the problem when the corrected tender is still less than that of the next lowest tender although of course, if the corrected tender is then above that of the second lowest tender the contract will of course be placed with the latter. Figure 5.5 shows an example of the covering letter for tender documents.

The other problem, which not infrequently arises, is when the tender is greater than anticipated and exceeds the clients' authorized expenditure. The Code provides in this instance that reductions must always be negotiated only with the lowest tenderer and only if negotiations breakdown should an attempt be made to negotiate a lower tender with the second lowest. If however the reductions necessary are so great as to have materially changed the scope of the work, then the best course is to prepare a new set of tender documents and invite further tenders from the same or if appropriate, another selected list of contractors.

Contractors must always be told that 'qualified' tenders, such as those offering an alternative contract period or being 'subject to the availability of labour and materials' will be automatically rejected, as should those including substitutes for those plant species or sizes specified, although the Code provides for them to be considered, if submitted as supplementary or additional tenders to that submitted in accordance with the tender documents.

In landscape contracts, it is also essential to state in the tender documents the anticipated contract commencement date (having allowed four weeks for acceptance and a further four weeks during which the contractor can mobilize and allocate the necessary labour, plant and materials) since the cost of any upkeep required to be included for after practical completion will vary considerably dependent on the time of year i.e. six months upkeep during the summer months costs the contractor considerably more than six months during the winter.

Reporting on tenders
Only after the date and time for the submission of tenders has passed –

usually noon on Monday, to allow for contractors' estimators to work over the weekend and, due to the uncertainties of postal deliveries, for tenders to be delivered by hand - should tenders be opened, those being delivered late being marked 'returned – received out of time' and returned unopened (Figure 5.6)

A full list of the names and tender sums received can then be prepared including the names of those invited to tender but who had subsequently declined or did not submit (with the reasons where known). At this stage the Code requires all but the lowest two or three to be notified that their tender is unlikely to be recommended for acceptance but without giving any indication of the other tenders received nor their amounts.

A financial analysis and arithmetic check only on the lowest should then follow to establish that the tender has been fairly, accurately and consistently priced and is free from major arithmetical errors, any that are found being corrected by which ever alternative has been previously chosen.

This having been done it is then possible to prepare a report for the client containing:

1 a list of the names and amounts of the tenders received and in whose presence they were opened, together with the names and reasons if known of those not submitted;
2 any qualifications and confirmation that they had been withdrawn;
3 any amendments to the tender documents made during the tender period;
4 any corrections required as a result of arithmetical errors;
5 confirmation that the tender has been fairly, accurately and consistently priced;
6 any savings to be made to bring the tender within the authorized expenditure or any revised budget; and
7 confirmation of the ability of the contractor to commence and complete the work within the time and to the standards required.

If the procedures laid down in the Code have been followed, only rarely will the recommendation for acceptance of a tender, other than the lowest, be justified.

When, and only when, approval for acceptance of a tender has been confirmed by the client should the other tenderers be formally notified of the results of all the tenders submitted, including both confirmation of their own and that accepted. This can be achieved by a standard letter which lists the amounts of tenders received in ascending order so that they cannot be identified with a particular firm. Names of firms can also be included if required but they should be listed alphabetically to preserve confidentiality.

Tender for ...Landscape...Improvements.,..Forest..Glades...

To ...I.C...Green.,..Landscape...Architects..Dept...Ambershire
District Council, High St, Amberham

Sir(s)

I/We having read the conditions of contract specification and
schedules of quantity delivered to me/us and having examined the
drawings attached thereto do hereby offer to execute and complete
in accordance with the conditions of contract the whole of the
works described within the period specified from the date of
possession for the sum of £ Jb, 591 .... (Sixteen thousand, five ..
hundred.and.one. pounds).

I/We agree that should obvious pricing errors in arithmetic be
discovered before acceptance of this offer in the priced schedules
of quantity submitted by me/us these errors /will be dealt with
and adjusted (Alternative 1)/ will not be adjusted and we will
stand by our tender (Alternative 2)(1) in accordance with Section
6 of the current NJCC for Building Code of Procedure for Single
Stage Selective Tendering.

This tender remains open for consideration for 28/56/ days (2)
from the date fixed for the submission for lodgement of tenders.

Dated this twenty.third .... day of November .... 1987..

Name .... Doug..Potterton.&.Sons.......................

Address.......... Greenacre ....
.... Amberham ....

Signature .... Doug..P.Herton ....

REFERENCES: 1 Delete as appropriate before issuing.

             2 The period specified should not normally exceed
                28 days and only in exceptional circumstances
                should be extended to 56 days.

SUMMARY OF TENDER

Preliminaries	2 000.00
Hard landscape	7 329.00
Top soil	1 000.00
Grassed areas	1 120.00
Shrubs and herbaceous plants	2 647.00
Trees	2 405.00
	16 501.00

Figure 5.6 An example of a Form of Tender

6

Landscape Contracts and Contract Conditions

The meaning and essentials of a valid contract

Both the law of tort and the law of contract are derived from common law, but whereas tort involves a civil wrong or unreasonable behaviour and can be independent of any contract, the law of contract depends on a commercial bargain between two individuals or legal bodies. This is not to say however that the existence of a contract does not prevent one of the parties suing the other in tort, in the event of a dispute instead. To bring a case of negligence under contract however the plaintiff has to prove that the defendant owed him a duty of care, that there was a breach of that duty and that he suffered damages as a result.

Simple contracts do not have to be in any special form, they can be made orally and do not need to be in writing unless they are such as HP agreements, contracts of employment or are under seal. Even if not in writing, however, to be legal there has to be an offer and it has to be accepted. Only when accepted does the contract come into being, even though any formal contract documents may not yet have been signed.

To be legally binding there must also be benefit to both parties and a *consideration* (unless the contract is under seal). This usually takes the form of the payment of money although the consideration may be the provision of goods or services in return. The amount of the consideration even if only a penny, blatantly unjust as in the case of Shylock's bargain, or a contractor offering to carry out work for a price which must inevitably cost him more, still makes the contract binding. If he does not do it for the price agreed he must pay the other party to the contract damages. The price to be paid is irrelevant, once fixed and stated in the contract, and the courts cannot alter it. If the amount of the consideration is however not stated, the courts will fix a quantum meruit payment – £12 000 against the £64 000 claimed in *L. Obermeister* v. *London Rodwell Properties*, 1967.

Usually contracts contain express terms or conditions for the execution of the work and the method and time of payment. Even when not explicitly or expressly stated there are other terms which can be implied e.g. to carry out the duties required of him under a contract for landscape works there is an implied obligation on the contractor to give the landscape consultant (but not the client!) access to the site and for the employer to give possession of the site within a reasonable period. It can also be implied that the contractor will exercise all reasonable skill and care in the execution of the works unless expressly stated to the contrary and subject always to the provisions of the Unfair Contract Terms Act. If however the contractor has built something strictly in accordance with the drawings and it subsequently fails, it cannot be argued that he has any responsibility or implied warranty as to its fitness for the purpose for which it was designed (*Lynch* v. *Thorne*, 1956).

Privity of contract arises when only those directly concerned in the contract receive the benefits, have any liability under it and are bound by it. Contracts can be held not to be binding on the parties under certain circumstances, the most common being those arising from a mistake by one or both of the parties, when the mistake is undisputed and fundamental to the contract, e.g. in the ownership of the land on which the contract is to be executed. Equally, especially if arising from an ambiguity, if one or both of the parties believe they have entered into a contract with fundamentally different intentions, it can be held there is no binding contract.

Misrepresentation is also grounds for determining or rendering a contract void, when a statement which is induced into, but not a term of, the contract is found to be untrue if made fraudulently or innocently; and if the former will entitle the other party to damages in tort whether he opts to determine or not. Contracts which are against the law where the work contravenes the law, e.g. planning or building regulations or when one of the parties is legally precluded, are also unenforceable.

The discharge of most contracts occurs when both parties have *performed* all their obligations under the contract, the contractor has completed the work and made good all defects and the employer has paid the contractor all the monies due to him in full and final settlement. Equally, if one or other of the parties, usually the contractor, has been *frustrated,* not because what he has contracted to do is too expensive or proves to be impossible but if as rarely happens the contractual obligation becomes so radically different from what is in the contract, the parties may be discharged from their obligations also.

A *breach of contract* on the other hand, when a contractor refuses to obey an instruction to remove defective work or some event occurs for a reason not provided for in the contract, entitles the employer to consequential damages.

Repudiation of a contract arises when one or other of the parties refuses to discharge his contractual obligations and if it is so serious as to go to the root of the contract, is considered to be a fundamental breach, entitling the other for example to cease work and withdraw from the site or to refuse to pay for the work and claim damages for delay until the work is properly completed.

Most standard forms of contract envisage these situations and provide for them so that only the contractor's employment is determined and the parties remain bound by the contract conditions.

The types of contract for landscape works

There are six different types of contract currently used to procure buildings and landscape work in this country today:

1 Management
2 Cost plus
3 Approximate quantities
4 Lump sum
5 Design and build
6 Package deal.

There are also a variety of standard forms of contract for each for use by government departments and in both the public and private sectors. The choice of which depends on a variety of factors the most important being dependent on the client's priorities in respect of the time available for completion, the client's knowledge of his requirements at the outset and the need for cost of the work to be contained within the limits of the authorized expenditure.

Management

A management contract in which a landscape contractor is appointed to manage the construction of a landscape contract for a new work is usually the most suitable when the completion date is so important that the work on site must start before the client's requirements and the design are finalized and costs ascertained. The main contractor is employed only to manage the site without employing the subcontractors himself.

Cost plus

Cost plus contracts are also equally often used when the scope is unknown at the outset and the need for quality requires the client to choose some but not all of the specialist subcontractors but in this case are all actually engaged by the main contractor.

Approximate quantities

Approximate quantities contracts are possible when there is time to complete the design and most of the drawings before the work starts but not to measure them in detail. Quotations are then obtained based only on approximate quantities and specification and the contract is entered into on the basis of a tender sum before the work starts on site. The work is then remeasured after it has been completed on site and the 'ascertained final sum' valued in accordance with the rates in the bills.

Lump sum

Lump sum contracts are used when there is time to complete the tender documents with full drawings, specification and often complete bills of quantities, so that a lump sum for the work to be finished by a certain date, can be agreed at the outset. For local authority work and all other contracts where staying within the authorized expenditure is of prime importance, this is still the type of contract most often used for building and landscape work and can be let either on a fixed price or fluctuations basis if the duration of the work is more than 12 months.

Design and build

Design and build contracts are applicable when the scope of the work is relatively simple and no more than an adequate quality required. Under these circumstances the client may not need to choose the consultants or any of the subcontractors himself and finds it preferable for this to be left to the contractor, who then takes full responsibility for the satisfactory completion of the work, within the time stated and for the contract sum. In this instance variations are undesirable and expensive. If they arise many of the benefits of this type of contract are lost.

Package deal

Package deal contracts are really for a standard design and if not already built, at least similar in almost every respect to one on another site that the employer or contractor can visit and build, using the same design and details.

The relative advantages and disadvantages of each type of contract are illustrated diagramatically in Figure 6.1.

The JCLI Standard Form of Agreement for Landscape Works

The Landscape Institute first published a Standard Form of Agreement for Landscape Works for use without quantities in 1969. This closely followed the 1963 edition of the Standard Form of Building Contract, as did the Landscape edition for use with bills of quantities which was published in 1973. The two forms did not however incorporate subsequent Joint Contracts Tribunal (JCT) amendments and five years later in April 1978 the Joint Council for Landscape Industries with the co-operation of the Landscape Institute published a much shorter form. This with additional clauses appropriate for the planting aspects was almost identical to the then current JCT Form of Agreement for Minor Building Works which they had first published in 1968. This had been agreed with the JCT in the interest of conformity and ensured the acceptance of the JCLI Form by the local authority and county councils' associations who were represented as constituent members of the JCT.

Since the designation 'landscape architect' is not protected by legislation as is the architect, there is no need for the alternative 'contract administrator' as in the JCT contracts. Where the landscape work is under the direction of a local authority chief officer other than a landscape architect or under a landscape manager or scientist, their title should be entered accordingly in the First Recital and can thereafter be referred to as 'the landscape architect'. It is important to enter the office and not the name of the individual person, as this could cause difficulties should they leave the practice or the authority before the contract is completed.

The Form was revised in April 1981 to conform with the section headed format of JCT MW80 and was reprinted with minor corrections again in 1982. It was again revised in April 1985 by the insertion of an additional Clause 1.3 enabling the form to be used with full bills of quantities prepared in accordance with SMM and the JCLI Rules for the Measurement of Landscape Works, provision for the naming of a quantity surveyor having always been provided for in a 4th Recital if required. An addition to the end of the 1st Recital also enabled the form to be used under either English or Scottish law as appropriate. (See Appendix 3.)

It is now therefore the recommended Form of Agreement for all local authority and private sector landscape contracts with or without quantities in the United Kingdom, up to a value of at least £75 000 at 1981 prices. For works executed as a subcontract under a building contract or of a higher value other conditions are appropriate, e.g. NSC4 for subcontracts under JCT80 and IFC84 for landscape contracts of up to £250 000 which are discussed later in this chapter.

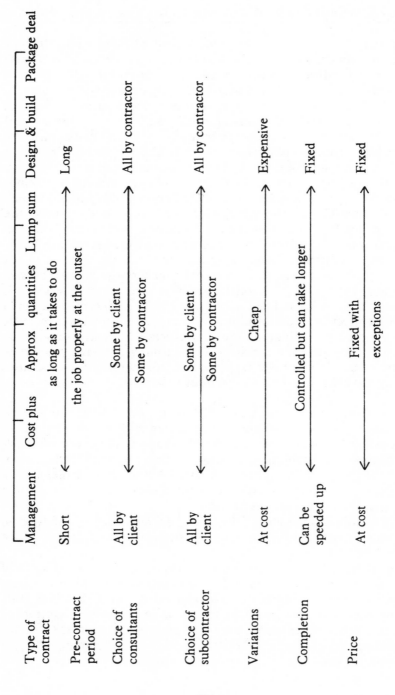

Figure 6.1 The advantages and disadvantages of different types of contract.

An explanation of the Form of Agreement is given below (see also Appendix 3). Provision is made at the head of the Form of Agreement for it to be dated and the names and addresses of the employer and the contractor to be filled in.

The recitals

There are 4 Recitals and 4 Articles in the Form.

The 1st Recital

Space is left for a short two-line description of the work to be carried out ('the Works') and the name of the (practice of) the landscape architect followed by the contract documents, namely the drawings, specification, schedules, schedules of rates, and/or bills of quantities – therein after referred to as 'the contract documents' with a footnote pointing out those not included to be deleted and concluding with the option of English or Scottish Law.

The 2nd Recital

This requires the contractor to price the contract documents.

The 3rd Recital

This requires the contract to be signed by both parties or their representatives.

The 4th Recital

This names the quantity surveyor (but with no mention in the subsequent conditions of what his duties are) with provision for the employer to nominate another, should he die or cease to be the quantity surveyor for the contract.

The 4 articles

Article 1

This obliges the contractor to carry out and complete the works.

Article 2

The other part of the 'bargain' – the amount in words and figures the employer will pay the contractor to carry out and complete the Works. It also states this to be exclusive of any value added tax and for which reason interim certificates are exclusive of VAT, which is the subject of a second invoice submitted by the contractor to the employer direct (but who may or may not want the landscape consultant to check it for him) although there is no mention of this in the LI Appointment.

Article 3

Space again for the insertion of the name of the landscape consultant and in the event of his death or ceasing to be the consultant, for the employer to nominate another within 14 days who will not have the power to disregard or overrule any certificate or instruction given by his predecessor.

Article 4

In the event of any dispute between the employer or landscape architect on his behalf for an arbitrator (who *does* have the power to disregard, or overrule any certificate or instruction) to be agreed or to be appointed by the President or Vice President of the Landscape Institute.

In addition, 1, to issuing certificates for interim payments and the final account, 2, at practical completion and when defects have been made good, 3, valuing variations, 4, extending the contract period for completion as may be reasonable and 5, issuing such instructions as are necessary for the proper carrying out of the works, the landscape consultant can, if the contractor does not comply with an instruction within seven days, instruct others to carry out the works and deduct the cost from the money due to the contractor. The case of *Sutcliffe* v. *Thakrah* in 1974 however confirmed that the consultant was not carrying out these duties as 'a quasi arbitrator', since his decisions could always be challenged, however 'fairly and reasonably' he was required to act. He was only an agent of the employer, and the contractor could always refer a decision of the employer and/or the landscape consultant on his behalf to the court.

The JCLI Conditions of Contract appear on four pages under eight headings as follows:

1 The intentions of the parties

1.1 The contractor's obligations

The first condition is the obligation of the contractor to carry out and complete the works with due diligence in accordance with the contract documents in a good and workmanlike manner. The only qualification being that where the quality of materials and standard of work are a matter for the opinion of the landscape consultants, this shall be to their reasonable satisfaction. Since the consequence of this is that having approved something, should it subsequently go wrong, the landscape contractor has quite rightly been relieved of further responsibility in the matter landscape consultants will reserve this right to themselves only when it is impracticable to specify the work or material sufficiently accurately otherwise.

1.2 The landscape consultant's duties

Under the contract these are relatively few (his own duties to his client under his conditions of engagement to 'monitor' the work being an entirely separate matter) namely the issue of certificates, valuations, extensions and instructions. The responsibility that he carries in their execution, and the consequences financial or otherwise to his client or the contractor in the event of his making a mistake, are considerable.

1.3 The contract bills

These must be prepared in accordance with SMM and the JCLI Rules for the Measurement of Soft Landscape Works, so that all the quantities are measured and prepared in a common form familiar to the estimators (particularly important in the age of computerized quantities). Also so that estimators can ensure that everything necessary is itemized and included in their tender, since if it is not in the Bill and is necessary whether shown on the drawings or not, the contractor is entitled to charge it as an extra. Departures from the rules are of course sometimes necessary due to special circumstances arising on a particular project and these of course are permissable, subject to the fact being expressly stated against the item concerned.

2 Commencement and completion

2.1 Dates

The date when the works may be commenced should be filled in the space provided. It should be noted that this is the date when the employer intends to hand the site over to the contractor, after which its safety and security is his responsibility. There is no obligation on the contractor however to start the work on site on this date (provided he still complies with the date for completion to be inserted on the following line). Contractors may wish to delay the actual start until they have received all the necessary plants and other material and arranged for the labour and plants required to be available, thereby reducing the amount of time they have to spend on site. A delayed actual start date is therefore a matter for mutual agreement. If however the delay in starting is caused by the employer then the contractor may be able to consider the whole contract frustrated and be entitled to renegotiate the contract sum.

2.2 Extensions

Extensions of contract period are made by the landscape consultant for such periods of time as may be reasonable, when completion of the work is delayed (not progress) for reasons beyond the control of the contractor. Neither in this Form of Contract nor in the JCT Minor Works is there any obligation on the contractor to notify the consultant of any delays nor to list the reasons for the delay which are beyond his control. Equally there is no timetable within which the landscape consultant must make his extension nor, when he does, to give the contractor his reasons or any breakdown of the period by which he has extended the contract. Clearly however the more information he can give the contractor, the less likely he is to challenge the decision and refer the matter to arbitration. Reasons beyond the control of the contractor are usually considered to be equivalent to the 12 'relevant events' set out in Clause 25 of JCT 80 (see Table 6.1).

2.3 Damages for non-completion

Damages for non-completion are provided to reimburse the employer for any damages he has suffered as a result of the landscape contractor not having completed the work within the contract period or any extended contract period. Forecasting the weekly sum that these damages are likely to amount to, must be evaluated as accurately as possible, always bearing in mind that if they are too low the employer will not be adequately compensated and if they are too high, not only will a court not enforce them on the grounds that they were not a true estimate (liquidated and ascertained) and were intended to be punitive, but also if they are too high tenders will be inflated to cover the cost of an event that arises all too often. Damages are normally considered to arise under three headings:-

1 notional loss of interest on capital;
2 inconvenience or any actual consequential loss; or
3 additional professional fees.

The calculation of the first is relatively easy, by the application of the formula:

$$\frac{\text{Contract sum}}{52 \text{ weeks}} \times \frac{\text{bank rate}}{100} = £\ldots\text{. per week.}$$

This is explained more fully in the JCLI Practice Note 3 attached to the back of the contract form (see Appendix 3) and compensates the employer for loss of use of the money that he has already paid under interim certificates to date, for which he has received no benefit and which could otherwise have been invested elsewhere and earning profit. The second heading, referring to inconvenience or any actual consequential loss, rarely arises in landscape contracts (it can be a considerable sum on certain commercial building projects). The third is often overlooked but the extra cost to the landscape consultant in visiting the site during the period of overrun and which will not be reflected in any increase in the value of work certified, often can amount to several hundreds of pounds spread over a number of months.There is no provision for the involvement of the landscape consultant, the clause simply providing that if the work is not completed by the due date the contractor *shall* pay or allow the employer the liquidated damages at the rate stated.

2.4 Completion date

The completion date is to be certified by the landscape consultant 'when in his opinion the works have reached Practical Completion'. This phrase has yet to be defined in the courts and hopefully never will be, since this might legally confine the way in which the landscape consultant arrived at his opinion. Every case must be decided on the merits of the particular situation prevailing in that instance, but it is generally considered practical completion (not practically – i.e. almost completed) to have been achieved when the works can safely be used for the purpose for which they were designed.

2.5 Defects liability

Defects liability covers the situation when after a period of use – usually six months in the case of building work and twelve months in the case of heating, electrical engineering services and landscape work – the work, material or plants, through no fault of the designer, are not performing as well as they could be expected to. The contract therefore provides for the work to be inspected at the .end of the period specified, and the defects to be made good by the contractor at his own expense, after which the landscape consultant will issue a further certificate when these defects have been properly made good.

2.6 Partial possession

Partial possession by the employer was not included in the JCT Minor Works Contract, it being thought unlikely to arise. In landscape works however the previously unforeseen possibility of part of the works being finished in advance of another which might have been delayed, and the employer wanting to use it if the contractor would agree, was thought to be more likely. Circumstances could arise when all the work was finished in the autumn but it was too late to sow the grassed areas, or conversely in the spring when all the hard landscape was finished but it was too late to plant bare root standard size trees. This is therefore provided for in Clause 2.6 which allows, while the contractor remains responsible for the balance of the site, a certificate of partial completion to be issued for that part handed over, the relevant proportion of retention to be released and the contractor relieved of responsibility for any liquidated and ascertained damages for the part handed over, for which he might otherwise be liable.

2.7 Plant failures

Failures of plants are not covered in the JCT Forms but are covered in the JCLI Form in Clause 2.7. All plants, other than those covered by Clause 6.5 i.e. stolen or subject to vandalism, found to be missing or defective prior to practical completion, are to be replaced by the contractor entirely at his own expense. If this is during the dormant season the landscape consultant will carry out his inspection six weeks after the planting has come into leaf.

Two alternative Sub-clauses 2.7A and 2.7B cover plants which subsequently die. The choice of clauses depends on whether subsequent maintenance after practical completion has been undertaken by the contractor or by the employer. Clause 2.7A covers the subsequent maintenance by the contractor and provides separate blank spaces, for various periods to be inserted, for making good grass, shrubs, plants, ordinary stock trees, advanced extra large nursery stock and semi-mature trees. Any found defective at the end of the periods inserted, to be replaced by the contractor entirely at his own cost unless the consultant instructs otherwise. When all necessary replacements have been provided the consultant issues a further certificate. If however all maintenance subsequent to practical completion is undertaken by the employer then clause 2.7B is to be used, which relieves the contractor of all further responsibility and any plants that subsequently die, whether due to inadequate maintenance by the employer or for any other reason, are his responsibility and he is then responsible for the costs of any replacements.

If plant failures at practical completion are greater than 10 per cent, their value is to be deducted from the penultimate certificate issued at that stage before releasing half the retention monies under Clause 4.3.

3 Control of the works

3.1 Assignment

Assignment of the whole contract by either the employer or the contractor to another without written consent, is precluded by Clause 3.1. This did not appear in the first addition in 1978 but was added in 1981 to conform to the new JCT 80 Minor Works when it was published.

3.2 Subcontracting

This clause prohibits the landscape contractor from subcontracting any part of the works without the written consent of the landscape consultant. It should be noted that this consent should not be reasonably withheld and there is no obligation on the part of the landscape contractor to inform the consultant of the name of the firm to whom he intends to subcontract the work. Under such circumstances it is suggested it would not be unreasonable for the consultant to withhold his consent until this information too had been provided. As soon as the name of the proposed subcontractor is known, it is always essential for the consultant to take up references from other landscape consultants for whom the subcontractor has previously worked, if the subcontractor is not known to the consultant already. It should also be noted that there is no provision in this contract for the contractor to allow direct employees of the client (artists and tradesmen) to carry out other work at the same time as the main contract works, whether described in the tender documents or not. He can of course 'nominate' such other firms to carry out work as a subcontract under Clause 3.7.

3.3 Contractor's representative

The contractor is to keep a competent person in charge on site at all reasonable hours i.e. during normal working hours and when work is being carried out. Any instructions issued to him are considered to have been issued to the landscape contractor in accordance with the terms of the contract.

Although the clause does not say that the representative should not be changed without the consultant's consent, this is important and no mere formality, since it safeguards the consultant from the possibility of mistakenly issuing an instruction to an employee of the contractor direct and assuming responsibility in the event of a subsequent accident. Such an accident occurred in the case of *Clayton* v. *Woodman* in 1962 when a consultant instructed a bricklayer to cut a chase in brickwork and who was injured when it subsequently collapsed due to lack of shoring.

3.4 Exclusion from the works

Exclusion from the site of certain employees of the contractor may be ordered by the consultant if he considers their behaviour to be offensive or detrimental to the works. He cannot of course require their dismissal from employment by the contractor, since this might conflict with the Employment Protection Act of 1975. This power should not be used lightly and then only with tact. Contractors' (and landscape consultants') choice of employees most competent to carry out the work is a matter entirely for their own discretion.

3.5 Landscape consultant's instructions

The power for the landscape consultant to issue instructions on the employer's behalf to the contractor is covered by Clause 3.5. All instructions are to be in writing (oral instructions to be confirmed within two days) and are to be complied with by the contractor 'forthwith' i.e. 'as soon as reasonably can be'.*

In 1981 the power to instruct others to carry out the work and deduct the cost from monies due to the contractor, if within seven days he had not complied with a written notice to do so, was added to follow JCT 80 Minor Works.

3.6 Variations

Instructions to vary the work covered by the contract documents, including the order in which they shall be carried out may be issued on behalf of the employer by the landscape consultant under Clause 3.6. The limits to scope are covered by the consultant's agreement with his client but whether the consultant has exceeded his authority or not, the contractor is obliged to carry them out and the employer must pay for them accordingly whether he wants them or not. They are to be valued by the landscape consultant (not the contractor) on a 'fair and reasonable basis' using where relevant the rates in the contract documents priced by the contractor as laid down in the First and Second Recitals. There is however a proviso in the clause that these rates shall not be applicable if the variation substantially varies the scope of the work and, instead of valuing the work as set out above, for the consultant (not the employer) and contractor to agree the price between themselves before the work is put in hand.

3.7 PC and provisional sums

The ability for the landscape consultant to include prime cost (PC)

---

*Osborne, P. G., *A Concise Law Dictionary,* 5th ed., Sweet and Maxwell, London, 1964.

and provisional sums in the contract and to issue the necessary instructions for their expenditure is covered by Clause 3.7. The definition of PC and provisional sums in the standard method of measurement SMM is as follows:

Provisional sums are for work or costs which cannot be entirely foreseen, defined or detailed at the time of issuing the tender documents. Prime cost (PC) sums are those for work by a nominated subcontractor, statutory authority, public undertaking, or materials or goods to be obtained from a nominated supplier, the sum to be exclusive of any profit required by the general contractor, for which provision should be made for it to be included in the tender.

It should be noted that there is no requirement for any cash discount for prompt payment to be allowed to the landscape contractor nor is there any reference to any obligatory procedures or documentation to be used when PC sums are used to enable the consultant to instruct the contractor to obtain the work from a single nominated subcontractor, or supplier.

JCLI however produced in 1986 a standard form of tender and subcontract, the use of which ensures that the subcontract conditions match those of the main contract. This form is suitable for both, those subcontractors chosen by the main contractor and those by the landscape consultant (see p.130).

Contingency sum. PC and provisional sum are not to be confused with 'contingency' sums which are separate amounts included in tender documents 'to be expended or deducted from the contract sum in whole or in part as instructed by the landscape architect'.

Depending on the complexity of the project it is inevitable that certain additional work of a larger or smaller amount will be required ranging from a relatively small number on a simple new project to several of a higher value on a large complex alteration scheme usually between 2½ and 7½ per cent of the estimated contract sum. These are covered both by the inclusion of a lump sum and also a notional amount of time and materials to be provided on a 'dayworks' basis which the contractor then has to price, thereby introducing a competitive element for variations to be valued in this way.

3.8 Objections to nomination

The acknowledgement of the fact that PC sums may be used for nomination is covered by Clause 3.8 which gives the landscape contractor the right to refuse to accept the nomination of any person

Table 6.1
Events leading to extension of the contract and to reimbursement

Relevant JCT 80 events justifying an extension to the contract period for the execution of the works	Circumstances under which the contractor is entitled to reimbursement of direct loss and expense
Clause 25 Relevant events	Clause 26 Direct loss and expenses
25.4. 1. Force majeure	26.4. —
2. Exceptionally adverse weather	—
3. Loss or damage by fire etc.	—
4. Civil commotion, strikes etc.	—
5. Compliance with architect's instructions on:	—
Discrepancies	.3
Variations	.7
PC and Prov Sums	.7
Postponement	.5
Antiquities	34.3
Nominated s/c	—
Nominated suppliers	
Opening up satisfactory work	.2
6. Not having received instructions in due time.	.1
7. Nominated subcontracts or suppliers.	—
8. Artists and tradesmen	.4
9. Government restrictions	—
10. Unforeseeable shortages of labour and materials.	—
11. Statutory undertakers.	—
12. Lack of ingress or egress	.6

against whom he may make a reasonable objection or who is imposing subcontract conditions at variance with those in the standard main or subcontract forms.

To reduce the likelihood of this occurring it is always advisable to include in the tender documents, when known, the name of the firm to whom the work is to be subcontracted or by whom the materials are to be supplied; the scope of the work; and wherever possible, the period the subcontractor requires to execute the work or deliver the materials (if they are known) at the date of tender. When this is done, it is always advisable to include in the tender documents, the requirement that should any tenderer wish to raise any objection against any of the firms named, he must do so no later than ten days before the latest date set for the submission of tenders.

When it is not considered necessary to select a single firm but nevertheless for quality reasons to restrict the main contractor's choice and the work is capable of being accurately described and specified, it is always possible to include the names of three or more firms to any one of whom the landscape contractor may subcontract the work.

3.9 Disturbance of regular progress

All standard building contracts, except the JCT Minor Works Form, provide for the main contractor to be reimbursed for any direct loss and expense he has incurred due to any disturbance of the regular progress of the work (even if completion is not delayed) caused by the employer, his agents or servants (which includes the landscape consultant) and any other delays arising from lack of instructions. JCLI Clause 3.9 requires in such an event that the landscape consultant should ascertain the amount of such loss and expense, and include it in any progress payments. While there is no obligation on the contractor to provide any details of such loss, it is clearly in his interest to do so, particularly as there are over 50 different headings under which a contractor can claim reimbursement.

4 Payment

4.1 Correction of inconsistencies

The possibility of the existence of inconsistencies within or between the contract documents discovered after the contract has been signed is acknowledged in Clause 4.1, which simply states that they will be corrected and if this involves a variation, instructions should be issued and it should be valued as such. This leaves every case to be treated on its merits. The clause goes on to say that the contract conditions take precedence over the other contract documents, in which it is generally accepted that drawings take precedence over the others in respect of matters affecting location, assembly and fixing, the specification with regard to quality and the bills or schedules for quantity e.g. if the drawings show five trees and the bills or schedules list only three the contractor is deemed only to have included for the three scheduled, although he will have to provide the five and be paid for them accordingly.

4.2 Progress payments

The contractor is allowed, at intervals of not less than four weeks or at the stages specified in tender documents, to request the landscape consultant to certify progress payments, on receipt of which, the consultant must issue a certificate for the value of work properly executed to date, less that which has been previously certified. The inclusion of the word 'properly' is considered to mean 'in accordance with the *terms* of the contract and not to imply that it is in accordance with the contract documents', since this is the contractor's responsibility under Clause 1.1. Should the consultant find at this stage that any work is unsatisfactory he must of course exclude it.

Progress payments are to include the value of variations and work executed under PC and provisional sums and any materials brought on site, but as yet unfixed, if this is reasonable and proper and they are adequately stored and protected. Since legally they may not become the property of the employer until they have been fixed, even if included in a certificate and paid for, it is usual to include in the tender documents, a request for the contractor to provide evidence that he has in fact paid for them himself and that they have therefore become his own property. There is no provision for the inclusion in a certificate for materials stored *off* site, e.g. in a landscape contractor's nursery or yard and it is unwise of a landscape consultant to do so, without at least ensuring that they are properly labelled as the property of the employer, with all necessary insurance against their subsequent damage.

The Clause also provides for the deduction of 5 per cent (or other such sum as had been included in the tender and inserted in the Clause) from each certificate to cover any defects which may subsequently arise and have to be made good under Clauses 2.5 and 2.7. The employer has to honour the certificate within 14 days of the date of its issue. Lack of compliance with this obligation entitles the contractor to terminate the contract under Clause 7.2. There is no express provision in the clause for the consultant to condemn work and/or its removal from site and replacement, nor for him to instruct the contractor to execute any remedial work to bring it up to specification. To issue instructions for the latter could make him responsible for its adequacy, which would be unwise.

4.3 The Penultimate Certificate

Within 14 days of issuing his Certificate of Practical Completion, the consultant has to issue a further certificate on the basis of 97½ per cent of the contract sum adjusted for the cost of variations, PC and provisional sums and any fluctuations to which the contractor is entitled, releasing half the retention. If it is apparent however that at this stage there are plant failures in excess of 10 per cent, their value shall be deducted accordingly. The clause also provides that where the landscape contractor is being paid under the contract for the subsequent maintenance during the defects liability period, the cost of this is to be excluded from the certificates also. Like progress payments, the penultimate certificate must also be honoured within 14 days of issue.

It is important that the valuation of this certificate is as accurate as possible since the contract does not provide for the issue of any other before the Final Certificate.

4.4 The Final Certificate

The landscape contractor now has three months (or such other date as has been inserted) in which to forward to the landscape consultant all the necessary details to enable him to prepare the Final Account and Certificate (see Figure 7.4, page 138). The landscape consultant then has 28 days in which to do this and issues his certificates as soon as the defects liability period has expired, defects have been made good and he has certified accordingly. The employer must then honour the certificate within 14 days of issue.

It must be remembered that certificates are always issued for the full value of work properly executed without the deduction of any liquidated and ascertained damages which the employer may wish to deduct.

Of the three cases to reach the High Court concerning the JCT/JCLI Contract two concerned arbitration (the first being *Pincot* v. *Fur Textile Care Ltd*, 1986) on the relationship between a main contractor and subcontractors. In *Oram Builders* v. *M. and C. Pemberton*, 1985 the court decided that where an arbitration clause such as that in Article 4 covering the appointment of an arbitrator who (even though the clause did not so state) could open up and review certificates that right did not apply to the courts or the official referee unless they were specifically appointed as an arbitrator.In

115

Crestar v. *Carr* (TLR 6/5/87) a firm of contractors, Crestar Ltd entered into a contract to alter a house in Essex and by the date of Practical Completion had issued Interim Certificates to the value of £77 698 at which time the contract envisaged a retention of only a further 5 per cent would become due. The Final Certificate was however issued 3 months later for £39 975 and when the building owners, Mr and Mrs Carr, attempted to refer the matter to arbitration they were told by the builder that this was not possible, since not having settled the certificate within 14 days he was now in breach of contract. The Court of Appeal however held that such a relatively large sum oustanding on the Final Certificate was not envisaged under the contract and the matter could therefore be referred to an arbitrator.

It is of course always good practice while not being influenced by the client to inform him of the imminence of a Final Certificate as it is to discuss the matter with the contractor and obtain his agreement wherever possible before its issue.

4.5 Contribution, levy and tax changes

The sudden imposition of tax changes, contributions and levies could impose a considerable burden on landscape contractors under a fixed price contract. Should this arise therefore, Clause 4.5 provides for its recovery by the contractor from the employer using the supplementary memorandum incorporated by reference. Since this covers only the cost of 'work people' and excludes site and head office supervisory staff, provision is made for an additional percentage to be added to cover them, 20 per cent being considered appropriate for contracts in excess of 12 months and 10 per cent for contracts of a shorter period. The whole clause can be deleted if the period is of such a limited duration as to be inappropriate.

4.6A Fixed price

When the duration of a landscape contract is 12 months or less, most contractors can reasonably accurately forecast any increases in the cost of labour and materials and therefore make such allowances in their tenders as they consider necessary or prudent. In such cases Clause 4.6A will apply which states that the contractor will not be entitled to any payment in respect of any increase or decrease in the cost to him of labour, materials, plant or other resources.

4.6B Fluctuations

It is however not unknown for some landscape contracts to have to extend over a period of more than 12 months, to cover two planting seasons, when future increased costs of labour or materials are more difficult to forecast. To reduce the risk to contractors and therefore the tenders submitted, it is often in the employer's interest to arrange for the landscape contractor to be reimbursed by payment of a sum more closely related to the actual increased costs that may or may not have been incurred. Clause 4.6B therefore incorporates for the calculation of increased costs by reference to part D of the Supplementary Memorandum setting out the use of the Formula Rules published by the RIBA, RICS and Building Employers Confederation (BEC), prepared in accordance with DoE. Circular 158/73 (313/73 in Wales and 2/74 in Scotland). These include a set of indices prepared monthly by the PSA and in the case of Category 48 – soft planting, based on information supplied monthly by the horticulture trade and published by HMSO and in *Building*. The amount of the increase being:

$$\frac{\text{Valuation month index} - \text{base month index} \times \text{value of work done in the month}}{\text{Base month index}}$$

Costs are based on June 1976 = 100

5 Statutory obligations

5.1 Statutory obligations, notes, fees and charges

Compliance with all statutory obligations, giving the necessary notices and paying all fees and charges is always the responsibility of the landscape contractor. Should he, during the progress of the work, consider anything that he has contracted to do conflicts, he must notify the landscape consultant and ask for instructions in writing. Provided however he has followed the contract documents and instructions, the landscape contractor cannot be held responsible for any divergence. If therefore work has to be carried out subsequently to make it comply he is entitled to be reimbursed accordingly.

5.2 Value added tax

The liability for the payment by the employer of value added tax is set out in Part B of the Supplementary Memorandum which describes the arrangement for its collection by the contractor direct from the employer, independently of any certificate and also the procedures the contractor must follow if the employer wishes to challenge any taxes which he considers have been incorrectly charged. Most landscape work is liable to tax at the standard rate and on the smaller contract many contractors delay its collection until the final account.

5.3 Statutory tax deduction scheme

The Finance (No. 2) Act of 1975 requires that contractors and subcontractors, particularly self-employed individuals who do not have a certificate of exemption from the Inland Revenue, must have 30 per cent tax deducted before payment is made and the tax forwarded by the employer to the Collector of Taxes direct. Should this not be done and the necessary tax due is not paid, the employer is still liable for payment to the Inland Revenue, even though he has in fact paid the contractor or subcontractor in full. The necessary details are set out in Part C of supplementary memorandum and it is clearly essential for all employers or landscape consultants to have sight of the relevant exemption certificates to ensure that they are current before any payments are made.

5.4 Fair wages resolution

The original 1946 Fair Wages Resolution of the House of Commons requiring contractors and subcontractors to pay no less than the current union rate was rescinded as being an anachronism in 1982. Although it may still remain in the standing orders of certain local authorities and councils and it has now been deleted from the contract conditions. On projects for the housing corporation however the corporation has directed that it should be deleted.

5.5 Prevention of corruption

Clause 5.5 is also applicable only if the employer is a local authority and entitles the employer to cancel the contract and to recover any loss as a result from the contractor if he offers, gives or agrees to give any gift or consideration which constitutes an offence under the 1889–1916 Prevention of Corruption Acts or the 1972 Local Government Act.

6 Injury, damage and insurance

6.1 Injury to or death of persons

The contractor is solely responsible under Clause 6.1 for the injury or death of any person which arises from the carrying out of work unless this is due to an act or neglect of the employer. He must indemnify the employer against any claim which may arise and to ensure that he has the financial resources to meet these obligations, he is therefore required to take out the necessary insurance.

6.2 Damage to property

While the contractor is equally solely responsible in this instance, it is only for that arising from his own negligence and for which he must take out the necessary insurance also. There is no provision for any minimum amount of insurance for damage to property, so that should employers doubt that he has sufficient cover, they should require him to submit the necessary evidence.

If the employer requires insurance for damage to adjoining property for which he is responsible, this is best covered by a provisional sum in the tender documents.

The MW80 Insurance Clauses were amended in November 1986 to bring them into line with the revisions made to JCT 80 at the same time and with current practice in the insurance market. Although it was thought unlikely that 'all risks' insurance would be applicable on the type of work for which the Form was intended, it was however necessary to amend Clauses 6.1, 6.2, and 6.3A/6.3B to cover the correction to the specified perils under 6.3A. In Clause 6.3A, for the insurance of new works against fire, the proviso was added that *if* the contractor had an all risks policy, that policy would recognize the employer as being 'jointly' insured.

6.3A Insurance of new work

Damage to the landscape works from the normal perils of fire, flooding etc. on contracts for new work is normally to be the responsibility of the contractor under Clause 6.3A. The policy should be endorsed to indicate the employer's interest for the full value of the works, together with landscape consultant's fees (for which space is left for the percentage to be inserted), loss of unfixed materials, the removal of debris, extra costs of reinstatement and any increased costs. Consequential loss to the employer and any damage to the contractor's temporary plant and buildings are normally excluded.

6.3B Insurance of alteration work

When the works are within an existing site or are to be added to existing work, it is clear that any damage might not be confined to the new work and insurance based solely on the value of the new work would be insufficient. Under these circumstances the alternative Clause 6.3B enables the employer, who no doubt already has the existing property insured, to add the new work to his present policy and cover the old and the new work together in a single policy.

6.4 Evidence of insurance

To ensure that the necessary contractor's policies are taken out and in force the employer is entitled to require evidence from the

119

contractor, which is usually provided by a formal 'Certificate of Insurance'. The contractor has similar rights when the employer includes the new work in his insurance under Clause 6.3B.

6.5A Malicious damage

Landscape work is particularly susceptible to malicious damage and so the JCLI has provided a clause specially to cover this eventuality. Malicious damage to the landscape works after practical completion is clearly the responsibility of the employer and that prior to practical completion, that of the landscape contractor, who is responsible for the overall security and protection of the site. This is covered by Clause 6.5A holding the contractor responsible for making good such damage entirely at his own expense.

6.5B High risk areas

Where this risk is considered to be abnormally high the option of a provisional sum to cover such damage is provided in 6.5B. While the contractor still has to take such steps as are reasonably necessary to protect the works, in the event of it occurring, the employer has the funds available to pay for no more and no less than the actual cost of the remedial work necessary.

7   Determination

The employment of the contractor (not the contract which is an entirely different matter) can be terminated i.e. determined by either the employer or the contractor for only a few specific reasons. Although apparently quite straightforward, legal advice is always essential before taking such a step, to ensure that the termination is to considered to be invalid on account of some purely technical formality.

7.1   Determination by the employer

This can be effected for only one of two reasons: first if the contractor without reasonable cause, fails to proceed diligently with the works or wholly suspends the carrying out of the works before completion. While 'lack of diligence', although a matter of opinion, is relatively simple to establish, 'wholly suspends', as distinct from 'partially suspends ' or 'postpones' is more difficult to establish and it is for just such reasons that legal advice is always desirable.

The second reason is if the contractor becomes bankrupt, winds up his business or has a receiver appointed. This is of course a matter of fact but it is not always easy to know when it has occurred, far less when it is imminent. When it does arise immediate action to secure the site, to safeguard the works and certified unfixed materials, plant and equipment etc. is essential.

In either case while the determination must not be made unreasonably, the employer is under no obligation to give the contractor any warning and provided the notice is served by registered post, the contractor's employment is determined forthwith. The contractor must then immediately give up possession of the site and the employer need make no payment until the work has been completed by others.

7.2 Determination by the contractor

In this instance there are four grounds for determination:

1 if the employer is more than 14 days late in making progress payments;
2 if the employer interferes with, or obstructs the works or fails to make the site available by the date stated;
3 if the employer suspends the execution of the work for over a month; or
4 if the employer becomes bankrupt etc. (an unlikely event but not impossible even in the case of local authorities).

However the contractor must give the employer seven days in which to rectify matters before the notice of determination takes effect and must be payed for all work completed up to the date of determination and the cost of removing his temporary buildings, plant and equipment.

8 Supplementary Memorandum

This sets out the detailed provisions in Part A for changes in tax levies and contributions, in Part B for the recovery from the employer of any value added tax due, in Part C for the statutory tax deductions under the 1975 Finance (No. 2) Act and for the recovery of fluctuations under the Formula Rules in Part D.

JCLI Practice Note 3 (April 1985)

The third practice note consolidates and supersedes the earlier notes 1 and 2 issued in April 1978 and April 1982, and explains the various points covered elsewhere in the preceeding chapters. It is issued with each form and is perforated to enable it to be detached before the form is signed by both parties.

The use of the form in Scotland

By inclusion of reference to the proper law under which the contract is carried out in the first recital, the form is suitable for use throughout the United Kingdom and even in some circumstances abroad, although it is also necessary to establish the place where the works are to be executed, so that the contractor can make himself familiar with any differences in statutory regulations and allow for them accordingly. This also applies to the arbitrations carried out under Article 4 although conformity to Scottish procedures if required causes no difficulty.

Notwithstanding its origins in Roman as distinct from Saxon and Norman Law, the reliance on Sheriffs for administrative and judicial duties, and the lack of distinction between equity and common law, apart from a difference in nomenclature (e.g. pursuer and defender instead of plaintiff and defendant and tort known as delict), Scottish practice and procedures differ from those in the rest of the UK in only three significant respects:

1 In Scottish law there is no need for a consideration to insure a binding contract. Tender documents therefore must refer to the execution of a formal contract in addition to that implied by the letter of acceptance. Nor is there any provision for contracts to be entered into under seal. *Jus quaesitum tertio* provisions in his own favour enforced by a third party and contrary to English partnerships, those in Scotland have a legal existence of their own enabling them to sue for debts in their own name (although the personal liability of the individual partners remains unaltered).
2 Delict (not to be confused with *in delicto veritas)* the righting of civil (not criminal) wrongs similar to but very different from the English law of tort and usually arising from negligence, requires careful study to identify the differences of detail.
3 Scottish property law however differs in many respects from English law, primarily on account of the feudal rights remaining from the Norman Conquest and power vested in the Sheriffs. These were rationalized and simplified by the Conveyancing and Feudal Reform (Scotland) Act 1970, the Land Tenure Reform (Scotland) Act 1974 and the Land Registration (Scotland) Act 1979.

The JCT Intermediate Form IFC84

Conditions in the JCT Minor Works Form made no provision for plant failures and malicious damage, nor did it cover partial possession, the valuation of variations using tender rates, PC sums and the ability to object to nominations, the payment of direct loss and expense due to disturbance of regular progress or fluctuations all of which were incorporated into the JCLI Contract.

The JCT however published in 1984 an Intermediate Form suitable for use on larger contracts of a value of up to £250 000 at 1981 prices. While still not covering plant failures or malicious damage, it did provide for the other circumstances previously omitted.

The JCLI has therefore prepared a single page supplement to IFC84 with an accompanying Practice Note 4, incorporating the two outstanding items covering plant failures and malicious damage, so that this form of contract can now also be used for the larger landscape contracts.

The Institute of Civil Engineers (ICE) Form of Contract

This form is applicable for the larger contract involving large quantities of ground works, movement of earth, roads and footpaths. It is not a fixed price lump sum contract but has quantities prepared in accordance with a simplified method of measurement and is a remeasurement contract, all work being remeasured on completion and paid for accordingly. The conditions are broadly similar but not identical to those under the JCLI Form, and the engineer has far wider powers with regard to the programme and sequence of work.

GC Works I (General conditions of government contracts for building and civil engineering works)

This form is used for all Government Property Services Agency projects, the provisions following closely those of the JCT Forms but with no insurance clauses, extensions granted in the event of any inclement weather, no reference to 'practical' completion but additional clauses to cover security items, the Official Secrets Act and such matters.

Summary

The main forms of contract and subcontract on which landscape consultants may be involved can be summarized as follows:

123

1 *ICE Form*. Designed for large civil engineering contracts (i.e. bridges, motorways, slagheaps, sewage works etc.). A very simple form for few trades with wide powers, i.e. engineer can dictate sequence of execution. Simple quantities, i.e. supply and fix 1 number manhole. All work remeasured as it proceeds.

2 *GC Works 1*. A very one-sided contract designed for government building (as distinct from local authority) contracts. Gives wide powers to the architect (SO). Comes about half way between ICE and SFBC.

3 *JCT SFBC*. Incorrectly known as RIBA Form or JCT80. By now a very complex document in a variety of forms, i.e. with/without quantities, private/local authorities (virtually the same), approximate quantities, phased completion, variants.

4 *JCT Clause 35 Form of Subcontract for Nominated Subcontractors*. Applicable to the majority of building contracts with the soft planting around buildings being carried out by a specially selected specialist enjoying special privileges with regard to direct interim payment if the main contractor defaults etc.

5 *IFC 84*. A JCT Form published in 1984 for both private sector and public sector building projects, with or without quantities, with provision for naming a single subcontractor and therefore suitable for the majority of medium-sized projects.

6 *JCT Minor Works*. The smaller version designed for 12-month contracts up to £75 000 value for use on private, local authority, new and alteration *fixed price* contracts. Very useful for a wide variety of projects. No standard form of subcontract.

7 *JCLI Form for Landscape Works and Landscape Subcontracts*. The LI variant of the above replacing the Institute of Landscape Architects (as it was then known) with and without quantities version of the SFBC but which had not been brought up to date for VAT etc. with special provision for increased costs, vandalism, dead plants etc.

Subcontracts

It is a regrettable fact that today much of the work of a contract is subcontracted to firms or individuals who are not on the payroll of the main contractor. Not only does the contract preclude both the contractor and the employer from assigning the contract to another, without the written consent of the other (Clause 3.1), but the contractor may not subcontract the work or any part of it without the written consent of the landscape consultant (Clause 3.2). This consent however shall not be unreasonably withheld and while the contract does not require the identity of the subcontractor requested to be disclosed, in order to be able to decide whether to consent or not, it is clearly incumbent on the consultant to know this, in order to decide whether the work can be entrusted to another of the contractor's choosing. Under these circumstances it is advisable for the contractor to inform the consultant not only of the identity of the subcontractor concerned but for him to provide the names of at least three other consultants for whom the subcontractor has previously worked, as references. It is then possible for the consultant to send a questionnaire such as that in Figure 6.2 (page 126) to the references provided for an indication of the subcontractor's competence and suitability for the work.

Consecutive direct contracts

It is sometimes possible and preferable to leave the completion of the landscape works until the building contractor has finished. It is clearly the simplest solution on projects such as those connected with industrial civil engineering or hospital work to delay the start of the planting, if the seasons permit, until the main contractor has finished and cleared up, before the landscape contractor starts. On other projects such as housing and schools, it is clearly essential to have all planting completed and well established before the buildings and their surroundings are occupied to minimize possible future vandalism.

Concurrent direct contracts

When it is not possible or desirable to carry out the landscape works after the main contractor has finished, it is sometimes possible for the work to be carried out at the same time as the building work. JCT 80 Clause 29 permits the employer to engage others of his own choosing to enter the site and undertake the landscape works while the main contractor is still on site, provided that this is made clear in the tender documents. Great care is however necessary to ensure that each does not blame the other for any errors or delays. Primarily intended to enable the employer to arrange for his own artists or tradesmen to work on site alongside the main contractor, it is equally appropriate when used for landscape contractors.

Domestic subcontracts

When the work is fully described in the tender documents and consent is given to the main contractor to subcontract the landscape works to specialists entirely of his own choosing, these are known as 'domestic sub-contracts'. Under these circumstances the main contractor remains entirely responsible for the quality of the subcontractors' work and any delays the subcontractors may cause him. There are therefore many advantages in this arrangement but it does require the landscape works to be fully designed, detailed and carefully specified to ensure the correct quality is provided. The main contractor can use a landscape contractor with whom he has developed a good working relationship in the past or with whom he has made special financial arrangements. The employer still has a reasonable right to object to the subcontractor proposed and the main contractor accepts full responsibility for any delays or substandard workmanship of the landscape subcontractor. He can also arrange for the work to be carried out at a time convenient to himself.

The BEC has published in conjunction with the Federation of Associations of Specialist Subcontractors (FASS) and the Committee of Specialist Engineering Contractors (CASEC), a standard form of subcontract (DOM1) for use, with the JCT 80 form of Building Contract, under these circumstances and which effectively transfers the obligations of the main contractor to the subcontractor, and is appropriate for engineering and landscape subcontracts alike. The subcontract contains four Recitals and three Articles in the usual way, with an arbitrator appointed by the President of the RICS, with 37 contract conditions running to 44 pages. An additional Clause 21.4.5 was published in August 1984 dealing with the transfer of ownership to the employer of unfixed materials on site.

Listed subcontractors

To ensure an adequate quality, it is sometimes preferable, instead of allowing the main contractor complete freedom of choice of the landscape subcontractor, to require that he subcontracts the work to one of at least three subcontractors named in the tender documents, this choice being entirely a matter for his discretion without further reference to the landscape consultant. It sometimes happens that he wishes to add to the list a subcontractor of his own choosing, which he is entitled under Clause 19 of JCT 80 to do, but consultants should require him to give notice of such an intention at least ten days before the date when tenders are due. It is essential to take up references on the landscape subcontractor proposed when this happens, using a standard letter such as that shown in Figure 6.2. The main contractor remains entirely responsible for the performance of a subcontractor selected in this way and cannot claim an extension to the contract period for any delays he may cause.

Named subcontractors

The Intermediate Form IFC 84 is unique in that it provides for the naming in the tender documents of a single landscape subcontractor which the main contractor must use without any option. To do this however, the landscape work must be fully described in sufficient detail for it to be priced and subcontract tenders obtained by the consultant, previously on a special form NAM/T which provides space for the insertion of any special attendance which the main contractor may be required to provide, subcontract commencement and completion dates etc.

Nominated subcontractors

Prior to the publication of JCT 80 nomination was the almost universal method of arranging for the execution of landscape subcontract works, when it was considered the work was of a too specialized nature to be entrusted to the main contractor and where he could not be left to select a subcontractor of his own choosing. The Banwell Report stated that nomination, namely when the employer retains the selection to a single subcontractor of his own choosing, was only justified to meet one of the following three requirements:

1 when special techniques are required,
2 when early ordering is necessary, or
3 when a particular quality of work is essential,

and this still holds true today.

In these instances it is often necessary to issue a letter of intent to the subcontractor concerned on the lines of that shown in Figure 6.3.

PC sums

Under these circumstances, when the landscape works are required under the JCT Form of Building Contract, a prime cost sum must be included in the tender documents accordingly and the subcontractor is then nominated under Clause 35. These procedures, which are set out in great detail, must be followed irrespective of whether the subcontract works are in connection with landscape, structural, steel or precast concrete, fixing metal windows, cladding, mechanical and electrical engineering works (even though the provision of shop drawings are unlikely to be required for landscape work).

Clause 35

When a subcontractor nominated under Clause 35 delays the completion of the work, the main contractor is entitled to an extension of the contract period and the employer loses his liquidated and ascertained damages as a consequence. If the main contractor defaults in handing over money included in Interim Certificates stated as being due to a landscape

CONFIDENTIAL:

FIRM:

WORKS CARRIED OUT:

Please enter details or tick box as appropriate:

YEARS

1. How long have you known this firm? ☐

2. What do you consider the maximum value of any one contract this firm is capable of executing?

AMOUNT

£ [   ]

How would you assess the following:

	POOR	REASONABLE	GOOD	EXCELLENT	COMMENTS
3. Their office organization and management capabilities.	☐	☐	☐	☐	
4. Their ability to formulate practical programmes.	☐	☐	☐	☐	
5. Their ability to maintain programme.	☐	☐	☐	☐	
6. Their standard of workmanship.	☐	☐	☐	☐	
7. Their site organization.	☐	☐	☐	☐	
8. Their conduct of labour relations.	☐	☐	☐	☐	
9. Their relationship with subcontractors and statutory authorities.	☐	☐	☐	☐	
10. Their attention to site welfare and safety.	☐	☐	☐	☐	
11. Their degree of co-operation	☐	☐	☐	☐	

	YES	NO
12. If the firm was the main contractor, did they rely extensively on subcontractors?	☐	☐
13. If the firm was the main contractor, were there any problems with payments to subcontractors and suppliers?	☐	☐
14. Were defects remedied promptly?	☐	☐
15. Were final accounts settled satisfactorily?	☐	☐
16. Would you use this firm again?	☐	☐

Figure 6.2   Standard letter for a reference on a sub contractor.

subcontractor, the subcontractor is entitled to payment from the employer direct.

NSC1

Under JCT 80 all nominated subcontract tenders must be obtained on the 12-page JCT Standard Form of Subcontract Tender. The second schedule on pages 9 and 10 are of the most concern to the landscape consultant.

The preceding first schedule is common to all subcontract tenders and enumerates the contract particulars, leaves space for the amount of tender and day work percentages, the required options and rates to establish fluctuations if they are required.

The second schedule sets out the particular conditions of the subcontract, the period for the carrying out of the subcontract works on and off site, the period required for the approval of drawings by the landscape consultant, the period for the submission of shop drawings if any, the notice required prior to commencement on site and the agreed programme details.

```
Dear Sirs
```

```
We are pleased to confirm that your quotation dated ...... in
the sum of ........ for .............. works at the above is
acceptable and the main contractor will be instructed to
enter into a subcontract with you after the main contract has
been entered into.

Would you therefore please proceed with the preparation of
the necessary shop and fabrication drawings/arrange for the
necessary labour and materials.

We enclose therefore a copy of an Employer/Subcontractor
Agreement for your signature and return for endorsement by
our client confirming our acceptance of any expense
reasonably and properly incurred by yourselves as a result
and your agreement to our client's subsequent use of them
without further obligation should the subcontract not be
proceeded with.
```

```
Yours faithfully
```

Figure 6.3   Letter of intent to nominated subcontractor

On the other side of the form are listed the subcontractor's attendance requirements with regard to the use of scaffolding, mechanical equipment and the proposed position of temporary accommodation.

The landscape consultant completes in duplicate the first part of the second schedule, inserting the periods he anticipates the work will be required on site and:

1 He sends it to the planting subcontractor.
2 Who in turn substitutes his own dates with the commencement and completion dates he anticipates will be required for the satisfactory execution of the work on site.
3 The subcontractor returns the form to the landscape consultant who then obtains the signature of the employer who keeps the original and signs it.
4 The landscape consultant sends one copy back to the landscape subcontractor and issues a preliminary notice to the contractor of his intended nomination, together with all necessary copies of NSC1 and NSC2.
5 The main contractor signs all three copies of NSC1 and sends them back to the landscape consultant.
6 The contractor and subcontractor then enter into the subcontract using NSC4.

Note. If NSC1 has not been used to obtain tenders then an alternative method using NSC2a/4a ensures that the same information passes between the main and subcontractors instead.

NSC2
The problem of loss of liquidated and ascertained damages is overcome in Clause 35 by the use of a separate employer/subcontractor agreement, in which the one contracts not to delay completion and the other to exercise all reasonable skill and care in the design of any part of the work.

NSC3
This is the preliminary notice of the intention to nominate a particular firm.

NSC4
As was said earlier this is the actual nominated subcontract, one copy of which has to be signed and attached to each subcontract let. It is obligatory for all nominated subcontracts and matches in every respect the clauses of the main form, particularly those relating to insurance, disturbance to progress, tax certificates and the like. The subcontract sets

Schedule 2: Particular Conditions

Note: When the Contractor receives Tender NSC/1 together with the Architect/Supervising Officer's preliminary notice of nomination under clause 35·7·1 of the Main Contract Conditions then the Contractor has to settle and complete any of the particular conditions which remain to be completed in this Schedule in agreement with the proposed Sub-Contractor. The completed Schedule should take account not only of the preliminary indications of the Sub-Contractor stated therein, but also of any particular conditions or requirements of the Contractor which he may wish to raise with the Sub-Contractor.

1.A Any stipulation as to the period/periods when Sub-Contract Works can be carried out on site:[s]

to be between _____ and _____

Period required by Architect to approve drawings after submission _____

1.B Preliminary programme details[t] (having regard to the information provided in the invitation to tender)

Periods required:

(1) for submission of all further sub-contractors drawings etc. *(co-ordination, installation, shop or builders' work, or other as appropriate)*[u]

_____

_____

_____

(2) for execution of Sub-Contract Works: off-site _____

on-site _____

Notice required to commence work on site _____

1.C Agreed programme details (including sub-contract completion date: see also Sub Contract NSC/4, clause 11·1)[v]

2. Order of Works to follow the requirements, if any, stated in Schedule 1, item 11[w]

Figure 6.4   Particular conditions for a subcontract using NSC1
(Reproduced with permission of RIBA Publications Ltd)

out the headings of the 34 main clauses on three contents pages followed by a further 39 pages making 42 in all. A ten-page BEC Guidance Note is available for reference but in general the provisions are the same as those in JCT 80. The right to set off is covered by Clauses 23 and 24, the payment of the costs of an arbitrator and of an adjudicator are covered and under Clause 29 for the architect to determine the subcontract, if he considers the subcontractor to be in default, if he becomes insolvent or if he has himself validly determined the subcontract. The architect, no doubt advised by the landscape consultants, then has to make a further nomination of another and if the determination by the subcontractor was valid, any extra cost to the employer arising from the result of the renomination has to be borne by the employer.

Subcontracts under the ICE form

The standard form of subcontract prepared by the ICE for use with their main form is relatively simple, covering only nineteen short clauses on seven pages followed by five schedules:

1 main contract particulars,
2 subcontract documents and the scope of the works,
3 price, retention and period for completion,
4 facilities provided by the contractor, and
5 insurance.

JCLI Standard Form of Tender and Conditions of Subcontract

This is for use on domestic named and nominated subcontracts alike under the JCLI Form and was published in January 1986 (Appendix 4). Section headed like the JCLI and JCT Minor Works Forms, it also provides all the main contract information needed by tenderers. The tender form includes day work charges, tender and subcontract period and, in addition to the normal seven sections for the intentions of the parties, commencement and completion etc., it includes also a final Section 8 'Temporary works and services, attendance and related works' covering accommodation, welfare facilities, temporary services, use of scaffolding, delivery and storage of material, removal of rubbish, cutting away and subsurfaces – all of particular interest to a subcontractor intent on submitting a keen price.

7
Landscape Contract Administration

Mobilizing resources

In addition to his obligations to his client to monitor the progress, cost and quality of the work, the contract conditions require the landscape consultant to undertake, as agent of the employer, the administration of the contract which calls for the highest standards of management, technical competence and administrative ability if the client is not to be put to unnecessary expense.

When the landscape consultants' recommendation to accept a tender has been confirmed by the client the tenderer should be informed immediately and arrangements made to put the work in hand on site. It is important to remember that the contractor should be allowed sufficient time to arrange for the appropriate site staff to be made available and to ensure that all labour and materials will be ready when required. On the other hand any delay in the start on site and consequently the completion of the work may well involve the client in additional costs particularly when the contract is on a 'fluctuation' basis.

Pre-contract meetings

When the client has confirmed agreement of the landscape consultants' recommendation on which of the tenders submitted to accept, a pre-contract meeting with the contractor and all others concerned should be arranged at which the following should be established:

1 *Names, addresses and telephone numbers.* It is always of assistance to all concerned if the names, addresses and telephone numbers of those involved: architect, quantity surveyor, engineering consultants, clerks of works and contractors' staff are identified and details issued either

with the agenda or the memorandum of the pre-contract meeting.

2 *Site.* The details of the site, any restrictions as to access, arrangements for operatives' car parking and contractors' working area should be confirmed at the outset.

3 *Contract documents.* The contract sum, dates for commencement and completion, documents to be attached to the Form of Contract, evidence and details of the Contract Bond, insurance and contractors' tax exemption certificates should all be agreed at this stage.

4 *Specifications and bills of quantities.* The numbers of copies of drawings specification and/or bills of quantities to be signed by the parties and by whom they are to be retained, together with requests for additional and blank copies and to whom they should be sent, should be agreed.

5 *Commissioning and maintenance.* Any requirements for commissioning and maintenance manuals and operation of any mechanical services or equipment either prior to or after practical completion, should be confirmed.

6 *Statutory obligations.* The need to comply with statutory requirements with regard to noise, building regulations, notices, confirmation of planning consent, tree preservation orders and any local restrictions should be noted.

7 *Contract administration.* The requirement for the contractor to supervise the works, to submit a progress chart, the frequency and responsibility for chairing subcontractors' co-ordination meetings and site inspections should be agreed. Also the consultant's arrangements for the promulgation and confirmation of oral instructions, the formal issue of written instructions, correspondence, valuations, dayworks and the recording of inclement weather should be confirmed.

8 *Temporary works.* The contractor's proposals for the location of spoil heaps, site hut, offices and sanitary accommodation, temporary services, and the style, size and position of any site notice boards both for the client and the contractor must be agreed.

9 *Quality control.* Requirements for samples both of materials and workmanship, e.g. bricks and pointing, concrete test cubes and grass seed mixes, arrangements for attendance during the spreading of herbicides, mulches and fertilizers should be confirmed.

10 *Engineering services.* Any arrangements for the co-ordination of inspections, instructions, further information and approvals of any other consultants and statutory authorities should be clarified.

11 *Subcontractors and suppliers.* The acceptance of responsibility by the landscape contractor for the performance of all subcontractors and suppliers, whether domestic, named or nominated must be emphasized (see also p. 125–126).

12 *Frequency and dates of meetings.* The frequency, dates and times of

visits by the consultants, whether daily, weekly or monthly progress meetings and valuations will depend entirely on the adequacy of the contract documents, the complexity of the work and the stage reached. Some degree of formality is however essential and it is normal to fix at the outset of each project the dates for at least the regular site visits and progress meetings.

Landscape consultants have then four specific contractual administrative duties which they are required to undertake, those relating to certification, instructions, subcontracts and extending the period for the completion of the works.

Certification

Progress payments

The contract conditions require a landscape consultant to certify progress payments at intervals of not less than four weeks (or at certain specified stages of the work) in respect of the value of work properly executed to date and which have to be honoured within 14 days. Should this not happen the contractor is entitled to determine his employment having given seven days' notice of his intention to do so.

The use of the words 'properly executed' should be noted. This enables a landscape consultant to deduct the value of any work improperly executed from an Interim Certificate. It can be argued that this does not imply that by including its value in an Interim Certificate the landscape consultant is certifying that the work in question has been properly executed.

All contracts envisage that the value of work certified may include 'latent' defects, the existence of which could not have been foreseen at the time of certification and which may only become apparent during the defects liability period or even after the final certificate. The larger forms of building contract include the phrase 'save as aforesaid' (i.e. except for items the consultant has reserved for his approval) 'no certificate shall of itself be conclusive evidence that any works, materials or goods to which it relates are in accordance with the Contract'. The apparent contradiction between these two clauses is explained by interpreting 'properly' as meaning properly executed in accordance with the contract *conditions* and not a reference to the quality of workmanship or materials.

Practical completion

The landscape consultant must also certify the date when in his opinion the works have reached 'practical completion'. A phrase that has never been defined in the courts but as has been said earlier is when the work is sufficiently complete to be safely used for the purpose for which it was designed. Although this is entirely a matter for the opinion of the landscape consultant, and for which he is under no obligation to give any reasons for his decision, it is clearly in the interests of the client for him to have the use of the work for which he has already paid as soon as is practicable, without waiting for every last shrub to be planted, or litter bin fixed. There is no obligation however for the landscape consultant to prepare a snagging list of defective items nor an extensive schedule of outstanding work, although regrettably these are often necessary.

Making good defects

Landscape contractors have also to make good any defects both in the hard landscape and plant failures within a specified period after practical completion, a percentage of the contract sum having been withheld to cover such eventualities. The landscape consultant has also a duty to certify when the contractor has made them good.

The Final Certificate

Having received from the contractor all the necessary documentation within three months or such other period as has been specified from the date of practical completion, the landscape consultant has to issue within a further 28 days, the Final Certificate covering the balance due to the contractor and which has also to be honoured within a further 14 days. While landscape consultants can certify accordingly by letter to the client the Landscape Institute has prepared forms (Figures 7.1, 7.2, 7.3 and 7.4) to enable them to discharge this duty accurately and expeditiously.

Instructions

Landscape contracts require the consultant, apart from issuing certificates, also to issue any further information necessary for the proper carrying out of the works and for all instructions to be in writing (Clause 1.2). These are to be carried out by the contractor 'forthwith' i.e. as soon as possible and in the event of his failing to do so, the landscape consultant can, after seven days' written notice if the contractor has not complied, instruct others to do it and deduct the cost from the balance of any money due to him.

Any instructions to the contractor that have been given by the landscape consultant orally must be confirmed in writing within two

Valuation and Current Financial Statement for Landscape Interim/Final Certificate

No.

Employer's name and address: E.O. Burlington Esq. Chiswick House, London W4.

Contractor's name and address: Town and Country Landscapes Ltd. Dukes Meadows Mortlake SW14

Contract: Improvements to Garden   Office reference: 17/36

AUTHORISED EXPENDITURE		ESTIMATED FINAL COST	
To amount of Contract	£ 7,500	To amount of Contract	£ 7,500
Additional authorised expenditure	£ 1,250	Less contingencies	£ 1,000
			£ 6,500
		Estimated value of Variations to date	+ £ 1,950
			£ 8,450
		Estimated value of Variations yet to be issued	± £ 150
			£ 8,600
Estimated increased costs (if allowable)	£ 750	Estimated increased costs (if allowable)	± £ 750
TOTAL AUTHORISED EXPENDITURE	£ 9,500	ESTIMATED TOTAL COST	£ 9,350

Signed: William W. Kent FLI   Landscape architect. Date: 3.2.85

Distribution: Client ☑   Quantity surveyor ☑   File ☑

Landscape architects name and address:
William W. Kent
12 Carlton House Terrace
London SW1Y 5AH

Landscape Architects
Interim/Final

Certificate

Employer's name and address:
E. O. Burlington Esq
CHISWICK HOUSE
London W4

Contractor's name and address:
Town & Country Landscapes Ltd.
Dukes Meadows
Mortlake SW14

Contract: Improvements to Garden

Reference: 17/36

I/We hereby certify that under the terms of the Contract

dated: _____

the sum of (words): 3rd February 1980

Two thousand and seventy five pounds

is due from the Employer to the Contractor

Certificate No.	FIVE
Date of Valuation	3.2.80
Date of Certificate	7.2.80
Valuation of work executed £	7,250.00
Value of materials on site £	1,250.00
£	8,500.00
Less retention £	425.00
Total to date £	7,075.00
Less amount previously certified £	5,000.00
	2,075.00

(Exclusive of any Value Added Tax)

Signed: William W. Kent FLI   Landscape architect   Date: 3.2.85

Distribution: Client ☐   Contractor ☐   Quantity surveyor ☐   File ☐

Figure 7.1 Landscape Interim/Final Certificate
(Reproduced with permission of the Landscape Institute)

137

Landscape Architect/

address

Employer
address

Works
situated at

Contractor
address

Contract dated

Certificate of

**Practical
Completion**

of Landscape Works

Job reference

Serial No.

Issue date

Under the terms of the above mentioned Contract,

I/We certify that Practical Completion was achieved and the works taken into
possesion on

_____ 19_____

the Defects Liability period
for faults other than plant failures will expire on

_____ 19_____

for shrubs, ordinary nursery stock trees and other plants will expire on

_____ 19_____

for semi mature and advanced nursery stock trees will expire on

_____ 19_____

The Employer should note that with effect from this date he becomes responsible
for the insurance of the works.

To be signed by or for   Signed _____
the issuer named
above.

Date _____

_____ 19_____

Distribution: Client ☐   Contractor ☐   Quantity surveyor ☐   Clerk of works ☐   File ☐

Figure 7.2 Landscape Practical Completion Certificate
(Reproduced with permission of the Landscape Institute)

Landscape Architect/

address

Employer
address

Works
situated at

Contractor
address

Contract dated

Certificate of
Completion of

**Making good
defects**

of Landscape Works

Job reference

Serial No.

Issue date

Under the terms of the above mentioned Contract,

I/We hereby certify that the defects, shrinkages and other faults specified
in the schedule of defects delivered to the Contractor as an instruction have
in my/our opinion been made good.

This Certificate refers to:

The Works described in the Certificate of Practical Completion
Serial No.   dated

Signed _____

Date _____

Distribution: Client ☐   Contractor ☐   Quantity surveyor ☐   Clerk of works ☐   File ☐

© 1987 The Landscape Institute

Figure 7.3   Landscape Certificate of Completion of Making Good Defects
(Reproduced with permission of the Landscape Institute)

Landscape Architect's name and address	MANNING CLAMP + PARTNERS 31-32 The Green RICHMOND Surrey	**Landscape Architects Instruction**

| Works | Elderly Person Housing
Dukes Road, |
| situate at | Richmond |

To contractor	Town & Country Landscapes Ltd. Dukes Meadows, Mortlake SW 14	Instruction no.	16
	Under the terms of the Contract	Date	

| dated | 3rd January 1985 |

I/We issue the following instructions. Where applicable the contract sum will be adjusted in accordance with the terms of the relevant Condition.

For office use: Approx costs
£ omit   £ add

	Instructions	

16.01

PLANTING

OMIT: The provisional sum of £500.00 and in lieu thereof place your order with Messrs Meadows Nurseries in accordance with their attached quotation dated 9th January 1985 in the sum of £978.46 subject to the following

i)	Substitute Taxus hibernica in lieu Malus	£26. 20.
ii)	Reduce climbers to one of each	41.90
iii)	Substitute Forsythia for Hamemelis	70.00
		£138.10
iv)	33% reduction in fertiliser and planting 33% x £220	70.00
		£208.10
v)	Omit watering and replanting	195.86
		403.96

Less VOP adjustment to contract base date 574.50
128.04

To AMOUNT OF REVISED TENDER   £446.46

Office reference

Signed_____ Landscape Architect

Notes	Amount of contract sum £ _____
	± Approximate value of previous instructions £ _____
	£ _____
	± Approximate value of this instruction £ _____
	Approximate adjusted total £ _____

Distribution: Client ☐   Contractor ☐ Quantity surveyor ☐   Clerk of works ☐   File ☐

Figure 7.4 Landscape architects instruction
(Reproduced with permission of the Landscape Institute)

days. To cover such eventualities consultants will either keep a duplicate pad on site, on which to confirm site instructions, or include written confirmation in memoranda of site visits and progress meetings. Instructions given by telephone can be confirmed by letter or by directions from the clerk of works if one has been appointed.

It is normally convenient to cover instructions which do not have any monetary significance in this way and confine those which do, to formal printed Variation Order (VO) or Architects Instructions (AI) Forms. When such an arrangement is adopted then it is useful to arrange for the contractor to notify the consultant of any instructions, not yet covered by a VO, if the contractor considers them to have a monetary value and that a VO is necessary.

Instructions must always be orderly and precise, unambiguous and indicate clearly by whom the action is required. While telephones can be used for simple instructions and resolving question and answer problems, subsequently confirmed in writing, they are never suitable for complicated, difficult or delicate ones, for which personal meetings are the only answer. Sufficient time can then be allocated for the problem to be investigated in depth and it will not have to be dealt with as an interruption to whatever the recipient of the telephone call was doing when the call was received.

Telephone messages left with the telephonist, even without specific requests to return the call, should always be recorded in writing and given to the individual concerned on their return to the office. Telephones should always be answered immediately and conversations kept brief and to the point. Telephones should not be used for lengthy or difficult discussions. Any call likely to last more than 10 minutes would be better covered by a letter or memorandum. Remember also that telephone calls nearly always interrupt the recipient who is usually engaged on other equally important tasks and it may well be better to put it in writing and wait for a considered reply.

Variations

Landscape consultants may issue instructions for the expenditure of any PC, provisional sums and any addition, omission or change in the works or the order or period in which they are to be carried out. These usually arise from a change in the employer's requirements (or lack of appreciation of what had been included in the contract) or from the realization by the landscape consultant that a particular problem could be resolved in a better way (or the realization that a certain problem had been overlooked or forgotten). In any event the ability for the consultant to instruct changes is an essential requirement in any one off project. It is very rare for a designer to invent a perfect prototype without the need for further instructions.

It is very important however to ensure that this ability for the landscape consultant to issue instructions to the contractor to vary the contract is not abused, either by not resisting the indulgence of second thoughts at too late a state ('wouldn't it be better if') or delaying the progress of the works, by delay in responding to a request for further information or instructions after the date on which the contractor had reasonably requested them.

The valuation of variations will rarely give a landscape contractor the proper recompense for the disruption and cost involved, the responsibility for their valuation on a fair and reasonable basis being solely that of the consultant, using where relevant the prices the contractor has provided in the contract documents. Although the contract provides for valuations to be agreed between the contractor and consultant prior to the work being carried out, this is all too rarely achieved. In practice a contractor will often price variations and submit them to the consultant who will if they appear to be reasonable, accept them without question. Contractually however it is the consultant's responsibility to value the variations, normally in accordance with the following building contract conventions viz:

1 the same work under similar conditions at the contract rates or prices;
2 similar work under different conditions based on contract rates;
3 different work for which no rates exist at fair and reasonable rates; or
4 work that cannot be measured at daywork rates.

If the variation involves a significant change in the scope or quantity of work, the contract provides for the effect of this on the contract rate or price to be taken into account.

Correspondence

All letters and drawings whether delivered to the office by post or hand should be formally stamped with the date of receipt and distributed to the partner or staff concerned in an orderly regular and not haphazard way. Whenever possible letters should be replied to on the date on which they are received and when acted upon, filed daily in chronological order by the individual or secretarial staff concerned.

Meetings

It is important to remember that the meetings in which landscape consultants are involved, are rarely 'committee' meetings wherein a number of people meet to reach a decision based on the majority vote of its members and from which the minority cannot disassociate themselves on a major point of issue without resigning, the chairman having a casting vote but not being individually responsible for the decisions reached.

Most consultants meetings, both 'design team' and progress meetings, are different in that subordinates and other consultants advise the lead consultant within their own individual sphere of responsibility so that he can come to a decision within the wider implications of the whole project.

Progress meetings are also 'information' meetings at which information about activities and operations can be exchanged, recorded, subsequently to be stated in a memorandum of the meeting confirming the decisions reached, what further action or information is required and from whom. Such memoranda are not minutes of a meeting attempting to precis and record the discussion. They should be confined solely to recording in a clear and factual way, the matters discussed.

Dayworks

These must always be authorized beforehand after reference to a quantity surveyor if necessary and it is important to check not only that the rates and prices are correct but that the quantity of labour and materials are reasonable also, the contractor still being required to carry out the work as expeditiously, efficiently and economically as possible.

The valuation of work on a daywork basis consists of the actual (prime) cost to the contractor of labour, materials and plant to which are added his incidental costs, overheads and profit evaluated and expressed as a percentage addition. The definitions of each are defined in their respective sections and published jointly by the RICS and BEC for the Building Industry *Definition of Prime Cost of Daywork carried out under a Building Contract* (December 1975 Edition) for building work and by the Federation of Civil Engineering Contractors for civil engineering works.

Variations valued on this basis must clearly be to a contractor's advantage since he will be imbursed his actual costs together with the profit to which he is entitled irrespective of the prices he is charging to the client, which he has included in his tender, and which may due to unforeseen circumstances now be less than the actual cost to himself. It is rare for contractors to suggest variations be valued on a dayworks basis when the reverse is the case!

There are however obviously situations such as, for example, locating existing underground services, site clearance to remove debris and large

143

stones arising from subsoiling and tree surgery, where there is no other equitable way of fairly and reasonably measuring the work.

The same principles apply to the evaluation and correction of any errors or inconsistencies within or between the contract documents which may come to light after the contract has commenced and which may or may not constitute a variation to the contract sum.

Most contracts provide for the appointment of a 'competent person in charge' to be on site at all reasonable times as the contractor's representative, with authority to accept such instructions. This must be strictly adhered to, if the problems of *Woodman* v. *Clayton* (1956) where the consultant was held to be liable having given instructions to a bricklayer direct and not through the contractor's site agent, are to be avoided.

Similar provisions are provided entitling the landscape consultant to issue instructions for the exclusion of any person from the works although this power must never be exercised lightly and only used in the most extreme circumstances.

PC and provisional sums

Circumstances also arise when the scope of some part of the work cannot be foreseen in the necessary detail at the outset, for example tree surgery, in which case contractors are instructed to include in their tender a provisional sum for the work inclusive of the contractor's profit and any attendance required. When at some later stage the full extent of the work is known, the consultant can then omit the *provisional sum* and instruct the contractor as to the full extent of the work required.

An appropriate prime cost (PC) sum can be included in the tender documents by a clause such as:

> Include the PC sum of £ . . . . . for . . . . work to be executed by a specialist subcontractor and allow . . . . . weeks for its execution at an appropriate stage in the contract. Add for profit and attendance

When the identity of the subcontractor is known at the time of preparation of the tender documents it is advisable if the name of the firm selected is stated also. Should this not be possible, then the contract provides for the right of reasonable objection to be exercised by the main contractor when either the identity of the subcontractor concerned is made known to him or if the subcontractor requires the incorporation of any conditions in the subcontract which may impose on the main contractor any conditions which are contrary to those incorporated into his own contract with the employer. To minimize the chances of this occurring the JCLI has produced a four-page Standard Form of Tender and Subcontract (Appendix 4) the conditions of which mirror exactly those of the JCLI Main Form.

When the contract is let, the amount of the PC sum is omitted by a Variation Order and instructions issued for the acceptance by the main contractor of the tender of the subcontractor selected.

Some contracts for landscape works are often part of a building contract and have to be carried out concurrently and as a subcontract under the building contractor. In that case the appropriate subcontract standard forms of tender and subcontract conditions must be followed and used. Applying to all building subcontracts the procedures for domestic, listed, named and nominated subcontract procedures are more detailed than those of JCLI and although the same principles apply, are covered in the relevant JCT, ICE and GC Works1 text books.

Extensions to the contract period and disturbance of regular progress

Landscape contracts provide for the contractor to notify the consultant 'if it becomes apparent the works will not be completed by the Contract Completion date for reasons beyond the control of the contractor'.

In building contracts there are twelve such relevant events beyond the control of the contractor, the most important of which are:

1 force majeure (caused by Acts of God?),
2 loss or damage to the works by fire, storm or flood etc.,
3 civil commotion or strikes,
4 compliance with the landscape consultant's instructions,
5 delays in the receipt of such instructions, and
6 delays by nominated subcontractors.

These constitute a sound basis for evaluating 'reasons beyond the control of the contractor'. Should any of these arise then the contractor must notify the consultant who then makes in writing such extension of the time for completion as may be reasonable (Clause 2.2). In addition, should the contractor notify the consultant of any direct loss and expense incurred by reason of the *progress* of the work having been delayed for reasons that were within the control of the employer, then the consultant must ascertain the amount of such loss and expense involved and include it in any progress payments due.

The exercise of this judgement calls for considerable skill and experience on the part of the landscape consultant, bearing in mind that

145

extensions involve only delays to completion not progress, many delays are concurrent and not consecutive, some are on the critical path and some are not, some within and some outside the control of the contractor. It must also be remembered that while the consultant should notify the contractor of the extension granted and advise him of the events he has taken into account as soon as he is able, he is under no obligation to give any reasons nor the individual amounts of the delays he has taken into account.

The advantages of coming to a decision while the events are still fresh in everyone's mind are obvious but it is equally essential to give a decision before the contract date for completion so that the contractor knows where he stands and can arrange accordingly, also to prevent damages to become 'at large' thereby obliging the employer to prove the loss or damage he has suffered instead of being able to rely on the 'pre-estimate' fixed beforehand and included in the contract accordingly.

Should however the consultant be of the opinion that completion was not delayed for reasons beyond the control of the contractor or progress not be delayed on account of any action of the employer, then the employer is entitled to deduct such liquidated damages as have been stated in the contract conditions as having been due for each week or part of a week that the works remain uncompleted beyond the contract completion date.

Should the consultant reject an application for an extension or for the reimbursement of direct loss and expense, it should be remembered that the latest conditions of appointment provide for the reimbursement by the client of the consultant's time involved. It is also the responsibility of the consultant to ensure that the amount of liquidated and ascertained damages per week provides not only for the reimbursement to the client of his financial costs incurred in payments already made, without his having the use of the works, but also for the landscape consultant's costs incurred in additional site visits until practical completion is achieved by the contractor.

Determination

The financial consequences of either the employer or the contractor determining the contract are great and should never be embarked on without competent and experienced legal advice.

The only grounds for the employer are the lack of diligence of the contractor, if he *wholly* suspends the carrying out of the works or if he becomes bankrupt.

There are similar grounds for the contractor namely: 1, the failure to make progress payments by the due date, 2, if the employer interferes with, obstructs the carrying out of the works or fails to make the site available, or 3, if the employer suspends the work or becomes bankrupt.

In any such case the decision is not a matter for the consultants although their opinion will no doubt be sought, but the employer or contractor, on the advice of their lawyers and there must be strict adherence to the proper procedures laid down with regard to matters such as notification.

Professional obligations to the client

In addition to his administrative duties under the contract, the landscape consultant has also the responsibilities under his appointment with his client to advise him:

1 if the contract period is likely to be exceeded,
2 if the contract sum is likely to be increased, and
3 that the quality of workmanship and materials is generally in accordance with the contract.

Progress of the work

If the contract period is likely to be exceeded

The speed of construction and arrangements for the supply of the necessary labour and materials are solely matters under the control of the landscape contractor, whether or not delays are caused by the employer and therefore justify an extension of the contract period for completion of the works. The provision of a master programme on which is indicated the critical path of several concurrent activities which must be completed before the next can be commenced, is an essential tool in any contract both for the contractor in properly managing the project and for the landscape consultant in monitoring its progress. Regular visits to site to compare the progress actually achieved with that which was intended, also make it relatively simple for the landscape consultant to advise his client, if in his opinion the date for completion of the works is unlikely to be met. It is therefore useful to require the contractor to submit, a few days before each regular progress meeting, a report such as that indicated in Figure 7.5, which the landscape consultant can then discuss and check with the contractor on site.

Financial control (if the authorized expenditure is likely to be exceeded)

The only person who can alter or control the cost of a landscape project is the consultant, since only he can instruct the contractor to vary the work

Document Ref.
K/CONPRO/Prelim.

Page No. ....

CONTRACTORS MONTHLY PROGRESS REPORT   for month of ....

Report No. ....

Contractor ....

Contract .... Contract Ref. No. ....

1. CONTRACT

Contract commencement date .... Contract completion date ....
Contract duration   .... Target completion date   ....
Weeks elapsed   .... Weeks remaining   ....
Contract sum   .... Value certified to date   ....

Inclement weather: rain/frost this month .... total to date ....
Extension claimed .... days. Extension agreed .... days.

2. PROGRESS

REF:	ITEM:	% work programmed	% work achieved	weeks ahead/ behind	reason for change/ delay action taken

Overall percentage work programmed to date .... %
                       work completed to date .... %

Figure 7.5   Contractor's progress report

148

3. Shortages of labour, plant and materials   Action taken

4. Subcontract difficulties and delays   Action taken

5. Monthly Schedule of Outstanding Information Required

REF: ITEM: Date required   Date received

Date: Prepared by:

Figure 7.5 Contractor's progress report (*concluded*)

and it is he who is responsible for the valuation of such variations in accordance with the rules laid down.

If landscape consultants complete and forward to the client the upper part of the financial statement attached to each LI Form of Interim Certificate (Figure 7.1) for progress payments, few problems should arise since the client will be continuously appraised of the estimated final cost of the project and able to take such action as is necessary, if it appears the authorized expenditure might be exceeded.

Quality inspections

While the provision of the necessary labour and materials in accordance with the contract documents, assembled and planted in the locations indicated on the contract drawings, is a matter entirely within the responsibility of the landscape contractor, in practice if he is to submit the lowest tender in competition, he can only include for the lowest standard of workmanship and materials necessary to meet the specification.

It is equally necessary therefore for the consultant, although not expected to be on site permanently, to visit the site at intervals, not to supervise but at least to monitor, inspect and check the work on the client's behalf, to ensure that the contractor and his workforce have interpreted the contract documents correctly.

While there is no specific provision for a clerk of works in the JCLI Contract, there is no reason why one should not be appointed, if it is considered constant supervision of the work is required. It must be remembered however that he is there solely as an inspector on behalf of the employer, and has no responsibility to the contractor for quality control nor any powers to give any instructions to the contractor. When a clerk of works is considered necessary, it is normally better for him to be employed by the client direct although working under the direction of the landscape consultant to avoid any responsibility for any errors he might make being transferred to the landscape consultant, who is still responsible for setting the minimum standards which the contractor should meet.

Inspections carried out by landscape consultants at regular intervals are not sufficient to ensure compliance with the contract requirements and flexibility is essential to ensure attendance on site at the crucial stages of a project, particularly for those items which are to be covered up subsequently. Such inspections should be made on a predictive basis, the stages being listed in the contract documents, with the requirement that the contractor should not be allowed to put the next in hand without at least 48 hours' prior notice to the landscape consultant, that the previous stage has been completed, and is ready for inspection. In this way the contractor will not be held up. Suggested stages for landscape projects are the following:

1 setting out,
2 excavation to remove top soil and formation levels,
3 collection and spreading materials already on site,
4 testing, spreading top soil and applying herbicides,
5 ground preparation and the application of fertilizer,
6 grass seeding,
7 hardcore beds for paving,
8 laying concrete and paving,
9 excavation of tree pits,
10 delivery and temporary storage of plants and other materials on site,
11 watering, and
12 maintenance visits.

Other items such as tree surgery, plants, brickwork and pointing, which are difficult to describe or specify accurately, can only be achieved by restricting their execution to certain subcontractors or suppliers of the consultant's choosing or to restrict the approval of the particular item of the work himself. Since this then relieves the contractor of any further responsibility for its adequacy, such items should be kept to the absolute minimum necessary.

The stage at which these approvals are given will depend on the individual circumstances. Some can and should be given at the moment of their construction or delivery to site, others only after a sufficient period of time to establish their survival, efficacy or performance in use, or at the end of the defects liability or maintenance period.

Such approvals must, however, be given as soon as it is possible to do so if the contractor is not to be unfairly penalized by condemning, at a later stage, some item which could have been rejected much earlier before it was incorporated in the works, covered up or planted. It is equally important that a decision once given should not be reversed without a subsequent very good and valid reason.

Some specified landscape items particularly herbicides, fertilizers, polymers and chemicals are difficult to identify after they have been applied, without subsequent expensive analysis and tests. Since it is neither fair to other tenderers nor right for the employer to pay for an inferior substitute or something which they have not received at all, particular care should be taken over such items.

Specification clauses for such items should therefore require proof of their purchase to be provided and prior notice of their delivery to site and subsequent application. Advice of delivery and delivery notes should be verified at the time of delivery, copies of purchase being inadequate. Delivery notes must always include the name of the contractor, the type, quality and quantity of the material supplied and the name of the particular contract for which they are intended, if double presentation of the same certificate on different contracts is to be avoided.

References

Clamp, H., *The Shorter Forms of Building Contract*, Granada, London, 1984.

Clamp, H., *Spon's Landscape Contract Manual*, Spon, London, 1986.

Harte, J.D.C., *Landscape, Land Use and the Law*, Spon, London, 1985.

Joint Council for Landscape Industries, *The JCLI Standard Form of Agreement for Landscape Works*, Landscape Institute, London, April 1987.

Keating, D., *Law and Practice of Building Contracts*,

Landscape Institute, *The Landscape Consultant's Appointment*, Landscape Institute, London, March 1988.

Speight, A., Stone, G., *A J Legal Handbook*, 4th ed., The Architectural Press, London, 1985.

Uff, J., *Construction Law*, 4th ed., Sweet and Maxwell, London, 1985.

Appendices

Appendices 1 to 4 are reproduced by permission of the Landscape Institute.

155

THE LANDSCAPE INSTITUTE

12 Carlton House Terrace, London, SW1Y 5AH
tel: 01·839·4044
Registrar Peter Bird

CODE OF PROFESSIONAL CONDUCT OF THE LANDSCAPE INSTITUTE

19TH MAY 1986

1. The object of this Code is to promote the standard of professional conduct and self-discipline required by members of the Landscape Institute. Members of the Institute are governed by its Constitution, By-Laws and Code of Professional Conduct; they shall conduct themselves in such a manner as will not prejudice the objects of the Institute as set out in the Constitution and repeated below:

    OBJECTS

    The objects of the Institute are the advancement of the art of landscape architecture; the theory and practice of landscape design; the promotion of research and education therein; the creation and maintenance of a high standard of professional qualification; and the promotion of the highest standard of professional service in the application of the arts and sciences of landscape architecture and management.

2. Members appointed to control the professional work of a public or private undertaking shall inform their employers of this Code and shall advise that the business of such an undertaking insofar as it relates to landscape is conducted in accordance with this Code.

The Professional Institute for Landscape Architects, Landscape Managers and Landscape Scientists

3. Members shall act impartially in all cases in which they are acting between parties and shall interpret the conditions of contract with fairness as between their client or employer and contractor.

4. Members may be principals, partners, directors and employees of any trade or undertaking, including those connected with landscape architecture, sciences or management, provided always that they inform their client in writing at the outset of the full extent of their interest in any undertakings connected with landscape.

5. Members shall agree with their client, in writing, at the outset of a commission, the terms and conditions for the professional services to be supplied.

6. Members may promote and advertise their services provided always that the information presented is factual, relevant, and neither misleading nor discreditable to the profession.

7. Members shall not have in partnership or other direct association any person who is suspended or expelled from membership. Members shall not disregard the professional obligations or qualifications of those from whom they receive or to whom they give authority, responsibility or employment nor of those with whom they are professionally associated.

8. Members on being approached to proceed with professional work on which to their knowledge another member is employed shall notify the fact to that member. Members of one division or grade of membership shall not misrepresent themselves as being qualified to perform the work of another.

9. This Code of Professional Conduct may only be amended by resolution passed by a two-thirds majority of the professional members present in person or by proxy who are entitled to vote and do vote at a specially convened General Meeting of the Institute of which due notice to the members, containing the proposed amendments, shall have been given.

The Landscape Consultant's Appointment

The Landscape Institute
12 Carlton House Terrace
LONDON SW1Y 5AH
01-839 4044

FOREWORD

This document has been designed to advise Landscape Consultants and their Clients in the execution of landscape commissions. It has been registered with the Office of Fair Trading under the terms of the Restrictive Trade Practices Act, 1976.

The Landscape Institute is the professional association for Landscape Architects, Landscape Managers and Landscape Scientists. One of its objects is to promote the highest standard of professional service in the application of the arts and sciences of landscape architecture and management. All members of the Institute, collectively referred to in this document as Landscape Consultants, are governed by the Institute's Code of Professional Conduct, but the rules of the members of the three different landscape disciplines vary in accordance with their education and experience.

Landscape Architects identify and solve problems using design techniques based on an understanding of the external environment, knowledge of the functional and aesthetic characteristics of landscape materials, and of the organisation of land-scape elements, external spaces and activities.

Landscape Managers are concerned with the long term care and development of new and existing landscapes and also with policy and planning for future manage-ment and use. This involves them in the organisation of man power, machinery and materials and requires a working knowledge of statutory measures and Grant Aid Schemes in order to preserve and enhance the quality of the landscape.

Landscape Scientists are specialists in the physical and biological aspects of landscape design and management. Relating scientific expertise to the practical problems of designers and managers, they may work in any of the many scientific subjects that are relevant to landscape, especially botany, ecology and soil surveys.

Any question on or arising out of the information contained herein may be referred to the Registrar, The Landscape Institute, 12, Carlton House Terrace, London SW1Y 5AH. Tel: 01-839 4044.

0   INTRODUCTION

0.1   The Landscape Consultant's professional responsibility is to act as the Client's adviser, understanding clearly his requirements, and, as the agent in any contract between the Client and Contractor, to administer the contract impartially and fairly. A good working relationship between the Client and Consultant is therefore essential when proceeding with a commission.
The Clients also have an important role. They must provide adequate information on the project, site and budget and fully understand and approve the Landscape Consultant's proposals at various stages of the work as it proceeds.

0.2   The most successful relationships are those which proceed in an atmos-phere of mutual trust and goodwill. An understanding of the Client's and the Consultant's respective obligations by both parties is fundamental to the creation of such an atmosphere. The Landscpape Institute therefore advises its members that before accepting a commission for professional services, they should agree with the Client the terms of the commission including the scope of the services, the allocation of responsibilities and any limitation of liability, the payment of fees including the rates and methods of calculation and the provisions for termination.

0.3   The Institute therefore advises its members to use the Schedules of Services and Memorandum of Agreement, samples of which are included in the appendices to this document. Alternatively, letters of agreement could also serve the purpose, provided that the services, responsibilities and fee basis are fully defined. If the agreement is not comprehensive it is likely to create uncertainties for either or both parties as the commission progresses.

0.4   The Landscape Consultant's Appointment. This document consists of three related parts as under.

0.4.1   *Part 1 - Landscape Consultant's Services.* The work which a Landscape Consultant normally undertakes after accepting a commission is primarily concerned with landscape design, construction (including planting), and management. It comprises Preliminary Services and Basic Services, sub-divided into Work Stages as follows:

— Preliminary Services   Work Stage A– Inception
Work Stage B– Feasibility

— Basic Services   Work Stage C– Outline Proposals
Work Stage D– Sketch Scheme Proposals
Work Stage E– Detailed Proposals
Work Stage F – Production Information •
Work Stage G– Bills of Quantities

Work Stage H– Tender Action
Work Stage J – Contract Preparation
Work Stage K– Operations on Site
Work Stage L – Completion

The Landscape Consultant may also provide services outside the design, construction and management process, for example Public Inquiry Commissions, Landscape Planning Issues, Environmental Impact Assessment, Landscape Appraisal and Evaluation.

0.4.2   *Part 2 – Other Services.* Many commissions will require Other Services additional to the Preliminary and Basic Services and it may be necessary to obtain and incorporate advice from various different consultants.

0.4.3   *Part 3 – Conditions of Appointment.* This part describes conditions which normally apply when a Landscape Consultant is commissioned.

0.5   The Parts are described in detail in succeeding sections of this document. In addition, the samples of the Schedule of Services and Memorandum of Agreement can be found in the Appendices.

0.6   Guidance on the various types of fee arrangement and their appropriate use is currently the subject of further discussion with the Office of Fair Trading.

PART 1	**1**	**LANDSCAPE CONSULTANT'S SERVICES**

1.1   This Part describes the Preliminary and Basic Services which a Landscape Consultant will normally provide. These services are common to large and small commissions and none should be omitted if the commission is to be completed successfully. However, it may be prudent to vary the sequence of the Work Stages or to combine two or more stages to suit the particular circumstances. Where, for any reason, partial services only are to be provided, the agreement between the Client and the Consultant should indicate precisely the extent of those services. Preliminary Services comprise Work Stages A and B; Basic Services comprise Work Stages C to L inclusive. Other Services are described in Part 2.

Work Stage A   **1.2**   **Preliminary Services – Work Stage A: Inception**

Brief   1.2.1   Discuss and assess the Client's requirements including the timescale and financial limits; advise the Client on how to proceed; agree the Landscape Consultant's services and the terms of engagement and fee payment basis, confirming these in writing with the Client.

Information which may be provided by the Client   1.2.2   Obtain from the Client information on ownership, other legal interests in the site, existing features, including underground services, and any other matters which may influence the development or management requirements.

Site Appraisal   1.2.3   Visit the site and carry out an initial appraisal.

Advice on other Consultants, Specialist Firms and Site Staff   1.2.4   Advise on the need for other consultants' services and the extent ot these services; advise on the need for specialist contractors or suppliers to execute the works; advise on the need for site staff.

Programme   1.2.5   Advise on outline programme and fee basis for further services, and obtain the Client's agreement thereto.

Work Stage B   **1.3**   **Preliminary Services – Work Stage B: Feasibility**

Feasibility Studies   1.3.1   Undertake such studies as are necessary to determine the feasibility of the Client's requirements; discuss with the Client alternative solutions and their technical and financial implications; advise on the need to obtain planning permissions and other statutory requirements.

Landscape Consultant's Range of Services	1.3.2	In the light of the Feasibility Studies, agree with the Client the detailed extent of Basic and Other Services required.

Work Stage C   **1.4**   **Basic Services – Works Stage C: Outline Proposals**

Outline Proposals	1.4.1	Broadly analyse the Client's requirements, prepare outline proposals and approximate estimate of the cost of executing the proposals for the Client's approval with other Consultants where appointed.

Work Stage D   **1.5**   **Basic Services - Work Stage D: Sketch Scheme Proposals**

Sketch Scheme Proposals	1.5.1	Develop the sketch scheme proposals from those agreed in outline, taking into account any changes requested by the Client, prepare cost estimates and programme for implementation with other Consultants where appointed. The sketch scheme proposals should indicate the size and character of the project in sufficient detail to enable the Client to agree the spatial arrangements, materials and appearance.
Changes in Scheme Proposals	1.5.2	Advise the Client of the implications of any changes in the cost and timing for executing the proposals and obtain approval for such changes.
Outline Planning Application	1.5.3	If appropriate, consult with the Planning Authority and submit any necessary application for outline planning permission.
Other Approvals	1.5.4	Similarly, make application for any other approvals from statutory bodies, where these are not dependent on detailed proposals being available.

Work Stage E   **1.6**   **Basic Services – Work Stage E: Detailed Proposals**

Detailed Proposals	1.6.1	Develop the proposals in sufficient detail to obtain the Client's approval of the proposed materials, techniques and standards of workmanship; and, when acting as design team leader, co-ordinate with the proposals made by other consultants, specialist contractors or suppliers, obtain quotations and other information in relation to specialist work.

Cost Checks and Changes in Detailed Proposals	1.6.2	Carry out cost checks where necessary and advise the Client of the consequences of any changes on the estimated cost and programme. Obtain the Client's consent to proceed.
Detailed Statutory Approvals	1.6.3	Make detailed applications for approvals under the planning and building legislation where necessary.

Work Stages F & G **1.7** **Basic Services – Work Stages F and G: Production Information and Bills of Quantities**

Production Information	1.7.1	Prepare all production drawings, schedules and specification of materials and workmanship required for the execution of the work.
Bills of Quantities	1.7.2	Provide information for bills of quantities to be prepared by others. All information to be supplied in sufficient detail to enable a contract to be negotiated or competitive tenders to be invited. See also 2.6.1

Work Stages H & J **1.8** **Basic Services – Work Stages H and J: Tender Action and Contract Preparation**

Other Contracts	1.8.1	Where necessary, arrange for other contracts to be let in advance of the Contractor starting work.
Tender Lists	1.8.2	With the Client's participation advise on suitable contractors and obtain approval of a final list of tenderers.
Tender Action or Negotiation	1.8.3	Invite tenders from approved contractors; appraise and advise on tenders submitted. Alternatively, arrange for a price to be negotiated with a contractor.
Contract Document Preparation	1.8.4	Advise the Client on the appointment of the Contractor and on the responsibilities of the Client, the Contractor and the Landscape Consultant under the terms of the contract; prepare the contract and arrange for it to be signed by the Client and the Contractor; provide production information as required by the contract.

Work Stage K **1.9** **Basic Services – Work Stage K: Operations on Site**

Contract Administration	1.9.1	Administer the contract during operations on site including control of the Clerk of Works where appointed.

Inspections	1.9.2	Visit the site at intervals appropriate to the contractor's programmed activities to inspect the progress and quality of the works. Frequency of the inspection shall be agreed with the Client.
Accounts	1.9.3	Check and certify the authenticity of accounts.
Financial Appraisal and Programme	1.9.4	Make periodic financial reports to the Client, identifying any variation in the cost of the works with other consultants where appointed, and in the expected duration of the contract.
Work Stage L	**1.10**	**Basic Services – Work Stage L: Completion**
Completion of Works	1.10.1	Administer the terms of the contract relating to the completion of the works and give general guidance on activities after completion of contract.
PART 2	**2**	**OTHER SERVICES**
	2.1	This Part describes services which may be provided by the Landscape Consultant by prior agreement with the Client to augment the Preliminary and Basic Services described in Part 1 or which may be the subject of a separate appointment. The list of services is not exhaustive.
	2.2	**Surveys and Investigations**
Site Evaluation	2.2.1	Advise on the selection and suitability of sites; conduct negotiations concerned with sites and their features.
Measured Surveys	2.2.2	Make measured surveys, take levels and prepare plans of sites and their features, including any existing buildings.
Site Investigation	2.2.3	Undertake investigations into, prepare reports and schedules, and give advice on the nature and condition of the vegetation, soil or other features of the site. Investigate failures, arrange and supervise exploratory work by contractors or specialists.
Maintenance and Management Cost in Use	2.2.4	Survey and analyse the usage, management and maintenance of a site, undertake cost in use studies, and analyse the need for additional design work.

Environmental Impact Appraisal	2.2.5	Undertake studies into the environmental impact of development proposals and land use changes.
Development Plans	2.2.6	Prepare development plans for sites, where development of part of the whole site will not be immediate.
Demolition and Clearance	2.2.7	Provide services in connection with demolition and clearance works.
Special Drawings and Models	2.2.8	Prepare special drawings, models or technical information for the use of the client for applications under planning or building regulations, or other statutory requirements, or for negotiations with ground landlords, adjoining owners, public authorities, licensing authorities, mortgagors and others; prepare plans for conveyancing, land registry and other legal or record purposes.
Prototype	2.2.9	Develop prototype proposals for repetitive use by the Client, but only when such repetitive use is specifically agreed by the Landscape Consultant and Client as appropriate
Site Furniture & Equipment	2.2.10	Design or advise on the selection of site furniture and equipment; arrange and inspect the fabrication of site furniture, arrange trials and training in use of equipment.
Multi-disciplinary Meetings	2.2.11	Attend multi-disciplinary meetings.
Public Meetings	2.2.12	Attend, prepare and organise material for public consultation and liaison.
Works of Art	2.2.13	Advise on the commissioning or selection of works of art in connection with landscape commissions.
Scientific Developments	2.2.14	Undertake research and conduct trials if necessary; especially where technical problems indicate that traditional solutions are inadequate.
Visits to Nurseries	2.2.15	Visit horticultural nurseries to ascertain the quantity, quality and cost of stock available for purchase.
	2.3	**Cost Estimating and Financial Advisory Services**
Cost Plans and Cash Flow Requirements	2.3.1	Carry out cost planning for a project, including the cost of professional fees; advise on cash flow requirements for fees, works and cost in use.

Schedules of Rates and Quantities	2.3.2	Prepare schedules of rates or bills of quantities for for tendering purposes; measure work executed.
Cost of Replacement and Reinstatement of Damaged Landscapes	2.3.3	Carry out inspections and surveys; prepare estimates for the replacement and reinstatement of damaged land-scapes; submit and negotiate claims.
Grant Applications	2.3.4	Provide information; make applications for and conduct negotiations for grants.

2.4   Planning Negotiations

Planning Applications; Exceptional Negotiations	2.4.1	Conduct detailed negotiations with a planning authority that become prolonged because of complexity.
Planning Appeals and Public Inquiries	2.4.2	Prepare and submit an appeal under planning acts; advise on other work in connection with planning appeals. Prepare and submit a proof of evidence for a public inquiry; appear as an expert witness at a public inquiry.
Royal Fine Art Commission	2.4.3	Make submissions to the Royal Fine Art Commission.
Building Regulations; Exceptional Negotiations	2.4.4	Conduct detailed negotiations for approvals under the building regulations; negotiate waivers or relaxations, all of which may become prolonged because of complexity.
Landlords Approvals	2.4.5	Submit plans of proposed works for the approval of landlords, mortgagors, freeholders or others.
Rights of Owners and Lessees	2.4.6	Advise on the rights and responsibilities of owners or lessees including rights of ways, rights of support, boundary, drainage and wayleave responsibilities etc., such advice shall always be subject to confirmation by the Client's legal advisor.

2.5   Additional Administration of Projects

Site Staff	2.5.1	Provide site staff for frequent or constant inspection of the works.

Project Management	2.5.2	Provide management from inception to completion; prepare briefs; appoint and co-ordinate consultants implementation managers, agents, suppliers and contractors; monitor time cost and agreed targets; monitor progress of the works, handover projects on completion.
Record Drawings	2.5.3	Provide the Client with a set of drawings showing the main elements of the scheme, arrange for drawings of other services to be provided as appropriate.
Landscape Management Plans	2.5.4	Prepare management plans and maintenance schedules; and operational manuals; assess cost and manpower implications of proposals.
Contract Claims	2.5.5	Carry out the administration, evaluation and settlement of contract claims.
Litigation and Arbitration	2.5.6	Prepare and give evidence; settle proofs; confer with solicitors and counsel; attend courts and arbitrations; appear before other tribunals; act as arbitrator.
	2.6	**Services normally provided by other Consultants**
Other Consultants' Services	2.6.1	Where services such as quantity surveying, architecture, civil, structural, mechanical or electrical engineering, town planning or graphic design are provided from within the Landscape Consultant's own office or by other consultants in association with the Landscape Consultants, it is recommended that the fees be separately agreed.
PART 3	**3**	**CONDITIONS OF APPOINTMENT**
	3.1	This Part describes the conditions which normally apply to a Landscape Consultant's appointment. If different or additional services are required they should be set out in the Schedule of Services, Memorandum of Agreement or letter of agreement.
Duty of Care	3.2	The Landscape Consultant will use reasonable skill, care and diligence in accordance with the normal standards of the profession.
Landscape Consultant's Authority	3.3	The Landscape Consultant will act on behalf of the Client in the matters set out or implied in the Landscape Consultant's appointment; the Landscape Consultant will obtain the authority of the Client before initiating any service or Work Stage.

Modifications	3.4	The Landscape Consultant shall not significantly alter an approved proposal without Client approval. Should changes be found to be necessary during implementation, the Client shall be informed and consent obtained without delay.
Revisions to the Conditions of Appointment	3.5	The agreement between a Client and a Landscape Consultant is deemed to allow for revisions due to changing circumstances. In long term commissions such changes will probably be due to unforeseen factors or matters beyond the control of the Landscape Consultant at the date of the appointment.
Project Control	3.6	The Landscape Consultant will report any significant variations in authorised expenditure or contract period.
Impartiality	3.7	The Landscape Consultant will be impartial in administering the terms of a contract between Client and Contractor.
Appointment of other Consultants	3.8	Consultants may be appointed either by the Client direct or by the Landscape Consultant subject to acceptance by each party.
Sub-letting	3.9	The Landscape Consultant shall not sub-contract any part of the commission without notifying the Client and receiving formal agreement on the division of responsibilities that will apply.
Liability of other Consultants	3.10	Where a Consultant is appointed under clause 3.8, the Landscape Consultant shall not be held liable for other Consultants' work, provided that in relation to the execution of such work under a contract between Client and Contractor nothing in this case shall affect any responsibility of the Landscape Consultant to perform his duties under the terms of that contract.
Consultant Co-ordination	3.11	The Landscape Consultant will have the responsibility to co-ordinate and integrate into the overall design the services provided by any consultant, however employed.
Design work by Contractors/ Suppliers	3.12	A specialist contractor, sub-contractor or supplier who is employed by the Client and who supplies design draw ings to the Landscape Consultant for incorporation in the works may be appointed by agreement. The Landscape Consultant shall not be held liable for the execution and performance of this work. The Landscape Consultant will have the authority to integrate and co-ordinate this design information into the overall design.

Contractor Responsibility	3.13	The Client will employ a contractor under a separate agreement to undertake construction or other works not undertaken by the Landscape Consultant. The Client will hold the contractor, and not the Landscape Consultant, responsible for the contractor's operational methods and for the proper execution of the works.
Site Inspections	3.14	The Landscape Consultant will visit the site at intervals appropriate to the progress of the works. As these intervals will vary depending on the nature of the work, the Landscape Consultant will explain to the Client at the outset when inspections will be made and agree these with the Client. If more inspections/visits to the site are required by the Client, details, as an extension to the Basic Services, will be agreed in writing with the Client.
Site Staff and Resident Landscape Staff	3.15	Where frequent or constant professional inspection is agreed to be required, a resident professional shall be appointed on a full or part time basis by the Consultant under specific terms of appointment and remuneration.
Site Staff/ Clerk of Works	3.16	Where frequent or constant inspection of the works is required a Clerk of Works suitably qualified in the supervision of landscape operations shall be employed. The Clerk of Works may be employed by the Client, or the Landscape Consultant, but in either case will be under the control and direction of the Landscape Consultant.
Information from Client	3.17	The Client is required to provide the Landscape Consultant with such information and make such decisions as are necessary for the proper performance of the agreed service. The requirement and reasons for such timely action shall be explained to the Client by the Landscape Consultant so that the implications of delay are clearly understood by both parties.
Client Representative	3.18	The Client, if a firm or other body of persons, will, when requested by the Landscape Consultant, nominate a responsible representative through whom all instructions will be given.
Copyright	3.19	Copyright in all documents and drawings prepared by the Landscape Consultant shall unless otherwise agreed remain the property of the Consultant.
Copyright Entitlement	3.20	The Client will be entitled to use documents and drawings in executing the works for which they were prepared by the Landscape Consultant provided that:

a) All fees due to the Landscape Consultant have been submitted or paid.

b) The entitlement relates only to that site or part of the site for which the design was prepared.

This entitlement applies to the design, maintenance and management of the works.

Assignment	3.21	Neither the Client nor the Landscape Consultant shall assign the appointment in whole or in part without prior written agreement as to the division of responsibilities that apply.
Suspension by Client	3.22	The length of notice for suspension should be agreed in writing at the outset. The Client may suspend the Landscape Consultant's appointment in whole or in part, the notice given being in accordance with the agreed timing and in writing.
Suspension by Consultant	3.23	The Landscape Consultant will give immediate notice in writing to the Client of any situation arising from force majeure which makes it impractical to carry out any of the agreed services, and agree with the Client a suitable course of action.
Resumption of Service	3.24	Following the notice in accordance with clause 3.22 if no instruction has been received within 6 months, the Landscape Consultant shall make a written request for instructions. If no instruction is received within 30 days, the appointment shall be treated as terminated.
Termination	3.25	The Landscape Consultant's appointment may be terminated by either party in accordance with clause 3.22 or 3.23.
Death or Incapacity	3.26	If death or incapacity of a sole practitioner stops the Landscape Consultant from carrying out the agreed duties under this appointment, it shall be terminated. As soon as all outstanding fees have been submitted or paid, the Client will be entitled to use all data prepared on the project subject to the provisions in respect of copyright in accordance with clause 3.19 and 3.20.
Settlement of Disputes by Agreement	3.27	Nothing herein shall prevent the parties agreeing to settle any difference or dispute arising out of the appointment without recourse to arbitration.

Mediation	3.28	Should the Client and the Landscape Consultant dispute any matter arising from an appointment under this document they are free by agreement to invite a third party to act as mediator to effect mediation and settlement before exercising their rights to other means of resolving the dispute. This third party should be well versed in the processes of mediation.
Ruling on a Joint Statement	3.29	Any difference or dispute arising from a written appointment under this document may, by agreement, be referred to the Landscape Institute for a ruling by the President. The parties must agree:

— to prepare and submit with their submissions a joint statement of undisputed facts to reduce the area of dispute to a minimum.

— to accept the ruling as final and binding.

Arbitration	3.30	Any difference or dispute arising out of the appointment which cannot be resolved in accordance with either clause 3.28 or 3.29 shall be referred to arbitration by a person to be agreed between the parties or, failing agreement within 21 days after either party has given to the other a written request to concur in the appointment of an arbitrator, a person to be appointed at the request of either party by the President or a Vice-President for the time being of the Chartered Institute of Arbitrators.

In Scotland, any difference or dispute arising out of the appointment which cannot be resolved in accordance with clause 3.28 or 3.29 shall be referred to arbitration by a person to be agreed between the parties or, failing agreement within 21 days after either party has given to the other a written request to concur in the appointment of an arbiter, a person to be nominated at the request of either party by the Chairman for the time being of the Scottish Branch of the Chartered Institute of Arbitrators.

Governing Laws England and Wales	3.31	The application of these conditions shall be governed by the laws of England and Wales.

or

Alternative for Scotland	3.32	The application of these conditions shall be governed by the laws of Scotland.

or

Alternative for Northern Ireland	3.33	The application of these conditions shall be governed by the laws of Northern Ireland.

MEMORANDUM OF AGREEMENT

between Client and Landscape Consultant for use with the Landscape Consultants Appointment.

This Agreement

is made on the

............day of .... 19 ....

between

....
(insert name of Client)

of

....

....
(hereinafter called the 'Client')

and

....
(insert name of Landscape Consultant and firm of Landscape Consulttants

of

....

....
(hereinafter called the Landscape Consultant)

NOW IT IS HEREBY AGREED

that upon the Conditions of the Landscape Consultants Appointment a copy of which is attached hereto,

save as excepted or varied by the parties hereto in the attached Schedule of Services and Fees, hereinafter called the 'Schedule',

and subject to any special conditions set out or referred to in the Schedule:

1.   The Landscape Consultant will perform for the Client the services listed in the Schedule in respect of

....
(insert general description of project)

at...
(insert location of project)

174

2.   the Client will pay the Landscape Consultant on demand for the services, fees and expenses indicated in the Schedule;

3.   other consultants will be appointed as indicated in the Schedule;

4.   site staff will be appointed as indicated in the Schedule;

5.   any difference or dispute arising out of this Agreement shall be referable to arbitration.

AS WITNESS the hands of the parties the day and year first above written.

Signatures: Client..

Landscape Consultant..

Witnesses: Name...........................Name................................

Address.........................Address..............................

Description...................Description...........................

SCHEDULE OF SERVICES AND FEES

Referred to in the Memorandum of Agreement dated.......

between   ....
            (insert name of Client)

and   ....
            insert of Landscape Consultant)

for   ....
            (insert description of project)

Unless otherwise stated the services listed in the conditions of appointment will be described in the Landscape Consultants Appointment (................Revision), issued by the L.I. Clause references relate to that document.

S1 SERVICES

Service	Clause	Fee basis (State whether percentage, time or lump sum)	Clause
Preliminary Services			
Basic Services			
Other Services			

S2 SPECIAL CONDITIONS   Insert any conditions which are to apply to the appointment

CONDITIONS NOT TO APPLY

Insert any clauses which are not to apply to this appointment

PERCENTAGE FEES

Fees based on a percentage of the total construction cost shall be calculated as follows:

LUMP SUM FEES

Interim payments for percentage and lump sum fees shall be * paid monthly/quarterly/half yearly: * paid at completion of work stages as follows:

Work stage	Proportion of fee	Cumulative total

Notwithstanding these, fees in respect of
Work Stage: _____ shall be paid in instalments proportionate to the drawings and other work completed or the value of works certified.

* Delete whichever is inapplicable

TIME CHARGE FEES

Rates for fees charged on a time basis shall be:

.1   for principals £_____ per hour

.2   for staff: —— p per £100 of gross annual income for office based staff.

177

**EXPENSES AND
DISBURSEMENTS**

* The fees charged are inclusive of all expenses and disbursements.

or

* Expenses and disbursements shall be charged

* Delete whichever
is inapplicable

Mileage rates shall be:

Signed: Client   Landscape Consultant

Date:

APPENDIX 3: The JCLI Standard Form of Agreement for Landscape Works

This Agreement is made the _____ day of _____ 19___

between _____

of_____
(hereinafter called 'the Employer')

of the one part AND _____

of (or whose registered office is at)_____

_____
(hereinafter called 'the Contractor') of the other part.

Whereas

Recitals

1st   the Employer wishes the following work_____

_____

_____

(hereinafter called "the Works") to be carried out under the direction of

_____

(hereinafter called "Landscape Architect") and has caused drawings
numbered
(hereinafter called "the Contract Drawings") [a] and/or a Specification (hereinafter
called "the Contract Specification") [a] and/or schedules [a] and/or schedules of rates
[a] and/or Bills of Quantities [a] which documents are together with the Conditions
annexed hereto (hereinafter called "the Contract Documents") showing and describing
the works to be prepared and which are attached to this Agreement.

The law of England/Scotland shall be the proper law of this Agreement [a].

2nd   The Contractor has priced the Specification [a] or the schedules [a] or Bills of
Quantities [a] or provided a schedule of rates [a];

3rd   the Contract Documents have been signed by or on behalf of the parties hereto;

4th   [a] the quantity surveyor appointed in connection with this contract shall mean

_____

or in the event of his death or ceasing to be the quantity surveyor for this purpose such
other person as the Employer nominates for that purpose;

[a]   Delete as appropriate

179

Now it is hereby agreed as follows

Article 1
For the consideration hereinafter mentioned the Contractor will in accordance with the Contract Documents carry out and complete the Works.

Article 2
The Employer will pay to the Contractor the sum of _____

_____

_____ (£ _____)

exclusive of VAT or such other sum as shall become payable hereunder at the times and in the manner specified in the Contract Documents.

Article 3
The term "Landscape Architect" in the said Conditions shall mean

_____

or in the event of his death or ceasing to be the Landscape Architect for the purpose of this Contract such other person as the Employer shall within 14 days of the death or cessation as aforesaid nominate for that purpose, provided that no person subsequently appointed to be the Landscape Architect under this Contract shall be entitled to disregard or overrule any certificate or instruction given by the Landscape Architect for the time being.

Article 4
If any dispute or difference concerning this Contract shall arise between the Employer or the Landscape Architect on his behalf and the Contractor such dispute or difference shall be and is hereby referred to the arbitration and final decision of a person to be agreed between the parties or, failing agreement within 14 days after either party has given to the other a written request to concur in the appointment of an arbitrator, a person to be appointed on the request of either party by the President or a Vice-President for the time being of the Landscape Institute.

As witness the hands of the parties hereto

Signed for and on behalf of the Employer _____
                                                   (For the Employer)

in the presence of _____
                                                   (Witness)

Signed for and on behalf of the Contractor _____
                                                   (For the Contractor)

in the presence of _____
                                                   (Witness)

Contents

Note:
Clauses marked * should be completed/deleted
as appropriate
†*see note on page 8*

Conditions hereinbefore referred to

1.0 Intentions of the parties

Contractor's obligation

1·1 The Contractor shall with due diligence and in a good and workmanlike manner carry out and complete the Works in accordance with the Contract Documents using materials and workmanship of the quality and standards therein specified provided that where and to the extent that approval of the quality of materials or of the standards of workmanship is a matter for the opinion of the Landscape Architect such quality and standards shall be to the reasonable satisfaction of the Landscape Architect.

Landscape Architect's duties

1·2 The Landscape Architect shall issue any further information necessary for the proper carrying out of the Works, issue all certificates and confirm all instructions in writing in accordance with these Conditions.

Contract Bills and SMM

1·3 Where the Contract Documents include Contract Bills, the Contract Bills unless otherwise expressly stated therein in respect of any specified item or items are to have been prepared in accordance with the Standard Method of Measurement of Building Works, 6th Edition, published by the Royal Institution of Chartered Surveyors and the Building Employers Confederation (formerly National Federation of Building Trades Employers) and the Joint Council for Landscape Industries Rules for the Measurement of Soft Landscape Works.

2·0 Commencement and completion

Commencement and completion

2·1 The Works may be commenced on

. . . .

and shall be completed by

. . . .

Extension of contract period

2·2 If it becomes apparent that the Works will not be completed by the date for completion inserted in clause 2·1 hereof (or any later date fixed in accordance with the provisions of this clause 2·2) for reasons beyond the control of the Contractor, then the Contractor shall so notify the Landscape Architect who shall make, in writing, such extension of the time for completion as may be reasonable.

Damages for non-completion

2·3 If the Works are not completed by the completion date inserted in clause 2·1 hereof or by any later completion date fixed under clause 2·2 hereof then the Contractor shall pay or allow to the Employer liquidated damages at the rate of £ . . . . .per week for every week or part of a week during which the Works remain uncompleted.

Completion date

2·4 The Landscape Architect shall certify the date when in his opinion the Works have reached practical completion.

Defects liability

2·5 Any defects, excessive shrinkages or other faults, other than tree, shrub, grass and other plant failures, which appear within three

months [b] . . . . of the date of practical completion and are due to materials or workmanship not in accordance with the Contract or frost occurring before practical completion shall be made good by the Contractor entirely at his own cost unless the Landscape Architect shall otherwise instruct.
The Landscape Architect shall certify the date when in his opinion the Contractor's obligations under this clause 2·5 have been discharged.

Partial Possession by Employer

†2·6 If before practical completion of the Works the Employer with the consent of the Contractor shall take possession of any part then:
The date for possession of the part shall be the date of practical completion of the part and clause 4·3 shall apply to the part.
In lieu of the sum to be paid by the Contractor under clause 2·3 for any period during which the Works remain uncompleted after the Employers possession of any part the sum paid shall bear the same ratio to the sum stated in clause 2·3 as does the Contract Sum less the value of the part to the Contract Sum.

Failures of Plants (Pre-Practical Completion)

†2·7 Any trees, shrubs, grass or other plants, other than those found to be missing or defective as a result of theft or malicious damage and which shall be replaced as set out in clause 6·5 of these conditions, which are found to be defective at practical completion of the works shall be replaced by the Contractor entirely at his own cost unless the Landscape Architect shall otherwise instruct. The Landscape Architect shall certify the dates when in his opinion the Contractor's obligations under this clause have been discharged.

(Post-Practical Completion)

*A The maintenance of trees, shrubs, grass and other plants after the date of the said certificate will be carried out by the Contractor for the duration of the periods stated in accordance with the programme and in the manner specified in the Contract Documents. Any grass which is found to be defective within . . . . months, any shrubs, ordinary nursery stock trees ot other plants found to be defective within . . . . months and any trees, semi-mature advanced or extra large nursery stock found to be defective within . . . . months of the date of Practical Completion and are due to materials or workmanship not in accordance with the contract shall be replaced by the Contractor entirely at his own cost unless the Landscape Architect shall otherwise instruct. The Landscape Architect shall certify the dates when in his opinion the Contractor's obligations under this clause have been discharged.

*B The maintenance of the trees, shrubs, grass and other plants after the date of the said certificate will be undertaken by the Employer who will be responsible for the replacement of any trees, shrubs, grass or other plants which are subsequently defective.

3·0 Control of the Works

Assignment

3·1 Neither the Employer nor the Contractor shall, without the written consent of the other, assign this Contract.

[b] If a different period is required delete 'three months' and insert the appropriate period.

Delete (A) or (B) as appropriate.

182

Sub-contracting
3·2 The Contractor shall not sub-contract the Works or any part thereof without the written consent of the Landscape Architect whose consent shall not unreasonably be withheld.

Contractor's representative
3·3 The Contractor shall at all reasonable times keep upon the Works a competent person in charge and any instructions given to him by the Landscape Architect shall be deemed to have been issued to the Contractor.

Exclusion from the Works
3·4 The Landscape Architect may (but not unreasonably or vexatiously) issue instructions requiring the exclusion from the Works of any person employed thereon.

Landscape Architect's instructions
3·5 The Landscape Architect may issue written instructions which the Contractor shall forthwith carry out. If instructions are given orally they shall, in two days, be confirmed in writing by the Landscape Architect.
If within 7 days after receipt of a written notice from the Landscape Architect requiring compliance with an instruction the Contractor does not comply therewith then the Employer may employ and pay other persons to carry out the work and all costs incurred thereby may be deducted by him from any monies due or to become due to the Contractor under this Contract or shall be recoverable from the Contractor by the Employer as a debt.

Variations
†3·6 The Landscape Architect may, without invalidating the contract, order an addition to or omission from or other change in the Works or the order or period in which they are to be carried out and any such instruction shall be valued by the Landscape Architect on a fair and reasonable basis, using where relevant prices in the priced specification/schedules/Bills of Quantity/schedule of rates [c].
If any omission substantially varies the scope of the work such valuations shall take due account of the effect on any remaining items of work.
† Instead of the valuation referred to above, the price may be agreed between the Landscape Architect and the Contractor prior to the Contractor carrying out any such instruction.

P.C. and Provisional sums
3·7 The Landscape Architect shall issue instructions as to the expenditure of any P.C. and provisional sums and such instructions shall be valued in accordance with clause 3·6 hereof.

Objections to a Nomination
†3·8 The Landscape Architect shall not nominate any person as a nominated sub-contractor against whom the Contractor shall make reasonable objection or who will not enter into a sub-contract that applies the appropriate provisions of these conditions.

Disturbance of Regular Progress
†3·9 If upon written application being made to him by the Contractor within a reasonable time of it becoming apparent, the Landscape Architect is of the opinion that the Contractor has been involved in direct loss and/or expense for which he would not be reimbursed by a payment under any other provisions of this contract by reason of the regular progress of the Works or part of the Works having been materially affected by reasons within the control of the Employer, his agents or servants, then the Landscape Architect shall ascertain such loss and expense and include it in any payments due under clause 4·2.

4.0 Payment

Correction of inconsistencies
4·1 Any inconsistency in or between the Contract Drawings [c] and the Contract Specification [c] and the schedules [c] shall be corrected and any such correction which results in an addition, omission or other change shall be treated as a variation under clause 3·6 hereof. Nothing contained in the Contract Drawings [c] or the Contract Specification [c] or the schedules or the Bills of Quantity [c] or the Schedule of Rates [c] shall override, modify or affect in any way whatsoever the application or interpretation of that which is contained in these Conditions.

Progress payments and retention
4·2* The Landscape Architect shall if requested by the Contractor, at intervals of not less than four weeks calculated from the date for commencement subject to any agreement between the parties as to stage payments, certify progress payments to the Contractor, in respect of the value of the Works properly executed, including any amounts either ascertained or agreed under clauses 3·6 and 3·7 hereof, and the value of any materials and goods which have been reasonably and properly brought upon the site for the purpose of the Works and which are adequately stored and protected against the weather and other casualties less a retention of 5% (. . . . . %) [e] and less any sums previously certified, and the Employer shall pay to the Contractor the amount so certified within 14 days of the date of the certificate.

Penultimate certificate
†4·3 The Landscape Architect shall within 14 days after the date of practical completion certified under clause 2·4 hereof certify payment to the Contractor of 97½% of the total amount to be paid to the Contractor under this contract so far as that amount is ascertainable at the date of practical completion, including any amounts either ascertained or agreed under clauses 3·6 and 3·7 hereof less the amount of any progress payments previously certified to the Employer, and less the cost of any subsequent maintenance included in the contract in accordance with Clause 2·7A unless the failures of plants as set out in clause 2·7 are in excess of 10% in which case the amount retained shall be adjusted accordingly, and the Employer shall pay to the Contractor the amount so certified within 14 days of that certificate.

Final certificate
4·4 The Contractor shall supply within three months/ . . . . [d] from the date of practical completion all documentation reasonably required for the computation of the amount to be finally certified by the Landscape Architect and the Landscape Architect shall within 28 days of receipt of such documentation, provided that the Landscape Architect has issued the certificate under clause 2·5 and 2·7A hereof, issue a final certificate certifying the amount remaining due to the Contractor or due to the Employer as the case may be and such

[c]	Delete as appropriate to follow any deletions in the recitals on page 1.
[d]	If a different period is required delete 'three months' and insert the appropriate percentage period.
[e]	If a different percentage is required delete 5% and insert the appropriate retention %.

sum shall as from the fourteenth day after the date of the final certificate be a debt payable as the case may be by the Employer to the Contractor or by the Contractor to the Employer.

Contribution, levy and tax changes [**f**]
4·5 Contribution, levy and tax changes shall be dealt with by the application of Part A of the Supplementary Memorandum to the Agreement for Landscape Works. The percentage addition under part A, clause A5 is .... % [**e**].

Fixed price [**f**]
4·6A No account shall be taken in any payment to the Contractor under this Contract of any change in the cost to the Contractor of the labour, materials, plant and other resources employed in carrying out the Works except as provided in clause 4·5 hereof, if applicable.

Fluctuations [**f**]
4·6B The Contract sum shall be adjusted in accordance with the provisions of Part D of the Supplementary Memorandum and the Formula Rules current at the date stated in the tender documents, and which shall be incorporated in all certificates except those relating to the release of retention and shall be exclusive of any Value Added Tax. These provisions shall also be incorporated as appropriate in any sub contract agreement.

5.0 Statutory obligations

Statutory obligations, notices, fees and charges
5·1 The Contractor shall comply with, and give all notices required by, any statute, any statutory instrument, rule or order or any regulation or byelaw applicable to the Works (hereinafter called 'the statutory requirements') and shall pay all fees and charges in respect of the Works legally recoverable from him. If the Contractor finds any divergence between the statutory requirements and the contract documents or between the statutory requirements and any instruction of the Landscape Architect he shall immediately give to the Landscape Architect, a written notice specifying the divergence. Subject to this latter obligation, the Contractor shall not be liable to the Employer under this Contract if the Works do not comply with the statutory requirements where and to the extent that such non-compliance of the Work results from the Contractor having carried out work in accordance with the Contract Documents or any instruction of the Landscape Architect.

Value Added Tax
5·2 The sum or sums due to the Contractor under Article 2 hereof this Agreement shall be exclusive of any Value Added Tax and the Employer shall pay to the Contractor any Value Added Tax properly chargeable by the Commissioners of Custom and Excise on the supply to the Employer of any goods and services by the Contractor under this Contract in the manner set out in Part B of the Supplementary Memorandum to the Agreement for Landscape Works.

Statutory tax deduction scheme
5·3 Where at the date of tender the Employer was a 'contractor', or where at any time up to the issue and payment of the final certificate the Employer becomes a 'contractor', for the purposes of the statutory tax deduction scheme referred to in Part C of the Supplementary Memorandum to the Agreement for Landscape Works, Part C of that Memorandum shall be operated.

Fair Wages Resolution
5·4 If the Employer is a local authority the contractor shall in respect of all persons employed by him (whether in the execution of this contract or otherwise) in every factory, workshop or place occupied or used by him for the executions of this contract comply with the conditions of Fair Wages Resolutions.

Prevention of corruption
5·5 If the Employer is a local authority he shall be entitled to cancel this contract and to recover from the Contractor the amount of any loss resulting from such cancellation, if the Contractor shall have offered or given or agreed to give to any person any gift or consideration of any kind or if the Contractor shall have committed any offence under the Prevention of Corruption Acts 1889 to 1916 or shall have given any fee or reward the receipt of which is an offence under sub-section (2) of section 117 of the Local Government Act 1972 or any re-enactment thereof.

6.0 Injury, damage and insurance

Injury to or death of persons
6·1 The Contractor shall be liable for and shall indemnify the Employer against any expense, liability, loss, claim or proceedings whatsoever arising under any statute or at common law in respect of personal injury to or death of any person whomsoever arising out of or in the course of or caused by the carrying out of the Works, unless due to any act or neglect of the Employer or of any person for whom the Employer is responsible. Without prejudice to his liability to indemnify the Employer the Contractor shall maintain and shall cause any sub-contractor to maintain such insurances as are necessary to cover the liability of the Contractor, or, as the case may be, of such sub-contractor, in respect of personal injury or death arising out of or in the course of or caused by the carrying out of the Works. Provided that nothing in this clause contained shall impose any liability on the sub-contractor in respect of negligence or breach of duty on the part of the Employer, the Contractor, his other sub-contractors or their respective servants or agents.

Damage to property
6·2 The Contractor shall, subject to clause 6·3A.B[**g**], be liable for and indemnify the Employer against and insure and cause any sub-contractor to insure against any expense, liability, loss, claim or proceedings in respect of any damage whatsoever to any property real or personal insofar as such damage arises out of or in the course of or by reason of the carrying out of the Works and is due to any negligence, omission or default of the Contractor or any person for whom the Contractor is responsible or of any sub-contractor or person for whom the sub-contractor is responsible.

Insurance of the Works – Fire etc. – New Works
6·3A The Contractor shall in the joint names of Employer and Contractor insure against loss and damage by fire, lightning, explosion, storm, tempest, flood, bursting or overflowing of water tanks, apparatus or pipes, earthquake, aircraft and other aerial devices or articles dropped therefrom, riot and civil commotion, for the full value of the Works thereof plus .... % [**h**] to

[**f**]   Delete clause 4·5 if the contract period is of such limited duration as to make the provisions of part A of the Supplementary Memorandum to this agreement inapplicable.
[**g**]   Delete 6·3A or 6·3B as appropriate.
[**h**]   Percentage to be inserted.
[**e**]   Normally 10%.

cover professional fees all work executed and all unfixed materials and goods intended for, delivered to, placed on or adjacent to the Works and intended therefore (except temporary buildings, plant, tools and equipment owned or hired by the Contractor and his sub-contractors). Upon acceptance of any claim under the insurance mentioned in this clause 6·3A the Contractor shall with due diligence restore or replace work or materials or goods damaged and dispose of any debris and proceed with and complete the Works. The Contractor shall not be entitled to any payment in respect of work or materials or goods damaged other than the monies received under the said insurance (less the percentage to cover professional fees) and such monies shall be paid to the Contractor under certificates of the Landscape Architect at the periods stated in clause 4·0 hereof.

Insurance of the Works — Fire, etc. — Existing structure [j]

6·3B The Works (and the existing structures together with the contents thereof owned by him and for which he is responsible) and all unfixed materials and goods intended for, delivered to, placed on or adjacent to the Works and intended therefor (except temporary buildings, plant, tools and equipment owned or hired by the Contractor or any sub-contractor) shall be at the sole risk of the Employer as regards loss or damage by fire, lightning, explosion, storm, tempest, flood, burst or overflowing of water tanks, apparatus or pipes, earthquake, aircraft and other aerial devices or articles dropped therefrom, riot and civil commotion, and the Employer shall maintain adequate insurance against that risk.
If any loss or damage as referred to in this clause occurs then the Landscape Architect shall issue instructions for the reinstatement and making good of such loss or damage in accordance with clause 3·5 hereof.

Evidence of insurance

6·4 The Contractor shall produce, and shall cause any sub-contractor to produce, such evidence as the Employer may reasonably require that the insurances referred to in clauses 6·1 and 6·2 and, where applicable 6·3A, hereof have been taken out and are in force at all material times. Where clause 6·3B hereof is applicable the Employer shall produce such evidence as the Contractor may reasonably require that the insurance referred to therein has been taken out and is in force at all material times.

Malicious Damage or Theft (before Practical Completion)

†6·5A All loss or damage arising from any theft or malicious damage prior to practical completion shall be made good by the Contractor at his own expense.

B The Contract sum shall include the provisional sum of £ . . . .* to be expended as instructed by the Landscape Architect in respect of the cost of all work arising from any theft or malicious damage to the works beyond the control of the Contractor prior to practical completion of the works.

7·0 Determination

Determination by Employer

7·1 The Employer may but not unreasonably or vexatiously by notice by registered post or recorded delivery to the Contractor forthwith determine the employment of the Contractor under this Contract if the Contractor shall make default in any one or more of the following respects:

1 if the Contractor without reasonable cause fails to proceed diligently with the Works or wholly suspends the carrying out of the Works before completion;
2 if the Contractor becomes bankrupt or makes any composition or arrangement with his creditors or has a winding up order made or (except for the purposes of reconstruction) a resolution for voluntary winding up passed or a receiver or manager of his business or undertaking is duly appointed or possession is taken by or on behalf of any creditor of any property the subject of a charge.

In the event of the Employer determining the employment of the Contractor as aforesaid the Contractor shall immediately give up possession of the site of the Works and the Employer shall not be bound to make any further payment to the Contractor until after completion of the Works. Provided always that the right determination shall be without prejudice to any other rights or remedies which the Employer may possess.

Determination by Contractor

7·2 The Contractor may but not unreasonably or vexatiously by notice by registered post or recorded delivery to the Employer forthwith determine the employment of the Contractor under this Contract if the Employer shall make default in any one or more of the following respects:

1 if the Employer fails to make any progress payment due under the provisions of Clause 4·2 hereof within 14 days of such payment being due;
2 if the Employer or any person for whom he is responsible interferes with or obstructs the carrying out of the Works or fails to make the site of the Works available for the Contractor in accordance with clause 2·1 hereof;
3 if the Employer suspends the carrying out of the Works for a continuous period of at least one month;
4 if the Employer becomes bankrupt or makes a composition or arrangement with his creditors, or has a winding up order made or a resolution for voluntary winding up passed on a receiver or manager of his business is appointed or possession is taken by or on behalf of any creditor of any property the subject of a charge.

Provided that the employment of the Contractor shall not be determined under clauses 7·2·1, 7·2·2 or 7·2·3 hereof unless the Employer has continued the default for seven days after receipt by registered post or recorded delivery of a notice from the Contractor specifying such default.
In the event of the Contractor determining the Employment of the Contractor as aforesaid the Employer shall pay to the Contractor, after taking into account amounts previously paid, such sum as shall be fair and reasonable for the value of work begun and executed, materials on site and the removal of all temporary buildings, plant, tools and equipment. Provided always that the right of determination shall be without prejudice to any other rights or remedies which the Contractor may possess.

8·0 Supplementary Memorandum

Meaning of references in 4·5, 4·6, 5·2 and 5·3

8·1 The references in clauses 4·5, 4·6, 5·2 and 5·3 to the Supplementary Memorandum to the Agreement for Landscape Works are to that issued for use with this Form by the Joint Council for Landscape Industries as endorsed hereon.

The amount to be inserted should take account of the Works and the place where they are carried out. Delete [A] or [B] as appropriate.

The Joint Council of Landscape Industries has issued a Supplementary Memorandum for use with this Form, where applicable, as referred to in the list of Contents on page 3 and in clause 8·1. The Supplementary Memorandum is attached.

The Council previously issued Practice Note No. 1 and Practice Note No. 2, but both are superseded by Practice Note No. 3 which is attached.

**The complete document now comprises 3 items:
Form of Agreement for Landscape Works.
Supplementary Memorandum.
JCLI Practice Note No. 3.
The Supplementary Memorandum and
Practice Note No. 3 may be torn off as convenient.**

Dated _____ 19 __

Agreement for Landscape Works

(In Scotland when English Law is not to apply supplementary clauses in respect of Building Regulations and Arbitration may be required)

First issued April 1978, revised April 1981 reprinted with corrections April 1982 revised April 1985, reprinted with corrections September 1986.

Between _____

_____

and _____

_____

This Form is issued by the Joint Council for Landscape Industries comprising:-

Landscape Institute
Horticultural Trades Association
British Association Landscape Industries
National Farmers Unions
Institute of Leisure and Amenity Management.

†Note: All clauses other than those marked † are similar to those in the Joint Contracts Tribunal Agreement for Minor Building Works.

Published for the Joint Council for Landscape Industries by the Landscape Institute 12 Carlton House Terrace, London SW1Y 5AH and available from RIBA Publications Limited 66 Portland Place, London W1N 4AD. © JCLI April 1985

Printed by Duolith Ltd. Welwyn Garden City, Herts.

Issued September 1986

Agreement for Landscape Works: Supplementary Memorandum

This Memorandum is the Supplementary Memorandum referred to in the Joint Council for Landscape Industries "Agreement for Landscape Works", 1981 Edition, clauses 4·5, 4·6, 5·2 and 5·3.

Unless otherwise specifically stated, words and phrases in the Supplementary Memorandum have the same meaning as in the Agreement for Landscape Works.

PART A – CONTRIBUTION, LEVY AND TAX CHANGES

Deemed calculation of Contract Sum – rates of contribution etc.

A1 The sum referred to in Article 2 (in this clause called "the Contract Sum") shall be deemed to have been calculated in the manner set out below and shall be subject to adjustment in the events specified hereunder:

A1·1 The prices used or set out by the Contractor in the contract documents are based upon the types and rates of contribution, levy and tax payable by a person in his capacity as an employer and which at the date of the contract are payable by the Contractor. A type and rate so payable are in clause A1·2 referred to as a 'tender type' and a 'tender rate'.

Increases or decreases in rates of contribution etc. – payment or allowance

A1·2 If any of the tender rates other than a rate of levy payable by virtue of the Industrial Training Act 1964, is increased or decreased, or if a tender type ceases to be payable, or if a new type of contribution, levy or tax which is payable by a person in his capacity as an employer becomes payable after the date of tender, then in any such case the net amount of the difference between what the Contractor actually pays or will pay in respect of

·1 workpeople engaged upon or in connection with the Works either on or adjacent to the site of the Works, and

·2 workpeople directly employed by the Contractor who are engaged upon the production of materials or goods for use in or in connection with the Works and who operate neither on nor adjacent to the site of the Works and to the extent that they are so engaged

or because of his employment of such workpeople and what he would have paid had the alteration, cessation or new type of contribution, levy or tax not become effective, shall, as the case may be, be paid to or allowed by the Contractor.

Persons employed on site other than 'workpeople'

A1·3 There shall be added to the net amount paid to or allowed by the Contractor under clause A1·2 in respect of each person employed on the site by the Contractor for the Works and who is not within the definition of 'workpeople' in clause A4·6·3 the same amount as is payable or allowable in respect of a craftsman under clause A1·2 or such proportion of that amount as reflects the time (measured in whole working days) that each such person is so employed.

A1·4 For the purposes of clause A1·3

no period less than 2 whole working days in any week shall be taken into account and periods less than a whole working day shall not be aggregated to amount to a whole working day;

the phrase "the same amount as is payable or allowable in respect of a craftsman" shall refer to the amount in respect of a craftsman employed by the Contractor (or by any subcontractor under a sub-contract to which clause A3 refers) under the rules or decisions or agreements of the National Joint Council for the Building Industry or other wage-fixing body and, where the aforesaid rules or decisions or agreements provide for more than one rate of wage emolument or other expense for a craftsman, shall refer to the amount in respect of a craftsman employed as aforesaid to whom the highest rate is applicable; and

the phrase "employed . . . by the Contractor" shall mean an employment to which the Income Tax (Employment) Regulations 1973 (the PAYE Regulations) under section 204 of the Income and Corporation Taxes Act, 1970, apply.

Refunds and premiums

A1·5 The prices used or set out by the Contractor in the contract documents are based upon the types and rates of refund of the contributions, levies and taxes payable by a person in his capacity as an employer and upon the types and rates of premium receivable by a person in his capacity as an employer being in each case types and rates which at the date of tender are receivable by the Contractor. Such a type and such a rate are in clause A·6 referred to as a 'tender type' and a 'tender rate'.

A1·6 If any of the tender rates is increased or decreased or if a tender type ceases to be payable or if a new type of refund of any contribution levy or tax payable by a person in his capacity as an employer becomes receivable or if a new type of premium receivable by a person in his capacity as an employer becomes receivable after the date of tender, then in any such case the net amount of the difference between what the Contractor actually receives or will receive in respect of workpeople as referred to in clauses A1·2·1 and A1·2·2 or because of his employment of such workpeople and what he would have received had the alteration, cessation or new type of refund or premium not become effective, shall, as the case may be, be allowed by or paid to the Contractor.

A1·7 The references in clauses A1·5 and A1·6 to premiums shall be construed as meaning all payments howsoever they are described which are made under or by virtue of an Act of Parliament to a person in his capacity as an employer and which affect the cost to an employer of having persons in his employment.

Contracted-out employment

A1·8 Where employer's contributions are payable by the Contractor in respect of workpeople as referred to in clauses A1·2·1 and A1·2·2 whose employment is contracted-out employment within the meaning of the Social Security Pensions Act 1975 the Contractor shall for the purpose of recovery or allowance under this clause be deemed to pay employer's contributions as if that employment were not contracted-out employment.

Meaning of contribution etc.

A1·9 The references in clause A1 to contribution, levies and taxes shall be construed as meaning all impositions payable by a person in his capacity as an employer however they are described and whoever the recipient which are imposed under or by virtue of an Act of Parliament and which affect the cost to an employer of having persons in his employment.

Materials – duties and taxes

A2·1 The prices used or set out by the Contractor in the contract documents are based upon the types and rates of duty if any and tax if any (other than any value added tax which is treated, or is capable of being treated, as input tax (as referred to in the Finance Act 1972) by the Contractor) by whomsoever payable which at the date of tender are payable on the import, purchase, sale, appropriation, processing or use of the materials, goods, electricity and, where so specifically stated in the Contract Documents, fuels specified in the list attached thereto under or by virtue of any Act of Parliament. A type and a rate so payable are in clause A2·2 referred to as a 'tender type' and a 'tender rate'.

A2·2 If in relation to any materials or goods specified as aforesaid, or any electricity or fuels specified as aforesaid and consumed on site for the execution of the Works including temporary site installations for those Works, a tender rate is increased or decreased or a tender type ceases to be payable or a new type of duty or tax (other than value added tax which is treated, or is capable of being treated as input tax (as referred to in the Finance Act 1972) by the Contractor) becomes payable on the import, purchase, sale, appropriation, processing or use of those materials, goods, electricity or fuels, then in any such case the net amount of the difference between what the Contractor actually pays in respect of those materials, goods, electricity or fuels and what he would have paid in respect of them had the alteration, cessation or imposition not occurred, shall, as the case may be, be paid to or allowed by the Contractor. In clause A2 the expression 'a new type of duty or tax' includes an additional duty or tax and a duty or tax imposed in regard to specified materials, goods, electricity or fuels in respect of which no duty or tax whatever was previously payable (other than any value added tax which is treated, or is capable of being treated, as input tax (as referred to in the Finance Act 1972) by the Contractor)

Fluctuations — work sublet

A3·1   If the Contractor shall decide to sublet any portion of the Works he shall incorporate in the sub-contract provisions to the like effect as the provisions of

clauses A1, A4 and A5 including the percentage stated in clause 4·5 pursuant to clause A5

which are applicable for the purposes of this Contract.

A3·2   If the price payable under such a sub-contract as aforesaid is decreased below or increased above the price in such sub-contract by reason of the operation of the said incorporated provisions, then the net amount of such decrease or increase shall, as the case may be, be allowed by or paid to the Contractor under this Contract.

Provisions relating to clauses A1, A3 and A5

Written notice by Contractor
A4·1   The Contractor shall give a written notice to the Landscape Architect of the occurrence of any of the events referred to in such of the following provisions as are applicable for the purposes of this Contract:
 ·1 clause A1·2
 ·2 clause A1·6
 ·3 clause A2·2
 ·4 clause A3·2

Timing and effect of written notices
A4·2   Any notice required to be given by the preceding sub-clause shall be given within a reasonable time after the occurrence of the event to which the notice relates, and the giving of a written notice in that time shall be a condition precedent to any payment being made to the Contractor in respect of the event in question.

Agreement — Landscape Architect and Contractor
A4·3   The Landscape Architect and the Contractor may agree what shall be deemed for all the purposes of this Contract to be the net amount payable to or allowable by the Contractor in respect of the occurrence of any event such as is referred to in any of the provisions listed in clause A4·1.

Fluctuations added to or deducted from Contract Sum — provisions setting out conditions etc. to be fulfilled before such addition or deduction
A4·4   Any amount which from time to time becomes payable to or allowable to the Contractor by virtue of clause A1 or clause A3 shall, as the case may be, be added to or deducted from the Contract Sum:

Provided:

— evidence by Contractor —
·1 As soon as is reasonably practicable the Contractor shall provide such evidence as the Landscape Architect may reasonably require to enable the amount payable to or allowable by the Contractor by virtue of clause A1 or clause A3 to be ascertained: and in the case of amounts payable to or allowable by the sub-contractor under clause A4·1·3 (or clause A3 for amounts payable to or allowable by the sub-contractor under provisions in the sub-contract to the like effect as clauses A1·3 and A1·4) — employees other than workpeople — such evidence shall include a certificate signed by or on behalf of the Contractor each week certifying the validity of the evidence reasonably required to ascertain such amounts.

— actual payment by Contractor —
·2 No amount shall be included in or deducted from the amount which would otherwise be stated as due in progress payments by virtue of this clause unless on or before the date as at which the total value of work, materials and goods is ascertained for the purposes of any progress payment the Contractor shall have actually paid or received the sum which is payable by or to him in consequence of the event in respect of which the payment or allowance arises.

— no alteration to Contractor's profit —
·3 No addition to or subtraction from the Contract Sum made by virtue of this clause shall alter in any way the amount of profit of the Contractor included in that Sum.

— position where Contractor is in default over completion
·4·1 No amount shall be included in or deducted from the amount which would otherwise be stated as due in progress payments or in the final certificate in respect of amounts otherwise payable to or allowable by the Contractor by virtue of clause A1 or clause A3 if the event (as referred to in the provisions listed in clause A4·1) in respect of which the payment or allowance would be made occurs after the completion date fixed under clause 2.

·4.2 Clause A4·4·4·1 shall not operate unless:
 ·1 the printed text of clause 2 is unamended; and
 ·2 the Landscape Architect has, in respect of every written notification by the Contractor under clause 2 of the Agreement, fixed such Completion Date as he considered to be in accordance with that clause.

Work etc. to which clauses A1 and A3 are not applicable
A4·5   Clause A1 and clause A3 shall not apply in respect of:

·1 work for which the Contractor is allowed daywork rates in accordance with any such rates included in the Contract Documents;

·2 changes in the rate of value added tax charged on the supply of goods or services by the Contractor to the Employer under this Contract.

Definitions for use with clause A1
A4·6   In clause A1:

·1 the expression 'the date of the contract' means the date 10 days before the date when the Agreement is executed by the parties;

·2 the expressions 'materials' and 'goods' include timber used in formwork but do not include other consumable stores, plant and machinery except electricity and, where specifically so stated in the Contract Documents, fuels;

·3 the expression 'workpeople' means persons whose rates of wages and other emoluments (including holiday credits) are governed by the rules or decisions or agreements of the National Joint Council for the Building Industry or some other wage-fixing body for trades associated with the building industry;

·4 the expression 'wage-fixing body' means a body which lays down recognised terms and conditions of workers within the meaning of the Employment Protection Act 1975, Schedule II, paragraph 2(a).

Percentage addition to fluctuation payments or allowances

A5   There shall be added to the amount paid or allowed by the Contractor under
 ·1 clause A1·2
 ·2 clause A1·3
 ·3 clause A1·6
 ·4 clause A2·2
the percentage stated in clause 4·5.

PART B — VALUE ADDED TAX

B1   In this clause 'VAT' means the value added tax introduced by the Finance Act 1972 which is under the care and management of the Commissioners of Customs and Excise (hereinafter called 'the Commissioners').

B2·1   The Landscape Architect shall inform the Contractor of the amount certified under clause 4·2 and immediately the Contractor shall give to the Employer a written provisional assessment of the respective values of those supplies of goods and services for which the certificate is being issued and which will be chargeable at the relevant times of supply on the Contractor at any rate or rates of VAT (including zero). The Contractor shall also specify the rate or rates of VAT which are chargeable on those supplies.

B2·2   Upon receipt of the Contractor's written provisional assessment the Employer shall calculate the amount of VAT due by applying the rate or rates of VAT specified by the Contractor to the amount of the supplies included in his assessment, and shall remit the calculated amount of such VAT to the Contractor when making payment to him of the amount certified by the Landscape Architect under clause 4·2.

B3·1   After the issue by the Landscape Architect of his certificate of making good defects under clause 2·5 of the Agreement the Contractor shall, as soon as he can finally so ascertain, prepare and submit to the Employer a written final statement of the value of all supplies of goods and services for which certificates have been or will be issued which are chargeable on the Contractor at any rate or rates of VAT (including zero). The Contractor shall also specify the rate or rates of VAT which are chargeable on those supplies and shall state the grounds on which he considers such supplies are so chargeable. He shall also state the total amount of VAT already received by him.

B3·2 Upon receipt of the written final statement the Employer shall calculate the amount of VAT due by applying the rate or rates of VAT specified by the Contractor to the value of the supplies included in the statement and deducting therefrom the total amount of VAT already received by the Contractor and shall pay the balance of such VAT to the Contractor within 28 days from receipt of the statement.

B3·3 If the Employer finds that the total amount of VAT specified in the final statement as already paid by him exceeds the amount of VAT calculated under clause B3·2, he shall so notify the Contractor, who shall refund such excess to the Employer within 28 days of receipt of the notification together with a receipt under clause B4 hereof showing a correction of the amounts for which a receipt or receipts have previously been issued by the Contractor.

B4 Upon receipt of any VAT properly paid under the provisions of this clause the Contractor shall issue to the Employer an authenticated receipt.

B5·1 In calculating the amount of VAT to be paid to the Contractor under clause B2 and B3 hereof, the Employer shall disregard any sums which the Contractor may be liable to pay to the Employer as liquidated damges under clause 2·3.

B5·2 The Contractor shall likewise disregard such liquidated damages when stating the value of supplies of goods or services in his written final statement under clause B3·1.

B6·1 If the Employer disagrees with the final statement issued by the Contractor under clause B3·1 he may request the Contractor to obtain the decision of the Commissioners on the VAT properly chargeable on the Contractor for all supplies of goods and services under this contract and the Contractor shall forthwith request the Commissioners for such decision.

B6·2 If the Employer disagrees with such decision, then, provided he secures the Contractor against all costs and other expenses, the Contractor shall in accordance with the instructions of the Employer make all such appeals against the decision of the Commissioners as the Employer may request.

B6·3 Within 28 days of the date of the decision of the Commissioners (or of the final adjudication of an appeal) the Employer or the Contractor as the case may be, shall pay or refund to the other any VAT underpaid or overpaid in accordance with such decisions or adjudication. The Contractor shall also account to the Employer for any costs awarded in his favour. The provisions of clause B3·3 shall apply in regard to the provision of authenticated receipts.

B7 The provisions of clause 8 shall not apply to any matters to be dealt with under clause B6.

B8 If any dispute or difference between the Employer and the Contractor is referred to an Arbitrator appointed under Article 4 or to a Court, then insofar as any payment awarded in such arbitration or court proceedings varies amounts certified for payment of goods or services supplied by the Contractor to the Employer under this Contract or is an amount which ought to have been but was not so certified, then the provisions of this Part B shall so far as relevant and applicable apply to any such payments.

B9 Notwithstanding any provisions to the contrary elsewhere in the Agreement the Employer shall not be obliged to make any further payment to the Contractor if the Contractor is in default in providing the receipt referred to in clause B4; provided that this clause B9 shall only apply where the Employer can show that he requires such receipt to validate any claim for credit for tax paid or payable under this Agreement which the Employer is entitled to make to the Commissioners.

PART C – STATUTORY TAX DEDUCTION SCHEME – FINANCE (No.2) ACT 1975 [a]

C1 In this clause 'the Act' means the Finance (No.2) Act 1975; "the Regulations" means the Income Tax (Sub-Contractors in the Construction Industry) Regulations 1975 S.I. No. 1960; "contractor" means a person who is a contractor for the purposes of the Act and the Regulations; 'evidence' means such evidence as is required by the Regulations to be produced to a 'contractor' for the verification of a 'sub-contractor's' tax certificate; 'statutory deduction' means the deduction referred to in section 69(4) of the Act or such other deduction as may be in force at the relevant time; "'sub-contractor'" means a person who is a sub-contractor for the purposes of the Act and the Regulations; 'tax certificate' is a certificate issuable under section 70 of the Act.

Provision of evidence – tax certificate
C2·1 Not later than 21 days before the first payment becomes due under clause 4 or after the Employer becomes a 'contractor' as referred to in clause 5·3 the Contractor shall:

either

·1 próvide the Employer with the evidence that the Contractor is entitled to be paid without the statutory deduction;

or

·2 inform the Employer in writing, and send a duplicate copy to the Landscape Architect, that he is not entitled to be paid without the statutory deduction.

C2·2 If the Employer is not satisfied with the validity of the evidence submitted in accordance with clause C2·1·1 hereof, he shall within 14 days of the Contractor submitting such evidence notify the Contractor in writing that he intends to make the statutory deduction from payments due under this Contract to the Contractor who is 'a sub-contractor' and give his reasons for that decision. The Employer shall at the same time comply with clause C5·1.

Uncertificated Contractor obtains tax certificate
C3·1 Where clause C2·1·2 applies, the Contractor shall immediately inform the Employer if he obtains a tax certificate and thereupon clause C2·1·1 shall apply.

Expiry of tax certificate
C3·2 If the period for which the tax certificate has been issued to the Contractor expires before the final payment is made to the Contractor under this Contract the Contractor shall, not later than 28 days before the day of expiry:

either

·1 provide the Employer with evidence that the Contractor from the said date of expiry is entitled to be paid for a further period without the statutory deduction in which case the provisions of clause C2·2 hereof shall apply if the Employer is not satisfied with the evidence;

or

·2 inform the Employer in writing that he will not be entitled to be paid without the statutory deduction after the said date of expiry.

Cancellation of tax certificate
C3·3 The Contractor shall immediately inform the Employer in writing if his current tax certificate is cancelled and give the date of such cancellation.

Vouchers
C4 The Employer shall, as a 'contractor', in accordance with the Regulations, send promptly to the Inland Revenue any voucher which, in compliance with the Contractor's obligations as a 'sub-contractor' under the Regulations, the Contractor gives to the Employer.

Statutory deduction – direct cost of materials
C5·1 If at any time the Employer is of the opinion (whether because of the information given under clause C2·1·2 of this clause or of the expiry or cancellation of the Contractor's tax certificate or otherwise) that he will be required by the Act to make a statutory deduction from any payment due to be made the Employer shall immediately so notify the Contractor in writing and require the Contractor to state not later than 7 days before each future payment becomes due (or within 10 days of such notification if that is later) the amount to be included in such payment which represents the direct cost to the Contractor and any other person of materials used or to be used in carrying out the Works.

C5·2 Where the Contractor complies with clause C5·1 he shall indemnify the Employer against loss or expense caused to the Employer by any incorrect statement of the amount of direct cost referred to in that clause.

C5·3 Where the Contractor does not comply with clause C5·1 the Employer shall be entitled to make a fair estimate of the amount of direct cost referred to in that clause.

Correction of errors
C6 Where any error or omission has occured in calculating or making the statutory deduction the Employer shall correct that error or omission by repayment to, or by deduction from payments to, the Contractor as the case may be, subject only to any statutory obligation on the Employer not to make such correction.

[a] The application of the Tax Deduction scheme and these provisions is explained in JCT Practice Note No. 22.

Relation to other Clauses of Agreement

C7 If compliance with this clause involves the Employer or the Contractor in not complying with any other provisions of the Agreement, then the provisions of this clause shall prevail.

Application of Arbitration Agreement

C8 The provisions of Article 4 (arbitration) shall apply to any dispute or difference between the Employer or the Landscape Architect on his behalf and the Contractor as to the operation of this clause except where the Act or the Regulations or any other Act of Parliament or statutory instrument rule or order made under an Act of Parliament provide for some other method of resolving such dispute or difference.

PART D – FLUCTUATIONS
Procedure for the recovery from the Employer of any Fluctuations in the cost of labour and materials (*delete if not applicable*).

Adjustment of Contract Sum – NEDO Price Adjustment Formula for Landscape Contracts

D1·1 The Contract Sum shall be adjusted in accordance with the provisions of this clause and the Formula Rules current at the Date of Tender issued for use with this clause by the Joint Contracts Tribunal for the Standard Form of Building Contract hereinafter called 'the Formula Rules'.

D1·2 Any adjustment under this clause shall be to sums exclusive of value added tax and nothing in this clause shall affect in any way the operation of Clause 5·2 (value added tax) and Part B of this Memorandum.

D2 The Definitions in rule 3 of the Formula Rules shall apply to this clause.
The adjustment referred to in this clause shall be effected (after taking into account any Non-Adjustable Element) in all certificates for payment (other than those under Clause 4·2 of these Conditions (release of retention)) issued under the provisions of these Conditions.
If any correction of amounts of adjustment under this clause included in previous certiificates is required following any operation of rule 5 of the Formula Rules such correction shall be given effect in the next certificate for payment to be issued.

Fluctuations – Articles manufactured outside the United Kingdom

D3 For any article to which rule 4·2 of the Formula Rules applies the Contractor shall insert in a list attached to the Contract Documents the market price of the article in sterling (that is the price delivered to the site) current at the Date of Tender. If after that Date the market price of the article inserted in the aforesaid list increases or decreases then the net amount of the difference between the cost of purchasing at the market price inserted in the aforesaid list and the market price payable by the Contractor and current when the article is bought shall, as the case may be, be paid to or allowed by the Contractor. The reference to 'market price' in this clause shall be construed as including any duty or tax (other than any value added tax which is treated, or is capable of being treated, as input tax (as defined in the Finance Act 1972) by the Contractor) by whomsoever payable under or by virtue of any Act of Parliament on the import, purchase, sale, appropriation or use of the article specified as aforesaid.

Power to agree – Landscape Architect and Contractor

D4 The Landscape Architect and the Contractor may agree any alteration to the methods and procedures for ascertaining the amount of formula adjustment to be made under this clause and the amounts ascertained after the operation of such agreement shall be deemed for all the purposes of this Contract to be the amount of formula adjustment payable to or allowable by the Contractor in respect of the provisions of this Clause. Provided always:

D4·1 that no alteration to the methods and procedures shall be agreed as aforesaid unless it is reasonably expected that the amount of formula adjustment so ascertained will be the same or approximately the same as that ascertained in accordance with Part I or Part II of the Formula Rules whichever Part is stated to be applicable in the Contract Documents; and

D4·2 that any agreement under this sub-clause shall not have any effect on the determination of any adjustment payable by the Contractor to any sub-contractor.

Position where Monthly Bulletins are delayed, etc.

D5·1 If at any time prior to the issue of the Final Certificate under Clause 4·3 of these Conditions formula adjustment is not possible because of delay in or cessation of, the publication of the Monthly Bulletins, adjustment of the Contract Sum shall be made in each Interim Certificate during such period of delay on a fair and reasonable basis.

D5·2 If publication of the Monthly Bulletins is recommenced at any time prior to the issue of the Final Certificate under Clause 4·3 of these Conditions the provisions of this clause and· the Formula Rules shall operate for each Valuation Period as if no delay or cessation as aforesaid had occurred and the adjustment under this clause and the Formula Rules shall be substituted for any adjustment under paragraph D5·1 hereof.

D5·3 During any period of delay or cessation as aforesaid the Contractor and Employer shall operate such parts of this clause and the Formula Rules as will enable the amount of formula adjustment due to be readily calculated upon recommencement of publication of the Monthly Bulletins.

Formula Rules
Rule 3

E1·1 Base Month.................................. 19........
Non-Adjustable Element.............% (not to exceed 10%).

Rules 10 and 30(i)

*Part I/Part II of Section 2 of the Formula Rules is to apply.

---

* *Strike out according to which method of formula adjustment (Part I – Work Category Method or Part II – Work Group Method) has been notified in the Schedules of Quantity issued to tenderers.*

This Supplementary Memorandum is issued by the Joint Council for Landscape Industries comprising:-

Landscape Institute
Horticultural Trades Association
British Association Landscape Industries
National Farmers' Union
Institute of Leisure and Amenity Management

Published for the Joint Council for Landscape Industries by the Landscape Institute
12 Carlton House Terrace London SW1Y 5AH and available from RIBA Publications Limited
66 Portland Place London W1N 4AD
© JCLI April 1985

Printed by Duolith Ltd
Welwyn Garden City, Hertfordshire

Issued September 1986

Practice Note No. 3 (April 1985)
JCLI Standard Form of Agreement for Landscape Works

Note: The JCLI Practice Note 3 supersedes No. 1 issued April 1978 and No. 2 on April 1982.

1. **Schedules (1st Recital)** means a list of items giving quantities, as necessary, and descriptions of work required, prepared in accordance with an appropriate method of measurement, which will be priced by tenderers and subsequently form part of the contract. Detailed information on materials and workmanship shall be contained in the Specification.

   Bills of Quantity
   Provision is now made for the option of including in the contract documents Bills prepared in accordance with SMM and the JCLI Rules.

   4th recital
   This provides for the naming of a quantity surveyor; neither the Articles nor the Conditions mention him but the Employer or the Landscape Architect on his behalf may wish to appoint a quantity surveyor in connection with the project, for example, to assist with valuations.

   Article 2
   The reference to VAT is new.

   Article 4: Arbitration
   Follows clause 8 (1978).

   Page 3
   The top part of the page is left blank for the parties to seal the Agreement if so required.

2. **Liquidated and Ascertained Damages:**
   (Clause 2·3)

   In landscape work it is generally very difficult to define the loss an Employer will suffer when a contract is delayed by the Contractor.

   The method outlined below for assessing the damages to be included in the contract is based on a notional interest on employed capital for the period of delay.

   The value of the project is assessed and interest at 1% over Bank Minimum Lending Rate is charged. This is spread over the contract period which realises a rate per week.

   Example:
   Contract Sum £75,000
   Period   40 weeks
   M.L.R.   12½%
   Interest   13½%

   Liquidated
   and
   Ascertained
   Damages $\dfrac{£75,000 \times 13\cdot5}{52 \times 100} = £194.71$ per week

   The essence of this method is that the damages are both ascertainable and realistic, being based on capital employed and not on some arbitrary assessment. Note: It does not however make any allowance for any additional professional fees which may be incurred as a result of the extended contract period.

3. **Date of Practical Completion:**
   (Clause 2·4)

   The date of Practical Completion is that date when the Landscape Architect certifies that the Contractor has fulfilled his obligations under the terms of the Contract. This does not preclude partial possession (dealt with under Clause 2·4) but simply determines the commencement of the Defect Liability Period for sections of work.

4. **Defects Liability: (Clause 2·5)**

   Except for plants which are dealt with separately the Contractor is responsible for making good all defects which appear after Practical Completion within a period inserted in the contract. It is recommended that the liability periods for landscape work should differ for hard landscape, grass, shrubs and trees. It is recommended that for hard landscape this period should normally be 6 months. Where paving forms a minor element within a predominantly soft landscape then the period should be as for the associated planting. In all cases the period should begin on the date of Practical Completion.

5. **Plant Failures — at Practical Completion:**
   (Clause 2·7)

   All plants which have failed prior to Practical Completion or within 6 weeks of the first leafing out in the case of trees and shrubs or grass at the first cut and roll, whichever is the later, are to be replaced by the Contractor entirely at his own expense, unless it arises from theft or malicious damage after Practical Completion. At an appropriate time the Contractor and Landscape Architect should meet to establish the extent of any defects and failures. The Landscape Architect will then prepare a schedule of these defects and send it to the Contractor within 14 days. The Contractor will inform the Landscape Architect when the work has been rectified.

6. **Plant Failures — after Practical Completion:**
   (Clause 2·7(A) or (B))

   At the time of preparing the tender documents a decision must be made as to whether the Contractor or the Employer is to be responsible for Maintenance of trees, shrubs and grass areas after Practical Completion. Maintenance is defined as those operations carried out by the Contractor or Employer after Practical Completion.

   i. If the Employer is to be responsible for Maintenance following Practical Completion then 2·7(A) is deleted and 2·7(B) is used, the Contractor is then relieved of all further obligations to replace defective plants other than those items listed in the Schedule of Defects referred to in item 5 above.

191

ii. If Maintenance is to be carried out by the Contractor 2·7(B) is deleted and 2·7(A) is used and the Contractor is then responsible for making good all defective plants during the Period, and this maintenance is to be separately scheduled and priced in the Schedules of Quantity. The Landscape Architect must not state for example, 'the Contractor is to allow for all maintenance during the Defects Liability Period', but must specify the operations in the Schedules of Quantity so that the Contractor is fully aware of his commitments and can incorporate the cost of such work in the Contract Sum. This does not include the cost of making good defects at Practical Completion which is deemed to be incorporated in the Contractor's Contract Sum. When the Contractor is responsible for Maintenance the following Defects Liability Periods for plants are recommended:

Grass: 3 months after the first cut and roll.
Shrubs and Trees: 12 months after the first breaking of buds.
Semi mature and ELNS: 2 years after the first breaking of buds.

In all cases the period should begin on the date of Practical Completion.

It is recommended that where varying Defects Liability Periods are required by the Contract, work relating to each Period shall be kept separate under a suitable heading, which can be identified with the particular periods, and only that part of the retention monies proportional to the value of the part of the work certified as being practically complete should be released.

7. **P.C. Sums: (Clause 3·7)**
Particular attention is drawn to Clause 3·6 where it will be noted that no cash discount is allowable by sub-contractors or suppliers arising out of instructions issued by the Landscape Architect in respect of prime cost sums. As such quotations are accepted nett Contractors are deemed to have included for the lack of cash discount elsewhere in the Contract Sum.

8. **Correction of inconsistencies (Clause 4·1)**
This does not provide that every correction is to be treated as a variation but only any correction of an inconsistency which results in a change. Where the correction is not a change there is no variation. It may be necessary to determine which of two inconsistent documents is the ruling document or which of two inconsistent statements prevails. For example, if written descriptions appear on a drawing and it is stated in the Contract Documents that any figure in, a description shall prevail over any figures otherwise shown on a drawing there would only be a change if it were necessary to correct a figure in a description where the inconsistent figure on the drawing was actually required.

9. **Malicious Damage: (Clause 6·5)**
The cost of all making good arising from malicious damage or theft after Practical Completion is always the responsibility of the Employer. When the risk of such damage is considered small, if the Landscape Architect wishes such damage or theft prior to Practical Completion to be made good by the Contractor at no extra cost to the Contract as at present, Clause 6·5(A) should be used. The Contractor will then make his own assessment of the likely cost and include for it in his tender and which the Employer then pays whether any damage arises or not.

Of it is preferred to reimburse the Contractor only for the actual cost of such damage which arises prior to Practical Completion then a provisional sum should be included in the tender documents and Clause 6·5(B) used.

10. **Supplementary Memorandum (Clause 8·0)**
Part A of the Supplement, Tax etc. changes, corresponds with clause 38 of the JCT Standard Form of Building Contract (1980); Part B, VAT, corresponds with the VAT Agreement Supplement to the Standard Form; and Part C, Statutory Tax Deduction Scheme, corresponds with clause 31 of the Standard Form.

11. **Temporary Protection:**

If temporary protective measures including fencing are required, these must be clearly stated and quantified at tender stage. It is not sufficient to state the 'the Contractor is to allow for the erection of any temporary fencing which may be necessary to protect grass or shrub areas.' Ownership of temporary protection may often with advantage be transferred to the Employer if so stated in the tender documents otherwise it remains the property of the Contractor.

12. **Watering**

The tender and contract documents should state the frequency and quantity of water required to be provided by the Contractor. In drought conditions when the provision of water is restricted by legislation contractors and sub-contractors should be required to inform the Landscape Architect of the cost of second class water from a sewage works or other approved source and await instructions.

13. **Maintenance**

When Maintenance is the responsibility of the Contractor in accordance with Clause 2·7A the value of this work is excluded from that included in the penultimate certificate issued in accordance with clause 4·3.

This Practice Note is issued by the Joint Council for Landscape Industries comprising:-

Landscape Institute
Horticultural Trades Association
British Association Landscape Industries
National Farmers' Union
Institute of Leisure and Amenity Management

Published for the Joint Council for Landscape Industries by the Landscape Institute
12 Carlton House Terrace London SW1Y 5AH and available from RIBA Publications Limited
66 Portland Place London W1N 4AD
© JCLI April 1985

Printed by Duolith Ltd.
Welwyn Garden City, Hertfordshire

Issued September 1986

JCLI Agreement for Landscape Works
Amendment to Insurance provisions, June 1987

Delete section 6·0, clauses 6·1 to 6·3B inclusive and insert clauses 6·1 to 6·3B amended as shown below:

6·0 Injury, damage and insurance

Injury to or death of persons

6·1 The Contractor shall be liable for and shall indemnify the Employer against any expense, liability, loss, claim or proceedings whatsoever arising under any statute or at common law in respect of personal injury to or death of any person whomsoever arising out of or in the course of or caused by the carrying out of the Works, except to the extent that the same is due to any act or neglect of the Employer or of any person for whom the Employer is responsible. Without prejudice to his liability to indemnify the Employer the Contractor shall take out and maintain and shall cause any sub-contractor to take out and maintain insurance which, in respect of liability to employees or apprentices shall comply with the Employer's Liability (Compulsory Insurance) Act 1969 and any statutory orders made thereunder or any amendment or re-enactment thereof and in respect of any other liability for personal injury or death shall be such as is necessary to cover the liability of the Contractor, or, as the case may be, of such sub-contractor.

Injury or damage to property

6·2 The Contractor shall be liable for, and shall indemnify the Employer against, any expense, liability, loss, claim or proceedings in respect of any injury or damage whatsoever to any property real or personal (other than injury or damage to the Works) insofar as such injury or damage arises out of or in the course of or by reason of the carrying out of the Works and to the extent that the same is due to any negligence, breach of statutory duty, omission or default of the Contractor, his servants or agents, or of any person employed or engaged by the Contractor upon or in connection with the Works or any part thereof, his servants or agents. Without prejudice to his obligation to indemnify the Employer the Contractor shall take out and maintain and shall cause any sub-contractor to take out and maintain insurance in respect of the liability referred to above in respect of injury or damage to any property real or personal other than the Works which shall be for an amount not less than the sum stated below for any one occurrence or series of occurrences arising out of one event:

insurance cover referred to above to be not less than: £ _____

Insurance of the Works – Fire etc. – New Works [g]

6·3A The Contractor shall in the joint names of Employer and Contractor insure against loss and damage by fire, lightning, explosion, storm, tempest, flood, bursting or overflowing of water tanks, apparatus or pipes, earthquake, aircraft and other aerial devices or articles dropped therefrom, riot and civil commotion, for the full reinstatement value of the Works thereof plus .... % [h] to cover professional fees, all work executed and all unfixed materials and goods intended for, delivered to, placed on or adjacent to the Works and intended therefore. After any inspection required by the insurers in respect of a claim under the insurance mentioned in this clause 6·3A the Contractor shall with due diligence restore or replace work or materials or goods damaged and dispose of any debris and proceed with and complete the Works. The Contractor shall not be entitled to any in respect of work or materials or goods damaged or the disposal of any debris other than the monies received under the said insurance (less the percentage to cover professional fees) and such monies shall be paid to the Contractor under certificates of the Landscape Architect at the periods stated in clause 4·0 hereof.

Insurance of the Works – Fire, etc. – Existing structure [g]

6·3B The Employer shall in the joint names of Employer and Contractor insure against loss or damage to the existing strucutres (together with the contents owned by him or for which he is responsible) and to the Works and all unfixed materials and goods intended for, delivered to, placed on or adjacent to the Works and intended therefore by fire, lightning, explosion, storm, tempest, flood, bursting or overflowing of water tanks, apparatus or pipes, earthquake, aircraft and other aerial devices or articles dropped therefrom, riot and civil commotion.

If any loss or damage as referred to in this clause occurs then the Landscape Architect shall issue instructions for the reinstatement and making good of such loss or damage in accordance with clause 3·5 hereof and such instructions shall be valued under clause 3·6 hereof.

[f] Delete clause 4·5 if the contract period is of such limited duration as to make the provisions of part A of the Supplementary Memorandum to this agreement inapplicable.
[g] Delete 6·3A or 6·3B as appropriate.
Where the Contractor has in force an All Risks Policy which insures the Works against loss or damage by, inter alia, the perils referred to in clause 6·3A this Policy may be used to provide the insurance required by clause 6·3A provided the Policy recognises the Employer as a joint insured with the Contractor in respect of the Works and the Policy is maintained.
[h] Percentage to be inserted.

Revised clauses 6·1 to 6·3B shown overleaf incorporate the following detailed changes:

6·0 Injury, damage and insurance

Injury to or death of persons
6·1 Line 8, **delete** 'unless' **insert** 'except to the extent that the same is'.

Lines 12 and 13, before 'maintain' **insert** 'take out and' in each line.

Line 13,
delete 'such insurances as are'
insert insurance which, in respect of liability to employees or apprentices shall comply with the Employer's Liability (Compulsory Insurance) Act 1969 and any statutory orders made thereunder or any amendment or re-enactment thereof and in respect of any other liability for personal injury or death shall be such as is'.

Line 15, **insert** a full stop after 'sub-contractor.

Lines 16 to 18, **delete** 'in respect of ... of the Works'.

Lines 18 to end, **delete** sentence beginning 'Provided that'.

6·2 Delete existing heading and **insert**:
'*Injury or damage to property*'

Re-draft to read:
'The Contractor shall be liable for, and shall indemnify the Employer against, any expense, liability, loss, claim or proceedings in respect of any injury or damage whatsoever to any property real or personal (other than injury or damage to the Works) insofar as such injury or damage arises out of or in the course of or by reason of the carrying out of the Works and to the extent that the same is due to any negligence, breach of statutory duty, omission or deafult of the Contractor, his servants or agents, or of any person employed or engaged by the Contractor upon or in connection with the Works or any part thereof, his servants or agents. Without prejudice to his obligation to indemnify the Employer the Contractor shall take out and maintain and shall cause any sub-contractor to take out and maintain insurance in respect of the liability referred to above in respect of injury or damage to any property real or personal other than the Works which shall be for an amount not less than the sum stated below for any one occurrence or series of occurrences arising out of one event:

insurance cover referred to above to be not less than: £ _____

6·3A *Insurance of the Works – Fire etc. – New Works*

Heading **insert [g]**

Line 7, after 'full' **insert** 'reinstatement'.

Line 12 after 'therefore' **insert** full stop.

Lines 12 to 14 **delete** '(except temporary ... sub-contractors)'.

Second sentence
Line 1, **delete** 'Upon acceptance of any claim' **insert** 'After any inspection required by the insurers in respect of a claim'.

Line 8, after 'damaged' **insert** 'or the disposal of any debris'.

ADD new wording to footnote **[g]**
'Where the Contractor has in force an All Risks Policy which insures the Works against loss or damage by inter alia the perils referred to in clause 6·3A this Policy may be used to provide the insurance required by clause 6·3A provided the Policy recognises the Employer as a joint insured with the Contractor in respect of the Works and the Policy is maintained.'

6·3B *Insurance of the Work – Fire etc. – existing structures*

Re-draft first paragraph to read:
'The Employer shall in the joint names of Employer and Contractor insure against loss or damage to the existing structures (together with the contents owned by him or for which he is responsible) and to the Works and all unfixed materials and goods intended for, delivered to, placed on or adjacent to the Works and intended therefore by fire, lightning, explosion, storm, tempest, flood, bursting or overflowing of water tanks, apparatus or pipes, earthquake, aircraft and other aerial devices or articles dropped therefrom, riot and civil commotion.'

Second paragraph
ADD at end and such instructions shall be valued under clause 3·6 hereof'.

JCLI

Published for the Joint Council for Landscape Industries by the Landscape Institute
12 Carlton House Terrace, London SW1Y 5AH and available from RIBA Publications Limited
66 Portland Place, London W1N 4AD
© JCLI June 1985

Printed by Duolith Ltd.
Welwyn Garden City, Hertfordshire

Issued June 1987

APPENDIX 4

Form of Tender and Conditions of Subcontract

For use with the JCLI Agreement for Landscape Works.

Information for Tenderers

1. Contract name and location: ....

2. Employer: ....

3. Contractor: ....

4. Landscape Architect: ....

5. The Form of Contract is the JCLI Agreement for Landscape Works, completed as follows:

   Clause 2·1: The Works may be commenced on .... and shall be completed by ....

   Clause 2·3: Liquidated damages: £ .... per week or part of a week.

   Clause 2·5: Defects Liability Period: .... months

   Clause 2·7: Plant Failures grass .... months after Practical Completion

               shrubs and trees .... months after Practical Completion

               semi mature and ELNS trees .... months after Practical Completion

   Clause 4·4   Documents for Final Valuation ....

   Clause 4·5   Contributions levy and tax changes ....

   Clause 6·3 A/B Insurance against fire .... clause A/B deleted.

   Clause 6·3A   Percentage to cover professional fees ....

   Clause 6·5B   Provisional sum for malicious damage ....

   *Clause 6·3A will be deleted.
   *Clause 6·3B will be deleted, the insurance under clause 6·3A being the full value plus .... %

6. The Subcontractor shall, before tendering, visit the Site or otherwise make himself familiar with the extent of the Subcontract Works, the Site Conditions, and all local conditions and restrictions likely to affect the execution of the work. The Subcontractor may have access to any available drawings or work programmes relative to the preparation of his tender on request and by appointment.

7. Two copies of this Form are provided — One copy to be priced, signed by the Subcontractor and

   returned to .... the other is for his retention.

Form of Tender

1. Tender price for ....
   (The Enquirer should enter trade or brief description of Works)

   .... Total tender price

   The Tenderer should enter the amount of his tender in words and figures.

   2a The tender is to be adjusted for price fluctuations of labour only/materials only*/labour and materials* as set out in Subcontract Condition 4·4, a list of relevant basic prices being enclosed.

   2b The tender is to be adjusted for price fluctuations by use of the NEDO Price Adjustment Formula Indices (Category ....)/the Specialist Engineering Installation Indices (Category ....)*.

   *2c The tender is to be on a firm price basis.

3. **Schedule of Daywork Charges**
   The Subcontractor is requested to insert his hourly daywork rates in the space provided in the Schedule below. His rates for labour shall be deemed to include overheads and profit and all payments in connection with Holidays with Pay, Bonus and Pension Schemes, Subsistence Allowances, Fares and Travelling Time, Imported Labour Costs, Non-Productive Overtime Costs, and any other payments made under the Working Rule Agreement, any Regulation, Bye-law or Act of Parliament. The Subcontractor is also invited to insert in the space provided the percentage addition he will require for his overheads and profits on the nett cost of materials and on plant charges.

   (i) **Labour**

   Craftsmen @ ....£ .... per hour

   Labourers/Mates @ .... £ .... per hour

   (ii) **Materials and Plant**
   Materials invoice cost plus ....%

   Plant Charges plus ....%

4. Period of notice required before commencing the Subcontract Works: ....

   Time required to complete the Subcontract Works (the Subcontract Period unless agreed

   otherwise): ....

5. We, the undersigned, agree that this quotation will be open for acceptance within .... week(s) and that we have read and understand the terms and conditions printed overleaf and that should our quotation be accepted we will enter into a Subcontract in accordance with the said terms and conditions.

   For and on behalf of ....

   ....

   Signed .... Date ....

*Delete if not required.

This page may be torn off.

Conditions of Subcontract

1.0 Intentions

Subcontractor's Obligation

1.1 The Subcontractor shall with due diligence and in a good and workmanlike manner carry out and complete the Works in accordance with the Subcontract Documents using materials and workmanship of the quality and standards therein specified provided that where and to the extent that approval of the quality of materials or of the standards of workmanship is a matter for the opinion of the Landscape Architect such quality and standards shall be to the reasonable satisfaction of the Landscape Architect.

No approval expressed or implied by the Contractor and/or the Landscape Architect shall in any way relieve the Subcontractor of his responsibility for complying with the requirements of this Subcontract.

Principal Contract and Special Conditions

1.2 The Subcontractor is deemed to have full knowledge of, and so far as they are applicable to the Works agrees to comply with, the provisions of the Principal Contract as though the same were incorporated herein and the Main Contractor were the Employer and the Subcontractor were the Contractor. Any conditions contained in the Subcontractor's Tender shall be excluded.

Information provided by others

1.3 The Subcontractor must make written application to the Contractor for instructions, drawings, levels or other information at a date which is not unreasonably distant from nor unreasonably close to the date on which it is necessary for the Subcontractor to receive the same.

Information provided for others

1.4 Any instructions, drawings, levels or other information relating to the Works which is requested from the Subcontractor must be provided in due time and so as not to cause disruption or delay to the works to be performed under the Principal Contract.

2.0 Commencement and Completion

Progress and Completion

2.1 The Works are to be commenced within the period of notice stated on the Form of Tender and are to be completed within the Subcontract period subject only to such fair and reasonable extension of time as the Contractor shall allow. The Works are to be carried out diligently and in such order, manner and time as the Contractor may reasonably direct so as to ensure completion of the Principal Contract Works or any portion thereof by the completion date or such extended date as may be allowed under the Principal Contract. If the Subcontractor is in breach of the foregoing he shall pay or allow to the Contractor the amount of loss or damage suffered by the Contractor in consequence thereof.

Overtime

2.2 No overtime is to be worked without the Subcontractor first obtaining the consent in writing of the Contractor. No additional payment for overtime will be made unless the Subcontractor is so advised in writing by the Contractor and, if the Subcontractor is so advised, he will be reimbursed the net additional non-productive rate incurred, including any net additional cost of Employers' Liability and Third Party Insurances. The Subcontractor will be required to obtain any necessary overtime permit from the appropriate authority.

Annual Holidays

2.3 Under the Annual Holiday Agreement, the Site will be closed down for certain periods which may be whilst the Subcontractor's work is in progress. The Subcontractor will be deemed to have included in his Tender for any additional costs and time resulting from such closure.

Maintenance and Defects Liability

2.4 The Subcontractor will (1) maintain the Works at his own expense to the Contractor's and the Landscape Architect satisfaction both during the progress of the Works and until the Landscape Architect has issued a Certificate of Practical Completion including the Works and (2) make good at his own expense, and at a time to be decided by the Contractor, any defects or damage to the Works.

3.0 Control of the Works

Assignment

3.1 Neither the Contractor nor the Subcontractor shall, without the written consent of the other, assign this Contract.

Use of Site

3.2 The Site shall not be used for any purpose other than for the carrying out of the Works. Works to be executed outside the Main Contractor's Site boundary shall be carried out to suit the convenience of adjacent occupiers or Local Authorities at times to be agreed by the Contractor in writing.

Variations

3.3 No variation shall vitiate this Subcontract. The Subcontractor shall advise the Contractor in writing of all work involving a variation or extra work within 14 days of such variation or extra work becoming apparent, at the same time submiting detailed and priced calculations based upon this Subcontract showing such price adjustment, if any. Variations or extra work shall not be undertaken by the Subcontractor nor shall he receive payment for such variation or extra works without written authority from the Contractor.

Where variations or extra works cannot be valued by reference to this Subcontract then the value of such variations or extra works shall be subject to agreement between the Contractor and/or the Landscape Architect and the Subcontractor.

Dayworks

3·4 No daywork will be permitted except where in the opinion of the Contractor and/or the Landscape Architect, it would be unfair to value such work at other than daywork rates. Where the Subcontractor considers he has claim to daywork due notice must be given and valuation by daywork approved by the Contractor in writing prior to the execution of the work in question in order to facilitate checking the time and materials expended thereon. All daywork sheets shall be rendered by the end of the week during which the work is executed. All daywork will be paid for at the rates stated on the Form of Tender.

Adjustment for Provisional Sums

3·5 Instructions will be issued in respect of Provisional Sums. No loss of profit will be allowed in respect of such instructions.

4·0 Payments

Discount to the Contractor

4·1 The Subcontractor will allow for all payments to be made in full within 17 days of the date of the Landscape Architect's Certificate to the Employer without any cash discount for prompt payment. Any such discount included on the Form of Tender will be deducted from the tender sum before the order for the subcontract works is placed.

Progress Payments

4·2 Payment will, subject always to these terms and conditions, be made to the Subcontractor as and when the value of such Works under the terms of the Principal Contract is included in a Certificate to the Contractor and the Contractor receives the monies due thereunder. Applications for payment are to be rendered to the Contractor in duplicate by the Subcontractor.
Payment shall be by instalments of the rate of:
95% of the value executed as the Works proceed.
2½% upon practical complete of the Works.
2½% on satisfactory completion of making good defects under the Principal Contract or as soon as the final account for all Works executed under this Subcontract shall have been agreed, whichever may last happen.
Progress payments shall be on account only and shall not be held to signify approval by the Contractor and/or the Landscape Architect of the whole or any part of the Works executed nor shall any final payment prejudice any claim the Contractor may have in respect of any defects in the Works whenever such defects may appear.

Estimates of Loss, etc.

4·3 In addition to the Contractor' Common Law rights of set off, if the Subcontractor shall cause the Contractor loss by reason of any breach of this Contract or by any tortious act or by any breach of statutory duty giving rise to a claim for damages or indemnity or contribution by the Contractor against the Subcontractor, or the Contractor shall

become entitled to payment from the Subcontractor under this Contract, then without prejudice to and pending the final determination or agreement between the parties, the Contractor shall bona fide estimate the amount of such loss, indemnity or contribution or payment, such estimate to be binding and conclusive upon the Subcontractor until such final determination or agreement.

Fluctuations (to apply only if item 2a of the Form of Tender is completed).

4·4 The sum or sums referred to in this Subcontract shall be based upon the rates of wages and such other emoluments, allowances and expenses (including the cost of Employers' Liability and Third Party Insurances) as are properly payable by the Subcontractor to work-people engaged upon or in connection with the Works in acccordance with the rules or decisions of the wage fixing body of the trade or trades concerned applicable to the Works. Such rates of wages and the prices of materials shall be as detailed in the Basic Price List as provided by the Subcontractor and attached hereto.
Should any fluctuations from the Basic Price List occur during the currency of this Subcontract, the net additional cost actually and properly incurred or saving that ought to have been made, by such fluctuations shall be added to or be deducted from the total amount payable under the terms and conditions of this Subcontract. Fluctuations in the cost of materials will be adjusted net.
Provided always that immediate notice in writing shall be given of such fluctuations, and an approved weekly return submitted to the Contractor showing the total number of men and hours and the deliveries of materials effected for detailed checking by the Contractor and Landscape Architect.

5·0 Statutory Obligations:

Safety, Health and Welfare

5·1 The Subcontractor shall comply with the Contractor's requirements on matters affecting the safe conduct of work on the Site and all statutes, bye laws and regulations affecting the Works and the carrying out thereof.

Statutory Payments

5·2 The Subcontractor shall include in his quotation for any payments to be made under the Working Rule Agreement, all payments in connection with holidays with Pay, Bonus and Pension Schemes, National Insurance, Subsistence Allowances, Fares and Travelling Time, Imported Labour Costs or any payments required by Regulations, Bye-law or Act of Parliament.

6·0 Injury, Damage and Insurance

Responsibilities of the Subcontractor

6·1 The Subcontractor shall indemnify the Contractor against all claims, causes of action, costs, loss and expense whatsoever in respect of:

1. Personal injury or death of any person or injury or damage to any property real or personal arising out of or in the course of or caused by any works executed by the Subcontractor and/or the execution of such works (including but not restricted to the use of any plant, equipment or facilities whether in connection with such execution or otherwise) and/or any design undertaken by the Subcontractor and
2. Any negligence or breach of duty on the part of the Subcontractor, his Subcontractors, his or their servants or agents and
3. Any breach or non-performance or non-observance by the Subcontractor, his Subcontractors, his or their servants or agents of the provisions of the Principal Contract in so far as they relate or apply to the Works and are not inconsistent with the provisions of this Subcontract.
4. Any act, omission, default or neglect of the Subcontractor, his Subcontractors, his or their servants or agents which involves the Contractor in any liability under the Principal Contract.
5. Any damage, claim loss or expense to or involving any plant (whether of the type aforesaid or otherwise) hired or loaned or otherwise made available to the Subcontractor or operating for the Subcontractor's benefit.

Responsibilities of Others
6·2 The Subcontractor shall not be responsible for loss or damage caused by fire, storm, tempest, lightning, flood, bursting and overflowing of water tanks, apparatus or pipes, earthquake, aircraft or anything dropped therefrom, aerial objects, riot and civil commotion, to the Works or to any materials (other than temporary buildings, plant, tools, scaffolding and machinery provided by the Subcontractor, or any scaffolding or other plant which is loaned to him by the Contractor), properly upon the Site and in connection with and for the purpose of the Subcontract. In the event of any such loss or damage, the Subcontractor shall, if and when directed by the Contractor in writing, proceed immediately with the rectification or replacement of the damaged work and materials and the erection and completion of the Works in full accordance with the terms, provisions and conditions hereof, and expenses in respect of any of the matters referred to in sub-clause 6.1.1 and 6.1.2 above and shall on demand produce to the Contractor adequate evidence of such insurance.

Subcontractor's Work, Materials and Plant
6·3 The Works, materials, tools, plant, scaffolding, machinery and buildings of the Subcontractor, the subject of or used in connection with this Subcontract whether on Site or not, shall in every respect be at the Subcontractor's risk (except those risks for which the Subcontractor is not responsible under Clause 6·2).

Subcontractor's Insurance
6·4 The Subcontractor shall adequately insure:
1 His and the Contractor's liability in respect of any claims, causes of action, costs, losses and expenses in respect of any of the matters referred to in sub-clauses 6·1·1 and 6·1·2.

2 Against all Employers' Liability and Third Party (including Third Party Fire) risks arising out of the execution of the Works.
The Subcontractor shall produce on demand policies of such insurances, together with receipts for premiums, or other adequate evidence of such insurance.
In case of neglect by the Subcontractor to effect the insurances, the Contractor shall be at liberty to insure on behalf of the Subcontractor and to deduct the premium so paid from any monies due or becoming due to the Subcontractor.

7·0 **Determination**

Determination by the Contractor
7·1 The Contractor may without prejudice to any other of his rights or remedies determine the Subcontractor's employment under this Subcontract if the Subcontractor:-
1. fails forthwith upon notice from the Contractor to commence remedial work to any defective workmanship and/or materials or fails to proceed with the same with due diligence or to complete such remedial work to the satisfaction of the Contractor or the Landscape Architect within a set period as the Contractor may specify in the said notice or if none is so specified within a reasonable time.
2. fails to withdraw immediately, at the request of the Contractor, any one or more of his employees to whom the Contractor objects or whose presence on the Works may contravene the conditions of this or the Principal Contract, or may cause labour disputes in the Subcontractor's or any other trade, and to replace such employees within a reasonable time by others against whom there is no such objection.
3. makes any arrangements with his creditors, has a Receiving Order made against him, executes a Bill of Sale, or commits an act of bankruptcy or, being a limited company, goes into liquidation, or has a Receiver appointed.
4. fails within seven days' notice in writing from the Contractor to comply with any of the obligations on the part of the Subcontractor herein contained.

Upon determination by the Contractor the Subcontractor shall not remove any of his equipment, materials or property from the Site and, notwithstanding anything contained in these conditions, shall be entitled to no further payment until completion of the Works by the Contractor or by others whereupon the Subcontractor shall become entitled to payment for Works executed and materials provided by the Subcontractor subject always to the right of the Contractor to set off all losses expense and damages suffered or which may be suffered by the Contractor by reason of such determination and subject further to any other right of set off which the Contractor may have. For the purposes of such completion the Contractor shall have the right to use the Subcontractor's equipment, materials and property on the Site and to any materials or fabricated work lying at the Subcontractor's works or workshop which have been bought or fabricated for the purpose of this Subcontract.

Determination by the Subcontractor

7·2 The Subcontractor may without prejudice to any other of his rights or remedies determine the Subcontractor's employment under this Subcontract if the Contractor:

1. fails to make any payments in accordance with this subcontract.

2. unreasonably attempts or obstructs the carrying out of the Subcontractor's Works

3. makes any arrangements with his creditors, has a Receiving Order made against him, executes a Bill of Sale, or commits an act of bankruptcy or, being a limited company, goes into liquidation, or has a Receiver appointed.

Upon determination by the Subcontractor the Contractor shall pay to the Subcontractor, after taking into account amounts previously paid, such sum as shall be fair and reasonable for the value of work begun and executed, materials on site and the removal of all temporary buildings, plant tools and equipment. Provided always that the right of determination shall be without prejudice to any other rights or remedies which the Subcontractor may possess.

8·0 Temporary Works and Services, Attendance, Related Works

Temporary Accommodation

8·1 The Subcontractor shall provide to the approval of the Contractor and at his own expense, any requisite temporary site office, workshop accommodation, together with the necessary equipment, lighting, power, fuel etc.

Welfare facilities

8·2 The Subcontractor shall, at his own risk have reasonable and free use of the temporary welfare accommodation and/or services (including First Aid facilities and treatment) which the Contractor or the Employer may provide on the Site in connection with the Works.

Temporary services

8·3 The Subcontractor shall, at his own risk, have reasonable and free use, in common with others engaged upon the Site, of the water supply, temporary plumbing, temporary lighting and temporary electric power. Electric power supply for small tools and equipment used on the Site shall not exceed 110V A.C. single phase. Any electrical equipment used to carry out the Works must be in good mechanical condition and suitable for the electric power supply and fittings made available and fitted with suitable plugs, sockets and connectors to BS4343 (CEE 17) or any other standard that the Contractor may direct.

Use of Scaffolding

8·4 The Subcontractor shall at his own risk and at such time(s) and for such period(s) as the Contractor may direct have free use of the Contractor's scaffolding, ladders and mechanical hoisting facilities which may be available on the Site or already in position.

Delivery and Storage of Materials

8·5 The Subcontractor shall provide all materials, package and carriage to and from the Site. He will be responsible for unloading during the progress of his Works, storing in the areas provided and moving his own materials at the Site. Any materials delivered prior to commencement on Site shall be off-loaded by the Contractor at the sole risk and cost of the Subcontractor.

Removal of Rubbish etc.

8·6 All rubbish and/or surplus materials and plant of the Subcontractor must be removed forthwith from the vicinity of the Works, paths, roads etc., to an approved position on the Site.

Cutting Away

8·7 In no circumstances whatsoever shall any cutting away be done without the prior written authority of the Contractor.

Sub-surfaces

8·8 The Subcontractor shall satisfy himself before commencing work, as to the suitability of any surfaces to which the Subcontractor is to fix, apply or lay his work.

This Form is issued by the
Joint Council for Landscape Industries
comprising:-

Landscape Institute
Horticultural Trades Association
British Association Landscape Industries
National Farmers Unions
Institute of Leisure and Amenity Management.

Published for the Joint Council for Landscape Industries by the Landscape Institute 12 Carlton House Terrace, London SW1Y 5AH and available from RIBA Publications Limited 66 Portland Place, London W1N 4AD.
© JCLI January 1986

Printed by Duolith Ltd.
Welwyn Garden City, Herts.

Issued January 1986

APPENDIX 5: Statutory Instruments relating to the Landscape 1980–1990

SI 1981	14	T&CP Tree Preservation Orders Amendment Regulations.
	369	T&CP Fees for Applications Regulations.
	1742	T&CP Enforcement Notices & Appeals Regulations.
	1743	T&CP Enforcement Enquiries Procedure Rules.
SI 1982	6	Compulsory Purchase of Land Regulations.
	209	Commons schemes Registration Regulations.
	975	T&CP Minerals Regulations.
	1346	Wildlife and Countryside Claims for compensation Regulations.
1983	21	Wildlife and Countryside Rights of Way Definitive Map Regulations.
	1190	T&CP Local Plans for greater London Regulations.
1984	6	T&CP (Structure and Local Plans Amendment) Regulations.
	421	T&CP Control of Advertisement Regulations.
	582	Control of Pollution Underground Water Regulations.
	1992	Control of Noise Code of Practice for Construction Sites Order.
	222	Ancient Monuments Class Consents Amendment Order.
	1285	Operations in forms of Archaeological Importance Terms of Notice Order.
	1286	Areas of Archaeological Importance Notification Exemption Order.
	2026	Environmentally Sensitive Areas Orders.
1985	1182	T&CP Fees for Applications Regulations.
	1981	T&CP GDO (Amendment No. 2) Order.
1986	8	T&CP National Parks AONB and Conservation Areas Order.
	148	Local Government Reorganisation of Property Order.
	854	Local Government Inspection of Documents Rights Order.
	1176	T&CP Agriculture Forestry Development in National Parks Order.
	1536	Land Registration Official Searches Rules.
	1856	Highways Road Humps Regulations.

1987	632	Forestry Felling of Trees Regulations.
	1730	Control of Noise Code of Practice for Construction and Open Sites Regulations.
	1750	T&CP Simplified Planning Zones Regulations.
	1760	T&CP Structure and Local Plans Amendment Regulations.
	1849	T&CP Simplified Planning Zones Excluded Development Order.

Index